How to Play a Bridge Hand

♣   ◇   ♡   ♠   ♣   ◇   ♡   ♠

by William S. Root

Introduction by Omar Sharif

Richard Pavlicek, Technical Consultant

Phillip Alder, Editor

CROWN PUBLISHERS, INC., New York

Other Books by William S. Root

Commonsense Bidding
Modern Bridge Conventions (co-authored
with Richard Pavlicek)

Published by Crown Publishers, Inc., 201 East 50th Street, New York, NY
10022.

CROWN is a trademark of Crown Publishers, Inc.

Library of Congress Cataloging-in-Publication Data
Root, William S.
      How to play a bridge hand / by
   William S. Root : introduction by Omar Sharif. — 1st ed.
      1. Contract bridge. I. Title.
GV1282.3.R5728 1990
795.41'53 — dc20   89-28919
ISBN: 0-517-57457-8
10 9 8 7 6 5 4 3 2
First Edition

To Vera

Contents

Introduction

♣   ◇   ♡   ♠   ♣   ◇   ♡   ♠

When my good friend Bill Root asked me to write this introduction to his new book, my first thought was: "Why another book on play?" Since the appearance of *Watson on Play* (1934), there's hardly a bridge writer who hasn't attempted to produce the ultimate book on the play of the cards.

Few, if any, have even come close. As far as I am concerned, only three books have stood the test of time: *Goren on Play and Defense, Card Play Technique* by Nico Gardener and Victor Mollo, and *Defensive Play Complete* by Eddie Kantar. All three have a common element: They are written by gifted writers, and those involved are both players of the highest caliber and outstanding teachers!

If it takes a combination of those factors to produce a classic on play, then this book is assured of that status. For Bill Root has not only represented the United States in World Championship competition many times, he has a proven track record as an author and is recognized as the world's premier teacher.

That piqued my curiosity. Although I am not given to reading bridge books, I decided to peruse the manuscript. It was all I expected it to be. Clearly written, well organized and, above all, easily understandable no matter what the level of one's skill.

Over the years, Bill has been able to accumulate an excellent collection of teaching hands. He puts this material to good use here. Each facet of play is broken down to its elements, then the illustrative hands make the theme crystal clear to the reader. And at the end of each chapter there is a quiz to test one's progress as one goes along.

Had the game of bridge been played centuries ago, Omar the Tentmaker would have recommended taking a bridge book into the wilderness. And if he were to come back today and decide to take up the game we all love so, it is quite likely that this would be the book he would choose. Certainly, Omar the Bridge Player enjoyed it.

Omar Sharif

Before You Read This Book

♣　　◇　　♡　　♠　　♣　　◇　　♡　　♠

Please read this section to familiarize yourself with the way tricks are counted in this book. The procedures for counting tricks at notrump contracts and trump contracts are treated separately, but first you must:

Think Before You Play

After the opening lead has been made and the dummy exposed, your first order of business as declarer is to count your tricks and plan your play.[1] This should be done *before you play a card from dummy*. It is not unreasonable to take up to one minute (perhaps longer with an occasional tough hand) before playing a card. Some irascible defenders may complain that you are taking too long, but the defenders themselves should be using the time to plan their defense. Of course you will be considered a slowpoke if you hesitate throughout the play of the hand, but not if you take a little extra time to think before you begin to play.

Counting Tricks at Notrump Contracts

The procedure at notrump contracts is to count the winning tricks in the combined hands and then try to figure out the safest way to develop any extra tricks needed to make your contract.

Here are two illustrations:

---

1. Your objective for the first eleven chapters is to make your bid; disregard overtricks if trying for them jeopardizes the contract.

#1   North
                                            ♠ A 5
                                            ♡ Q J 3
                                            ◊ K J 7 6 4
Contract: three notrump   ♣ 9 4 2

Opening Lead: queen of spades   South
                                            ♠ K 6 2
                                            ♡ A 7
                                            ◊ 10 9 8
                                            ♣ A K Q J 10

You have eight winning tricks: two spades, one heart, and five clubs. Do you see a sure way to get the ninth trick? The answer is to win the first trick in your hand with the king of spades and play the ace of hearts and another heart. The ace of spades will provide an entry to dummy and the queen of hearts will be your ninth trick. Your contract is safe no matter how the missing cards are divided.

If West has the queen of diamonds, you can take twelve tricks by finessing him for the queen. But if the diamond finesse fails, the opponents will have time to establish their spade suit and may win five tricks before you can win nine.

Notice how important it was to count your tricks. The knowledge that you have eight winners and need only one more to make your contract tells you to shun the long diamond suit and develop a sure ninth trick in hearts. If the bid were four, five, or six notrump, you would of course try to establish the diamond suit. The declarer's goal is to make his bid; he should not try for overtricks if it puts his contract in jeopardy.

#2   North
                                            ♠ 7 6 2
                                            ♡ K Q 10 7 3
                                            ◊ 8 7
Contract: three notrump   ♣ K 7 5

Opening Lead: queen of spades   South
                                            ♠ A K
                                            ♡ 8
                                            ◊ A 9 6 5 4 3
                                            ♣ A Q J 2

In this deal, you have seven winners: two spades, one diamond, and four clubs. You can afford to lose the lead only once, so you must ignore the diamond suit; the opponents will establish their spades before you can establish any diamond winners.

The only chance to develop the two needed tricks is to tackle the heart suit. Lead a heart toward dummy at trick two and, if West plays a low heart, *finesse the ten*. If East has the jack of hearts, you will be set (probably down two). If West has the jack of hearts, you will be able to develop two heart tricks and make your bid.

Note that if you play the king or queen of hearts on the first round, you will be limited to one heart trick (barring miracles) even if West has the jack. This would be the correct play if the bid were *two* notrump because it guarantees eight tricks. But in *three* notrump, you essentially would be playing safe to go down only one trick.

Counting Tricks at Trump Contracts

Counting tricks and planning the play are more complex in trump contracts because there are more ways to win (and lose) tricks. The best method for counting tricks in trump contracts is controversial: You may count the *winning* tricks in both hands as you do at notrump contracts, or count the possible *losing* tricks in one hand, or count *both* winners and losers. Few players can count both winners and losers without taking too much time and boring their opponents, so you probably should choose one way or the other unless your conscience tells you it is okay to take more time.

Although a matter of personal preference, I think that counting possible *losers* in one hand is a better teaching method. Therefore it will be used throughout this book. In a vast majority of cases the losers will be counted in the *declarer's* hand — typically the hand with the longer trumps. I shall explain the opposite, "Making Dummy the Master Hand," in Chapter 6.

Here are two examples of counting losers and planning the play:

#3	North
	♠ A 7 2
	♡ 9 8
	◊ 7 6 4
Contract: four spades	♣ Q 9 5 3 2
Opening Lead: king of diamonds	South
	♠ K Q J 10 9
	♡ A K 7 3
	◊ A J
	♣ 8 4

In your own hand (South), you have five losers: two hearts, one diamond, and two clubs. Since the three minor-suit losers are inevitable and you can afford to lose only three tricks, you should plan to dispose of your two heart losers by ruffing them in dummy.

Win the first trick with the ace of diamonds and, before drawing any trumps, cash the ace and king of hearts, and ruff a heart with the seven of spades. Unless hearts divide worse than 5-2, or East has a doubleton heart and the eight of spades (in which case he would overruff the dummy), the contract is cold. Assuming the seven of spades wins the trick, play the low spade from dummy to get to your hand and ruff your last heart with the ace of spades. You now have ten tricks: five spades, two hearts, two heart ruffs, and one diamond.

#4

Contract: four hearts

Opening Lead: king of spades

North
♠ 9 8 4 3
♡ 7 5 4
◇ A 10 2
♣ A 6 3

South
♠ A 10
♡ A K Q J 10
◇ 8 6 5
♣ K 9 2

West overcalls your one-heart opening bid with one spade, and you reach a contract of four hearts. You have four losing tricks: one spade, two diamonds, and one club. The challenge is to eliminate one of these, and this can be done by establishing the eight of spades to obtain a discard.

Here is the full deal with a play-by-play description:

North
♠ 9 8 4 3
♡ 7 5 4
◇ A 10 2
♣ A 6 3

West
♠ K Q J 7 2
♡ 9 6
◇ K Q 3
♣ 8 5 4

East
♠ 6 5
♡ 8 3 2
◇ J 9 7 4
♣ Q J 10 7

South
♠ A 10
♡ A K Q J 10
◇ 8 6 5
♣ K 9 2

Win the first trick with the ace of spades, draw trumps in three rounds, and lead the ten of spades to drive out the jack. Assume West switches to the king of diamonds (no defense is better) and you win with dummy's ace. Next, play the nine of spades and *discard a diamond* as West wins with the queen. West can cash the queen of diamonds, but that is the last trick for the defenders. You will discard your club loser on the eight of spades, which is now high.

1
How to Play Suit Combinations

♣   ◇   ♡   ♠   ♣   ◇   ♡   ♠

Before tackling how to play a bridge hand, it is appropriate to study how to play a single suit. There are thousands of suit combinations and only fifty-five illustrated in this chapter. It would be impractical for any bridge player to try to memorize the best way to play every suit combination; there are just too many of them, and some are so complex that you would be wasting your time trying to figure the odds. Furthermore, the percentage difference between one play and another is often very small. The best approach is to learn the important guidelines described in the following pages, and then try to figure things out for yourself at the table.

Clues from the opponents' bidding and plays are often helpful in deciding how to handle suit combinations, but they will be covered in later chapters. For now, we are concerned with a straightforward analysis of the best way to play a suit with no clues from the enemy.[1]

And just before we commence, if you would like to refer to it, the Percentage Table for Suit Distribution of Outstanding Cards can be found on page 172.

The Finesse

A finesse is an attempt to win a trick with a card that is not high. The correct procedure is to lead toward the high card (or high cards) with which you hope to win a trick (or tricks). Do not lead an *honor* card to take a finesse unless you will benefit if the next player covers.

Here are several examples:

---

[1]. The illustrations in this chapter are all suit combinations, as opposed to the full deals in all the other chapters. North is the dummy and South is the declarer. Unless you are notified otherwise, assume that there are unlimited entries to both hands; you may lead from either hand at will.

#1   North
                                            Q 7

                                            South
                                            A 4 3

Lead a low card from your hand toward the queen. If West has the king, the queen will win a trick; a 50-50 chance.

#2   North
                                            Q J 10

                                            South
                                            A 3 2

Lead the queen, jack, or ten intending to finesse through East for the king. If East has the king, you will win three tricks whether or not he covers your honor-card lead.

#3   North
                                            Q J 6

                                            South
                                            A 7 4 2

Your goal is to win three tricks. The correct play is to lead low from your hand *toward* the queen and jack; if you are allowed to win the first trick with the queen, return to your hand with a different suit and lead another low card toward the jack. If West has the king, you will win three tricks no matter how the suit divides; if East captures your queen with the king, you will need a 3-3 split.

This is a far better play than *leading* the queen or jack. East can cover if he has the king, or the finesse will lose if West has the king, so your only chance for three tricks is that the suit divides 3-3. When you are contemplating leading an honor card to take a finesse, ask yourself: What will I have left if the honor is covered? If you don't like the answer, don't lead the honor card.

#4   North
                                            J 6 5

                                            South
                                            A Q 10 3

The best chance to win four tricks is to lead a *low* card from dummy and, assuming East plays low, finesse the ten (or queen). If the finesse succeeds, return to dummy and lead a second *low* card intending to finesse the queen. It is *wrong* to lead the jack as it will cost you a trick if East has a singleton or doubleton king; he will cover your jack and limit you to three tricks. Leading low cards from dummy may gain a trick and cannot cost an extra trick no matter how the suit divides.

If you held A Q 10 9, it would be safe to lead the jack; if East covers with the king, you have the queen, ten, and *nine* left to win the rest of the tricks.

The correct way to play a suit combination depends on how many tricks you need. For example, how would you play the next combination to win four tricks? How would you play if you need only three tricks?

#5   North
                              A Q 6 3

                              South
                              J 5 4 2

The only chance to win four tricks is to find West with a doubleton king. So lead low from your hand and finesse the queen. If the queen wins, cash the ace and hope for the king to drop. Note that *leading the jack* is a hopeless play; West would cover with the king and there would be no chance for four tricks.

If your goal is to win three tricks, your first play should be the *ace*, in case East has a singleton king. You will always win three tricks if the suit divides 3-2, but cannot win more than two tricks if either defender has four to the king.

#6   North
                              A K 3 2

                              South
                              J 8

If your goal is to win three tricks, lead low from dummy toward the jack. You will win a trick with the jack if East has the queen.

#7   North
                              Q 10 5

                              South
                              K 7 4

If West has the jack, you can win two tricks by finessing the ten. However, your first play should be a low card from dummy as East may contribute the ace or jack and solve your problem. If East plays low when you lead from dummy, put up the king; whether your king wins this trick or West wins with the ace, you will be able to finesse the ten next time the suit is led.

#8   North
                              K J 2

                              South
                              7 6 5

Your first play should be to lead low from your hand to the jack. If East captures the jack with the queen, your next play should be to lead low from your hand to the king. This is the first illustration of a "double finesse." Several more will follow, so it is important that you know the odds. The ace and queen (or any two cards) can be divided four ways:

	West	East
1.	A-Q	—
2.	A	Q
3.	Q	A
4.	—	A-Q

If West has both honors, you will win two tricks; only one chance in four.

If West has one honor, you will win one trick; two chances in four.

If West has neither honor, you will win no tricks; one chance in four.

Note that you will win *at least* one trick in three cases out of four; the odds are 3-to-1 in your favor.

#9
North
A K 10

South
9 5 4

If West has both the queen and jack, you can win three tricks by leading low from your hand and finessing the ten—a double finesse. Since you must find two cards onside, you have only one chance in four; the odds are 3-to-1 against you.

#10
North
A 10 2

South
Q 7 5

Your goal is to win two tricks. The best chance is to lead low from dummy to your queen. If West captures the queen with the king, you should eventually lead low from your hand and finesse the ten. Unless West has the king and East the jack, you will win two tricks.

#11
North
A J 9

South
5 4 2

The best play to win two tricks is to lead low from your hand and finesse the nine—a "triple finesse." If East wins with the king or queen, you will next lead low from your hand and finesse the jack. If West has the king-ten, queen-ten, or king-queen-ten, you will win two tricks. The odds are against you; but the chances are much better than a first-round finesse of the jack, which would succeed only if West had the king and queen.

#12

North
Q 4 3 2

South
A 10 9 8

The best play to win three tricks is to take repeated finesses through East. Lead dummy's two to your ten (or nine or eight). Assuming West wins with the jack, you should eventually lead the queen to finesse through East again. You will succeed if East has either the king or jack (or both), 3-to-1 odds in your favor.

Note: With fewer cards between the two hands, you should still finesse twice through East. However, with *nine* total cards, the best play is to cash the ace first, and then lead toward the queen.

Lead Toward Honor Cards

#13

North
Q J 5 3

South
K 7 4

If the opponents capture the king, queen, or jack with the ace, your only chance to win three tricks is if the suit divides 3-3. If you can force out the ace without using one of your honor cards, you can win three tricks regardless of how the suit divides. The best play is to lead a low card from your hand toward the queen-jack and, if you are allowed to win this trick with the queen (or jack), come back to your hand *by playing a different suit* and lead another low card toward the jack. If West has a singleton or doubleton ace, he will have to play it and you will win three tricks even though the suit does not divide 3-3. Note that leading toward your king is not as good because you can do it only once.

#14

North
K 6 5 4

South
Q 7 3 2

The only chance to win three tricks with this combination is to find either opponent with a doubleton ace, but you must *guess* which way to play. If you decide West has the doubleton ace, lead low from your hand and, if West plays low, put up the king. If the king wins the trick, lead low from dummy and *duck* in your hand on the way back; do not play the queen. If West started with a doubleton, he will have to play his ace and you will have your three tricks. If you decide East has the doubleton ace, you should reverse this procedure; begin by leading a low card from dummy.

To Finesse, or to Play for the Drop

Sometimes you must decide whether to finesse for an honor, or to play for it to drop. The combined length of the suit enters the picture.

For example:

#15

North
A Q 10 5

South
K 2

Your goal here is to win four tricks and, after cashing the king, the question is whether to finesse the ten or play the ace-queen and hope the jack drops. The percentage play is to finesse the ten. Since the opponents began with seven cards in the suit, the 50-50 chance that the finesse will work is better than the hope that the defender with fewer than four cards has the jack.

#16

North
A Q 10 4

South
K 7 3

You cash the ace and king and the jack does not fall. Then you lead toward dummy's queen-ten and West follows with a low card. Since the opponents began with only six cards, the odds are slightly in favor that East has the jack; so playing the queen offers a better chance than the finesse.

#17

North
A 10 9 8

South
K J 5 2

You have two ways to finesse for the queen and must guess which defender has it, but your first play should be to cash the ace or king, in case the queen is singleton. Assuming the queen does not drop, lead toward the remaining honor (king or ace) with the intention of finessing if second hand follows suit with a low card. When there are five cards missing, the odds are strongly in favor of finessing, rather than cashing the ace-king and hoping the queen drops.

#18

North
K J 4

South
A 10 8 5 2

This may appear to be another two-way finesse, but the odds favor playing East for the queen because you can run the suit without losing a trick even if he has four to the queen. First cash the king and then lead the jack, intending to finesse. If East covers the jack with the queen, win with the ace. Then if West shows out, you will return to dummy in a different suit and finesse the eight.

Note that if your first play is the ace, you cannot pick up the suit if West started with four to the queen.

#19   North
                                      A K J 10 7 5

                                    South
                                    4 2

Again you are missing five cards including the queen and should finesse, but this time you should not cash the ace or king before you finesse, or else you will be able to finesse only once. If West has Q x x x you will have to finesse twice to pick up the suit, and this holding is much more likely than finding East with a singleton queen.

#20   North
                                      A K J 10 7 5

                                    South
                                    6 3 2

Your first play is to cash the ace (or king) in case the queen drops or East shows out. If both players follow with low cards, cash the king and hope that the queen will drop. Holding nine cards, the odds slightly favor playing to drop an outstanding queen.

#21   North
                                      A Q J 10 9

                                    South
                                    8 6 5 4 2

Suppose you lead a low card from your hand and West follows with a low card. You can avoid losing a trick by going up with the ace if East has a singleton king, or by finessing if East has a singleton spot card or a void suit. With ten cards in the combined hands, there are more combinations where the finesse will succeed; so the odds are substantially in favor of finessing.

#22   North
                                      A Q J 10 9

                                    South
                                    8 7 5 4 3 2

Once again you lead low from your hand, and West follows with the missing low card. You can avoid losing a trick by playing the ace if East has the king, or by finessing if he is void in the suit. It is almost a toss-up, but with eleven cards in the suit the odds slightly favor going up with the ace; two cards will divide 1-1 52 percent of the time and 2-0 48 percent of the time.

Since this is an easy one to understand, here is an explanation of the way the odds are figured. After West follows suit with the low card, he has 12 unknown cards left in his hand while East has 13. So there are 12 chances out of 25 (which equals 48 percent) that West has the king and 13 chances out of 25 (which equals 52 percent) that East has the king. These odds assume there is nothing revealing about the enemy distribution from the bidding or earlier plays in other suits.

#23   North
                                         A J 9 5 4

                                         South
                                         Q 7 6 3 2

As in illustration 21, you are missing three cards including the king, and the percentage play is to finesse. However, your first play should be to lead the queen to guard against West having K 10 8. If your first play were low to the jack, West would have a sure trick if his remaining cards were the king-ten. Here is a rare case where leading an unsupported honor may gain a trick and cannot lose.

Restricted Choice

#24   North
                                         A J 10

                                         South
                                         8 7 5

Here is a rather easy combination to play. By taking a double finesse, you can win two tricks if West has either or both missing honors — 3-to-1 odds in your favor.

Suppose you finesse the ten and East wins with the king. What are the odds that the second finesse will succeed?

Originally there were four possibilities: East could have king-queen, king, queen, or neither. However, once East wins the king there are only two possibilities left: East has the king-queen or just the king. Therefore, it appears that the chances of the second finesse working are about even. Actually they are roughly 2-to-1 in your favor.

These odds are based on the Principle of Restricted Choice, which states: If you lead a suit in which you are missing two *equivalent* cards (as the king-queen), the defender who first plays one of them is less likely to hold the other. To illustrate: If in 100 deals East holds the king and queen, he has a choice of plays; he might win with the king about 50 times and with the queen about 50 times. If in 100 deals East holds just the king, his choice is restricted; if he wants to win the trick, he must always play the king. Therefore, the fact that he won with the king makes it more likely that he did so from a holding without the queen. This reasoning may not convince you, but it is mathematically sound and has proven to be accurate in practice.

The next three combinations are further examples of restricted choice:

#25   North
                                 K 10 9

                                 South
                                 4 3 2

Your goal is to win one trick and the best play is to finesse through West for the queen and jack. Lead low from your hand and finesse the nine. Suppose East wins the queen or jack, and later you lead low toward the king-ten. Should you finesse the ten or put up the king? It may seem like a tossup, but the ten is the percentage play. The queen and jack are equivalent cards, so when East plays one of them, *West* is a favorite to have the other.

#26   North
                                 A Q 9 8

                                 South
                                 K 5 3

Your first two plays should be to cash the ace and king. If East does not drop the jack or ten, you have no choice but to cash the queen and hope for a 3-3 split.

Now suppose East does play the ten on the second lead, and West follows suit with a low card when you lead toward the queen-nine. East started with J 10 x or 10 x, and you must decide whether to go up with the queen or finesse the nine. Before reading further, which would you do?

Once again, it may seem like a tossup, but based on restricted choice the odds are substantially in favor of finessing. If East started with J 10 x, he may have played the ten or jack on the second lead; while if he started with 10 x, his choice was restricted to the ten. (Compare with illustration 16, which is not a restricted-choice situation.)

#27   North
                                 6 5 3 2

                                 South
                                 A K 10 9 8

Let's assume you cash the ace and West follows with the queen or jack. Your next play in the suit should be to lead from dummy and finesse East for the missing honor. Since the queen and jack are equals, the odds are roughly 2-to-1 that East holds the missing honor.

Safety Plays

When you play a suit in a manner that guards against a bad division of the enemy cards, it is called a "safety play." Sometimes this is nothing more than the correct percentage play to win the maximum number of tricks. For example:

#28   North
                                       A J 7 6 4

                                       South
                                       K 9 8 5 2

Your first play should be the king to guard against West having Q 10 3. Only if East has Q 10 3 will you lose a trick, in which case there is nothing you can do about it.

#29   North
                                       A K 10 6 5

                                       South
                                       Q 9 7 4

You can avoid losing a trick no matter how the suit divides if your first play is to cash the ace or king. If either defender shows out, you will be able to finesse the other out of his jack.
    Note that if you begin by leading the queen, you will lose a trick if East holds J 8 3 2.

#30   North
                                       A K 8 6 5

                                       South
                                       Q 9 7 4

This looks like the previous example, except now you are missing the ten as well as the jack. If your first play is the queen, you can avoid losing a trick if West has J 10 3 2; East will show out and you will have the marked double finesse with dummy's A K 8 6 behind West's J 10 3. There is no way to avoid losing a trick if East has J 10 3 2.
    Note that if your first play is the ace or king, you will lose a trick if either defender has J 10 3 2. It will be worth your while to compare examples 29 and 30.

#31   North
                                       J 5 3 2

                                       South
                                       K Q 8 7 6

If West has A 10 9 4, there is no way to avoid losing two tricks. If East has A 10 9 4, you can hold your losers to one trick if your first play is the jack. But you will lose two tricks if your first play is the king or queen.

There is another kind of safety play where you maneuver a suit combination in an unusual way to win a certain number of tricks, rather than always trying to win as many tricks as possible. This depends on how many tricks you need. You have already seen a case of this in example 5, and here are several more. So that you can challenge yourself before reading the explanations, the targeted number of tricks is given for examples 32 through 38.

#32   **North**
                                       Q 8 7 6 5
Target: four tricks
                                       South
                                       A 10 4 3 2

Suppose the contract is six notrump and you need four out of five tricks in this suit; the rest of the suits are solid. There is a safety play to guarantee the contract no matter how the suit divides.

Lead a low card from dummy: If East plays the nine, finesse the ten to guard against his holding K J 9. If East plays the king or jack, win with the ace. If East shows out (West has K J 9), go up with the ace and lead toward dummy's queen. You could also achieve your objective if your first play in the suit is a low card from your hand toward dummy's queen; but this is not as good as it needlessly loses an overtrick if East has the blank king.

If you need to win five tricks with this combination, the best play is to lay down the ace and hope to drop a singleton king; the odds are substantially against you, but it is your best chance. Note that if West has the blank jack, the winning play is to lead the queen; but logically it is better to play for *either* defender to have a blank king than for one defender to have a blank jack.

#33   **North**
                                       8 5 4 2
Target: four tricks
                                       South
                                       A Q 7 6 3

If you need four tricks to make your contract, there is no sure way — but there is a safety play to improve your chances. Cash the ace — in case West has a singleton king — and, if the king does not fall, cross over to dummy in a different suit and lead toward the queen. Unless West has three cards including the king, or the suit divides 4-0, you will win four tricks.

If you need five tricks, lead low from dummy and finesse the queen. You will succeed only if East started with a doubleton king.

#34   **North**
                                       Q J 3 2
Target: four tricks
                                       South
                                       A 9 6 5 4

The safety play to insure four tricks no matter how the suit divides is to lead a low card from your hand toward the queen-jack. If your first lead is the ace, you will lose two tricks if East has K 10 8 7. If your first lead is the queen or jack, you will lose two tricks if West has K 10 8 7.

If you need five tricks in the suit, lead the queen and hope East has a doubleton king or K 8 7.

#35   North
                                                  6 3
Target: five tricks
                                                  South
                                                  A K 10 9 7 2

If your goal is to win five tricks, there is a safety play to guard against any 4-1 break except if West has the Q J x x *behind* you. Start by cashing the ace (or king). Assuming the queen or jack does not show up, cross to dummy in a different suit and lead a low card toward your hand. If East plays low, finesse the ten. If East plays the queen or jack, win with the king.

To win six tricks you must be lucky. The best chance is to lead from dummy with the intention of taking a double finesse against East. You will succeed only if East has Q J or Q J x.

#36   North
                                                  J 6 5
Target: four tricks
                                                  South
                                                  A K 9 3 2

If you require four tricks, there is a safety play to guard against either defender having Q 10 x x. Cash the ace (or king) and, if both defenders follow with low cards, lead a low card from your hand toward the jack. If West shows out on the second lead, you will play the jack in dummy. East can win this trick with his queen, but you will eventually finesse him out of his ten.

If you need five tricks the odds are substantially against you, but the best play is to cash the ace and, unless the queen drops, continue with the king and hope the queen falls.

#37   North
                                                  K 9 3 2
Target: three tricks
                                                  South
                                                  A J 5 4

Again there is a safety play to insure three tricks if either defender has Q 10 x x. Cash the ace and lead a low card toward dummy. If West follows with a low card, finesse the nine. If West follows with the ten or queen, win with the king. If West shows out (East still has Q 10 x), go up with the king and lead toward your jack.

The best play to win four tricks is to lead low from dummy and finesse the jack (unless East plays the queen — then win with the ace and cash the jack). You will succeed if East has one, two, or three cards including the queen.

#38   North
                                       A J 4 3
Target: three tricks
                                       South
                                       K 5 2

The safety play to give you the best chance to win three tricks is to cash the ace and king—in that order—and then to lead toward the jack. This play gains when there is a doubleton queen behind the jack. Only if East has four or more cards including the queen can you be prevented from winning three tricks.

If your contract depends on winning four tricks, your chances are slim; the suit must divide 3-3 and West must have the queen. After cashing the king (nonessential, but good technique), finesse the jack.

When Entry Cards Are Limited

So far in this chapter it has been assumed that declarer has unlimited entries to both hands. The following four illustrations show how to play suit combinations when entries are a problem.

#39   North
                                       J 9 3

                                       South
                                       A Q 10 5

Suppose the lead is in dummy for the last time and you need four tricks in this suit. The correct play is to lead the *nine* as this will allow you to win four tricks if East has the king, no matter how many cards he has in the suit. If the nine wins, your next lead of the jack will allow the lead to remain in dummy for a third finesse, if it is necessary.

Note that if you lead the jack first and it wins the trick, you are left with the nine-three in dummy and ace-queen-ten in your hand. After the second finesse the lead will be in your hand. You cannot take a third finesse and will lose a trick if East still has the guarded king.

#40   North
                                       A 10 7

                                       South
                                       K Q 9 3 2

This time you have no side entries to your hand and need five tricks from this suit. To guard against East holding J x x x, your first play should be to cash the king (or queen) and unblock the *ten* from dummy. Then lead a low card to dummy's ace. If West shows out, East is left with J x. With the seven-spot in dummy and the Q 9 3 in your hand, you can finesse the nine and win five tricks. If you do not unblock, you will have the Q 9 3 in your hand and the *ten-spot* in dummy. When you lead the ten, East will not cover holding J x, and you will be limited to three tricks.

This hand illustrates a fundamental rule that is not always so obvious: When running a long suit, save a low card in the short hand to play last so you don't block the suit.

#41   North
                                         10 8 7 3

                                         South
                                         K J 9 5 2

This time there are no entries to dummy and the lead is in your hand. The only chance to win four tricks is to lead the king and hope there is a singleton queen.

#42   North
                                         7 3 2

                                         South
                                         Q J 8 6 5 4

Once again there are no entries to dummy and you must play the suit from your hand. Before reading further, which card would you lead first, and why? If the suit divides 2-2, or if either defender has A K 10 or A K 9, you will win the same number of tricks no matter which card you lead. But if either defender has a singleton ace or king, you can save a trick if your first lead is a *low* card. With the queen-jack still in your hand, you can limit the defender with ace-ten (or king-ten) to one more trick.

When an Opponent Leads the Suit

An enemy lead sometimes provides a chance to win a trick that you cannot win if you have to lead the suit yourself.

For example:

#43   North
                                         K 10 2
            West   East
            Q J 9 8   7 6 5
                                         South
                                         A 4 3

West leads the queen. You can now win three tricks by capturing the queen with your ace and finessing the ten.

#44   North
                                         K 4 2
            West   East
            Q 10 8 3   A 9 7
                                         South
                                         J 6 5

West leads the three. If your first play from dummy is a low card, you can be sure of one trick. As the cards lie, you cannot win a trick unless an opponent leads the suit.

The best way to play a suit combination is usually less challenging when an opponent leads the suit, but some skill may be required. In the following eleven illustrations, which card should you play from dummy at trick one?

#45   North
                                       A Q 2
West leads the three
                                       South
                                       10 5 4

Your first play from dummy should be the two. This allows you to win an extra trick if West has led from the jack or the king-jack. However, if you must win two tricks and cannot afford to lose the lead, play the queen.

#46   North
                                       A J 2
West leads the three
                                       South
                                       K 9 4

Again you should play the two from dummy. This gains a trick if West has led from the ten and East has the queen.

#47   North
                                       A 10 2
West leads the three
                                       South
                                       K 9 4

By playing low from dummy, you can win three tricks if West has led from the queen, jack, or queen-jack. Note that there is very little hope to win more than two tricks if you lead the suit yourself; you must find a singleton queen, a singleton jack, or a doubleton queen-jack — and even then you must guess how to play.

#48   North
                                       Q 2
West leads the three
                                       South
                                       A 10 4

By playing the two from dummy, you can win two tricks no matter how the cards lie. If East plays the jack, you win with the ace; then the queen and ten will ensure a second trick. If your first play is the queen, you will be limited to one trick if East has the king and West the jack.

#49   North
                                           Q 2
West leads the three
                                           South
                                           A 5 4

The only chance to win two tricks is to go up with dummy's queen and hope that West has led from the king. If your first play from dummy is the two, East will play the jack, ten, or nine, and your queen will be useless.

#50   North
                                           Q 4 2
West leads the three
                                           South
                                           A 6 5

Now that the dummy has a third card in the suit, the best play is not obvious. In most cases you should play low from dummy; you will still be able to win a trick with the queen if West has the king, with a few other chances. However, some contracts may hinge on keeping your ace to control the suit, in which case it would be right to play the queen immediately.

#51   North
                                           Q 10 2
West leads the three
                                           South
                                           A 5 4

With this combination you can win two tricks unless East has both the king and jack, provided you play an honor from dummy at trick one. In most cases playing the ten will work out as well or better, but playing the queen is right if you suspect that West has the king and you cannot afford to release the ace. If you play the ten and East covers with the jack, win with the ace; you can still win a trick with the queen if West has the king.

Note that it would be wrong to play low from dummy, as East would most likely play the eight or nine to drive out your ace. If you later lead toward the queen-ten and the honors are split (West has one and East has one), West will play low and you will have to *guess* whether to play the ten or queen.

#52   North
                                           J 2
West leads the three
                                           South
                                           A 5 4

The only chance to win a trick with the jack is to play it on the first trick and hope West has led from the king-queen. True, leading a low card when holding the king-queen is unlikely against a suit contract, but it is fairly common as an opening lead against a notrump contract.

#53   North
                                       J 10 2
West leads the three
                                       South
                                       A 5 4

Play the jack (or ten) from dummy. If East covers, win with the ace and eventually lead toward the ten. You will win two tricks unless East has both the king and queen.

#54   North
                                       J 9 2
West leads the three
                                       South
                                       A 5 4

The best play is the nine from dummy. You will win a second trick if West has led from the king-ten or queen-ten. If your first play from dummy is the jack, you will win two tricks only if West has led from the king-queen. Playing the nine gives you two chances instead of one.

#55   North
                                       K 2
West leads the three
                                       South
                                       J 4

If this is an opening lead versus a suit contract, you should play low from dummy; defenders rarely underlead aces at the first trick. At notrump, however, it is a close decision; West might have the ace. But it is still probably better to play low; my opinion is that good players are more likely to lead from Q x x x than A x x x.

Note: If West makes this lead with the dummy in view (after the opening lead), the above reasoning does not hold. It is then a pure guess.

Quiz for Chapter One

1.

North
♠ J 10 3
♡ 7 4
◇ A Q 9 5 4
♣ Q 8 6

South
♠ A K Q
♡ A 8 2
◇ K 10 6
♣ 5 4 3 2

West	North	East	South
			1 NT
Pass	3 NT	All Pass	

West leads the king of hearts.

2.

North
♠ A Q J 6 3
♡ K J 8 2
◇ K 7 4
♣ 5

South
♠ K
♡ Q 7 6 5 4
◇ A Q 10 2
♣ A Q 8

West	North	East	South
	1 ♠	Pass	2 ♡
Pass	4 ♡	Pass	4 NT
Pass	5 ◇	Pass	6 ♡
All Pass			

West leads the jack of clubs.

3.

North
♠ A 4
♡ A J 10 2
◇ K 9 4
♣ J 8 6 5

South
♠ K 7
♡ Q 6 5
◇ A 8 5 2
♣ A 7 4 2

West	North	East	South
			1 ◇
Pass	1 ♡	Pass	1 NT
Pass	3 NT	All Pass	

West leads the jack of spades.

4.

North
♠ A 8 5 4 3 2
♡ 9 5 2
◇ 4
♣ K 7 6

South
♠ 6
♡ K 3
◇ A K Q 10 7 5 2
♣ A 8 5

West	North	East	South
			1 ◇
Pass	1 ♠	Pass	3 NT
All Pass			

West leads the queen of clubs.

5.

North
♠ 9 6 3
♡ A Q 10
♢ K J 6 2
♣ 5 4 2

South
♠ A K
♡ K J 2
♢ Q 5 3
♣ A 9 8 7 6

West	*North*	*East*	*South*
			1 NT
Pass	3 NT	All Pass	

West leads the five of spades.

6.

North
♠ A 9 7
♡ K 8 5
♢ 6 3
♣ A K J 4 2

South
♠ K J 5 3 2
♡ A 4
♢ A K Q J
♣ 9 3

West	*North*	*East*	*South*
			1 ♠
Pass	2 ♣	Pass	2 ♢
Pass	3 ♠	Pass	4 NT
Pass	5 ♡	Pass	6 ♠
All Pass			

West leads the queen of hearts.

7.

North
♠ —
♡ 10 8 7 3
♢ Q 9 4
♣ A 10 8 6 5 2

South
♠ A J 10 7 6 5 2
♡ —
♢ A K J 10
♣ 4 3

West	*North*	*East*	*South*
			1 ♠
Pass	1 NT	Pass	4 ♠
All Pass			

West leads the king of hearts.

8.

North
♠ Q J
♡ 10 4 3
♢ K 9 7 6 5
♣ J 10 4

South
♠ A 8
♡ Q J 9 7
♢ A 10 4 2
♣ A K Q

West	*North*	*East*	*South*
			2 NT
Pass	3 NT	All Pass	

West leads the four of spades and East plays the king.

Answers to Quiz for Chapter One

1.   North
                     ♠ J 10 3
                     ♡ 7 4
                     ◇ A Q 9 5 4
                     ♣ Q 8 6

West   East
♠ 9 5   ♠ 8 7 6 4 2
♡ K Q J 10   ♡ 9 6 5 3
◇ J 8 3 2   ◇ 7
♣ K J 7   ♣ A 10 9

                     South
                     ♠ A K Q
                     ♡ A 8 2
                     ◇ K 10 6
                     ♣ 5 4 3 2

West	North	East	South
			1 NT
Pass	3 NT	All Pass	

West leads the king of hearts.

---

2.   North
                     ♠ A Q J 6 3
                     ♡ K J 8 2
                     ◇ K 7 4
                     ♣ 5

West   East
♠ 7 5 2   ♠ 10 9 8 4
♡ A 10 9 3   ♡ —
◇ 8 6 3   ◇ J 9 5
♣ J 10 9   ♣ K 7 6 4 3 2

                     South
                     ♠ K
                     ♡ Q 7 6 5 4
                     ◇ A Q 10 2
                     ♣ A Q 8

West	North	East	South
	1 ♠	Pass	2 ♡
Pass	4 ♡	Pass	4 NT
Pass	5 ◇	Pass	6 ♡
All Pass			

West leads the jack of clubs.

You need five diamond tricks to make three notrump; there is no other way. If diamonds divide 3-2, there is no problem; and if East has four to the jack, there is no chance. It is when West has four diamonds to the jack that it is still possible to win five tricks, but you must make a good unblocking play.

Hold-up plays in hearts would jeopardize your contract, so you win the first trick with the ace of hearts. Now lead the *ten* of diamonds to dummy's ace and return a low diamond to your king (or cash the king first and then lead the ten). When East shows out on the second diamond lead, you know that West still has the jack-eight. Since you have the six-spot in your hand and queen-nine-five in dummy, you can finesse the nine and run five diamond tricks.

Note that if your first two diamond plays from your hand are the six and the king (leaving yourself with the lone ten), you block the suit. Since there are no side entries to dummy, West can limit you to three diamond tricks by not covering with the jack when you lead the ten.

The only possible losers are hearts, so it is a cinch to make this slam if trumps divide 2-2 or 3-1. Only a 4-0 heart break poses a problem. As this happens about one time in ten, you should assume for the moment that it will happen and see if there is anything you can do about it.

If East has all four hearts, you will lose two tricks no matter how you play the suit. But if West has the four hearts, you can hold your losers to one trick by playing the *queen* of hearts first. If West covers your queen with his ace, you can win the rest of the tricks by taking a double finesse; the dummy is left with K J 8 behind his 10 9 3. If West ducks when you lead the queen of hearts, dummy is left with the K J 8 behind his A 10 9; again he can win only one trick.

Note that if your first heart play is the king or jack, you will be set.

You have six winners (two spades, one heart, two diamonds, and one club) and the heart finesse must work or you will be set. If West has four or more hearts including the king, you can win only three heart tricks no matter how you play; West will cover the queen when it is led. It is when West has one or two hearts that it makes a difference how you play the heart suit.

Win the first trick with the king of spades, play a *low* heart and finesse the ten (or jack). Return to your hand with a minor-suit ace and lead another *low* heart. Since West must play the king, you now have the four heart tricks you need to make your bid.

Note that leading low hearts cannot possibly cost a trick, but if you mistakenly lead the queen, West will cover with the king and limit you to three heart tricks.

3.

```
              North
              ♠ A 4
              ♡ A J 10 2
              ◇ K 9 4
              ♣ J 8 6 5
West                        East
♠ J 10 9 8 3                ♠ Q 6 5 2
♡ K 4                       ♡ 9 8 7 3
◇ Q 10 7 6                  ◇ J 3
♣ 9 3                       ♣ K Q 10
              South
              ♠ K 7
              ♡ Q 6 5
              ◇ A 8 5 2
              ♣ A 7 4 2
```

West	North	East	South
			1 ◇
Pass	1 ♡	Pass	1 NT
Pass	3 NT	All Pass	

West leads the jack of spades.

If diamonds divide 3-2 (or the jack is single-ton), you can run seven diamond tricks and make three notrump with an overtrick. But only *six* diamond tricks are needed to make your bid. In case it is necessary to give up a diamond trick, you have two things to consider: First, you will need an entry back to your hand to win the rest of your diamonds. Second, you must keep East off lead if possible, as a heart lead from him will set you if West has the ace.

To start, win the opening club lead with dummy's king and save the ace in case you need an entry to your hand. Now, to guard against East having four diamonds to the jack, lead a diamond and *finesse the ten*. Since the finesse works, you have ten tricks. If West has the jack of diamonds and wins the trick, the contract will be safe; regardless of what he returns, you will be able to run off at least nine tricks.

4.

```
              North
              ♠ A 8 5 4 3 2
              ♡ 9 5 2
              ◇ 4
              ♣ K 7 6
West                        East
♠ Q 10 9 7                  ♠ K J
♡ A 8 4                     ♡ Q J 10 7 6
◇ 6                         ◇ J 9 8 3
♣ Q J 10 9 3                ♣ 4 2
              South
              ♠ 6
              ♡ K 3
              ◇ A K Q 10 7 5 2
              ♣ A 8 5
```

West	North	East	South
			1 ◇
Pass	1 ♠	Pass	3 NT
All Pass			

West leads the queen of clubs.

5.
```
              North
              ♠ 9 6 3
              ♡ A Q 10
              ◇ K J 6 2
              ♣ 5 4 2
West                          East
♠ Q 10 7 5 4                  ♠ J 8 2
♡ 9 8 4 3                     ♡ 7 6 5
◇ A 7                         ◇ 10 9 8 4
♣ J 3                         ♣ K Q 10
              South
              ♠ A K
              ♡ K J 2
              ◇ Q 5 3
              ♣ A 9 8 7 6
```

West	North	East	South
			1 NT
Pass	3 NT	All Pass	

West leads the five of spades.

You have six winners (two spades, three hearts, and one club) and the only realistic chance to make your bid is to win three diamond tricks. If diamonds divide 3-3, the fourth diamond in dummy will provide the third trick. If the suit divides 4-2 or 5-1, the only chance is to force out the ace without playing one of your honor cards; then you can three tricks with the king, queen, and jack. The way to do this is to lead *toward* honor cards and hope that second hand goes up with the ace.

In this case the dummy has two diamond honors, so it is better to lead toward the dummy because you can do it twice. The idea is to make West play before the dummy; if he has a singleton or doubleton ace of diamonds (or greater length and foolishly rises with his ace), you will not waste an honor when the ace appears. After winning the opening spade lead, play a low diamond toward dummy and, assuming West plays low, win with the jack (or king).Now return to your hand with a heart and lead a second low diamond. With the cards as shown in the diagram, West must play the ace and you will make your bid. If the ace of diamonds does not appear on the first or second round, you will have no choice but to play a third diamond and hope for a 3-3 split.

6.
```
              North
              ♠ A 9 7
              ♡ K 8 5
              ◇ 6 3
              ♣ A K J 4 2
West                          East
♠ Q 10 8 4                    ♠ 6
♡ Q J 10 2                    ♡ 9 7 6 3
◇ 9 4                         ◇ 10 8 7 5 2
♣ 7 6 5                       ♣ Q 10 8
              South
              ♠ K J 5 3 2
              ♡ A 4
              ◇ A K Q J
              ♣ 9 3
```

West	North	East	South
			1 ♠
Pass	2 ♣	Pass	2 ◇
Pass	3 ♠	Pass	4 NT
Pass	5 ♡	Pass	6 ♠
All Pass			

West leads the queen of hearts.

You have no losers in the side suits, so your goal is to limit your trump losers to one trick. If spades divide 3-2, you cannot go wrong. It is when a defender holds Q 10 x x that you may lose two tricks—but there is a safety play to guard against any 4-1 split.

After winning the first trick, cash the *king* of spades and then lead a low spade toward dummy: (1) If West plays an honor, win with the ace. (2) If West follows with a low spade, finesse the *nine* to guard against West still having the queen and ten; if East wins with the queen or ten, it will be your only loser. (3) If West shows out (East still has Q 10 x), go up with dummy's ace and lead a third round of spades toward your jack; East can win only one trick with his queen.

7.

	North	
	♠ —	
	♡ 10 8 7 3	
	◇ Q 9 4	
	♣ A 10 8 6 5 2	
West		East
♠ K 4		♠ Q 9 8 3
♡ K Q J 6 4		♡ A 9 5 2
◇ 8 5 2		◇ 7 6 3
♣ Q 9 7		♣ K J
	South	
	♠ A J 10 7 6 5 2	
	♡ —	
	◇ A K J 10	
	♣ 4 3	

West	*North*	*East*	*South*
			1 ♠
Pass	1 NT	Pass	4 ♠
All Pass			

West leads the king of hearts.

Your goal here is to limit your spade losers to two tricks. If the suit divides 3-3, it is easy; but you can also succeed if the suit divides 4-2 provided the opponent with the doubleton has at least one honor.

After ruffing the first trick, cash the ace of spades and then lead a *low* spade. If you make the mistake of leading the jack or ten, you will be set unless the suit divides 3-3. With the cards as shown in the diagram, the low spade lead gets the money. After West wins with the king, East is left with queen-nine and you with J 10 x x. When you regain the lead, play the jack of spades to drive out East's queen; and eventually you will draw East's last trump with the ten.

8.

	North	
	♠ Q J	
	♡ 10 4 3	
	◇ K 9 7 6 5	
	♣ J 10 4	
West		East
♠ 10 9 6 4 3		♠ K 7 5 2
♡ K 6		♡ A 8 5 2
◇ Q J 8 3		◇ —
♣ 6 2		♣ 9 8 7 5 3
	South	
	♠ A 8	
	♡ Q J 9 7	
	◇ A 10 4 2	
	♣ A K Q	

West	*North*	*East*	*South*
			2 NT
Pass	3 NT	All Pass	

West leads the four of spades and East plays the king.

You have seven winners: two spades, two diamonds, and three clubs. With the spade lead, you do not have *time* to develop any heart tricks; however, the diamond suit will provide the two extra tricks you need. Since you need only four diamonds tricks, there is a safety play to guard against the only distribution than can hurt you: a 4-0 break. After capturing East's king of spades with the ace, lead a *low* diamond from your hand. If West follows with a low diamond, play the *nine* from dummy. If East shows out (as shown in the diagram), West is limited to one diamond trick. If West shows out on the first diamond lead, you can limit your diamond losers to one by winning with dummy's king and leading a diamond toward your hand. Finally, if East wins the first trick with the queen or jack (the suit does not divide 4-0), you are left with four sure diamond tricks.

With the cards as shown, you can also make this bid if your first diamond play is the ace, but that is wrong because you will be set if East has the four diamonds.

2

Blocking the Opponents' Communication

♣ ◇ ♡ ♠ ♣ ◇ ♡ ♠

In the course of developing the tricks you need to make your contract, it may be necessary to give up the lead one or more times. There are various ways to block the opponents' communication (so when they get the lead they cannot win enough tricks to set you), or at least to make it safe to give up the lead to one of the defenders. When one defender on lead can set you but the other cannot, you must keep the dangerous opponent from getting the lead if possible. Here's how to do it.

The Hold-Up Play at Notrump Contracts

One of the most common ways to block the opponents' communication is the hold-up play. It is most often used in notrump contracts to exhaust one defender's hand of all the cards he has in the suit that his side is leading. Then, if that defender ever gets the lead, he will be unable to play the suit. To get started, here is a fundamental example:

#1	North
	♠ K 7 2
	♡ A 6 5
	◇ 9 4
Contract: three notrump	♣ A Q 10 8 3
Opening Lead: six of diamonds	South
	♠ A Q 9
	♡ K 7 3
	◇ A 10 5
	♣ J 9 6 2

You have seven winners and must tackle the club suit to get the two extra tricks you need. Suppose East plays the queen of diamonds on the first trick: If you win with your ace, the contract is safe if diamonds divide 4-4, but you will be set if the club finesse fails and West started with five or six diamonds. So you should hold up your ace until the third time the suit is led in an effort to exhaust the East hand of diamonds. Then, you will make your bid even if West has five or six diamonds and the club finesse fails.

Suppose the four hands are:

```
                        North
                        ♠ K 7 2
                        ♡ A 6 5
                        ◇ 9 4
                        ♣ A Q 10 8 3
West                                        East
♠ J 6 4 3                                   ♠ 10 8 5
♡ 10 8 4                                    ♡ Q J 9 2
◇ K J 7 6 2                                 ◇ Q 8 3
♣ 5                                         ♣ K 7 4
                        South
                        ♠ A Q 9
                        ♡ K 7 3
                        ◇ A 10 5
                        ♣ J 9 6 2
```

Note that East will get the lead with the king of clubs before you can establish nine tricks. If you do not hold up twice in diamonds, you will be set; East will still have a diamond to lead and the opponents will win four diamond tricks.

In the last hand you had five cards in the enemy suit and it was clearly right to hold up your ace twice. When you have six cards in the enemy suit, it may be right to hold up your ace only once. For example:

```
#2                      North
                        ♠ 9 7 5
                        ♡ Q 3
                        ◇ K J 10 8 2
Contract: three notrump ♣ K J 9

Opening Lead: six of spades  South
                        ♠ A 4 3
                        ♡ A 7 5
                        ◇ Q 9 6
                        ♣ A Q 10 2
```

You have six winners and must develop the diamond suit to make your bid. When East plays the queen of spades on the first trick, you hold up. East then leads the ten of spades and you should win the second trick; do not hold up a second time. If West has a five-card spade suit and the ace of diamonds, the contract cannot be made no matter how many times you hold up. If spades divide 4-3, the contract is safe if you win the first or second spade lead; the opponents can win only three spade tricks. It is when West has a five-card spade suit and East has the ace of diamonds that it will make a difference; then, winning the second spade lead is the only way to insure the contract.

Look at the full deal to see what might happen if you hold up twice.

North
♠ 9 7 5
♡ Q 3
◇ K J 10 8 2
♣ K J 9

West
♠ K J 8 6 2
♡ J 10 4
◇ 5 3
♣ 8 6 4

East
♠ Q 10
♡ K 9 8 6 2
◇ A 7 4
♣ 7 5 3

South
♠ A 4 3
♡ A 7 5
◇ Q 9 6
♣ A Q 10 2

You may think it doesn't make any difference whether you win the second or third spade trick, but put yourself in the West seat to see what a good defender would do if you duck. With no entry in his hand it would be futile to lead a third round of spades, so he would win the second spade trick and switch to the jack of hearts. If East has the ace or king of hearts plus the right spot cards, heart tricks can be established. As the card lie, you would be set *three* tricks if you duck the second round of spades, while you would make three notrump with an overtrick if you win the second spade. Quite a difference.

The best way to block the opponents' communication may be *not* to hold up at all. For example:

#3

Contract: three notrump

Opening Lead: four of spades

North
♠ A 10
♡ Q 8 6
◇ A 9 7 4
♣ 10 5 3 2

South
♠ 9 6 5 2
♡ A K 4
◇ K 3
♣ K Q J 9

You must decide whether or not to hold up the ace on the first trick. You have six top tricks and can get the three additional tricks you need by driving out the ace of clubs and regaining the lead before the opponents can win five tricks. The opponents need four spade tricks to beat you, so you cannot be set if spades divide 4-3 whether you play the ace on the first or second trick. It is a 5-2 spade split that poses a problem. If you visualize the possible 5-2 holdings, you should rule out West having the king, queen, and jack; he would have led the king, not the four. So it is reasonable to assume that East has a doubleton honor. Now that you have a picture of how the spades are likely to divide, look at the four hands to see what happens if you hold up your ace, or if you win the first trick.

```
                        North
                        ♠ A 10
                        ♡ Q 8 6
                        ◇ A 9 7 4
                        ♣ 10 5 3 2
        West                            East
        ♠ K J 8 4 3                     ♠ Q 7
        ♡ 10 9 7                        ♡ J 5 3 2
        ◇ 6 5 2                         ◇ Q J 10 8
        ♣ A 8                           ♣ 7 6 4
                        South
                        ♠ 9 6 5 2
                        ♡ A K 4
                        ◇ K 3
                        ♣ K Q J 9
```

If you duck the first spade lead, East will win with his queen and return a spade to drive out your ace. Since West has the ace of clubs he will be able to run the spade suit and set you. Only if East has the ace of clubs can you make your bid, because he is out of spades.

If you win the first trick with the ace of spades, the contract is out of jeopardy no matter who has the ace of clubs (unless West has led from the four-three doubleton, or has made an unorthodox lead from K Q J 4 3). Suppose you lead a club at trick two. The defender with the ace wins the trick and leads a spade. If East is allowed to win the third trick with the queen of spades, he has no more spades to lead. If West wins the third trick with the king of spades, the queen falls and your nine of spades becomes a second stopper. Either way, the opponents cannot run the spade suit.

Here is a case where you should *not* hold up because you fear a switch to another suit.

#4

Contract: three notrump

Opening Lead: king of spades

```
                        North
                        ♠ 6
                        ♡ 7 5 4 2
                        ◇ K Q J 10
                        ♣ A K J 10

                        South
                        ♠ A J 5 4
                        ♡ A 3
                        ◇ 8 5 3 2
                        ♣ Q 9 7
```

West	North	East	South
1 ♠	Double	Pass	2 NT
Pass	3 NT	All Pass	

You have six winners and must develop three diamond tricks to make your bid. On the first trick East follows with the two of spades and you win with the ace—*do not hold up*. The bidding enters into the picture this time. West is a strong favorite to hold the ace of diamonds because of his opening bid. If you win the first trick with the ace of spades and lead a diamond, you are safe as long as East cannot get the lead; your jack of spades is a second stopper against West. The trouble with holding up the ace of spades at trick one is that West may switch to a heart.

Look at the four hands.

```
                          North
                          ♠ 6
                          ♡ 7 5 4 2
                          ◇ K Q J 10
                          ♣ A K J 10
         West                                   East
         ♠ K Q 10 8 3                           ♠ 9 7 2
         ♡ K Q 6                                ♡ J 10 9 8
         ◇ A 9 4                                ◇ 7 6
         ♣ 6 2                                  ♣ 8 5 4 3
                          South
                          ♠ A J 5 4
                          ♡ A 3
                          ◇ 8 5 3 2
                          ♣ Q 9 7
```

If you hold up your ace of spades, West should not lead another spade because his partner played the two—an indication that he does not have the ace or jack. Looking at the strong minor-suit holdings in the dummy, West should reason that the only chance to beat the contract is to find declarer with a doubleton heart. So he should switch to the king of hearts. If South holds up, he should continue with the queen of hearts. When West regains the lead with the ace of diamonds, there are enough heart tricks available to beat the contract by one trick.

When it will be necessary, or may be necessary, to give up the lead twice before you can win the required number of tricks, it is sometimes right to hold up with two stoppers. For example:

#5   North
                                          ♠ 7 6 4
                                          ♡ Q J 9 7
                                          ◇ A 5 2
Contract: three notrump   ♣ A Q 10

Opening Lead: nine of spades   South
                                          ♠ A Q 2
                                          ♡ 10 8 6
                                          ◇ K 9 8 7
                                          ♣ K J 6

West	North	East	South
			1 ◇
Pass	1 ♡	1 ♠	1 NT
Pass	3 NT	All Pass	

East plays the ten of spades on the first trick and you should let him win it; the bidding and the opening lead mark East with the king of spades, so you will not lose a trick by letting him win with the ten. You have only seven top tricks (two spades, two diamonds, and three clubs) and your plan is to drive out the ace and king of hearts to get the two extra tricks. You must hope that West has the ace or king of hearts (if East has both heart honors and at least five spades, the contract is hopeless).

Here are the four hands.

                            North
                            ♠ 7 6 4
                            ♡ Q J 9 7
                            ◇ A 5 2
                            ♣ A Q 10
        West   East
        ♠ 9 5   ♠ K J 10 8 3
        ♡ K 4 3   ♡ A 5 2
        ◇ 10 6 4   ◇ Q J 3
        ♣ 9 8 7 5 3   ♣ 4 2
                            South
                            ♠ A Q 2
                            ♡ 10 8 6
                            ◇ K 9 8 7
                            ♣ K J 6

East leads a spade at trick two and you finesse the queen. Now you play a heart. If West rises with his king, he has no more spades to lead. If East takes his ace, he can clear the spade suit, but he will not be able to regain the lead to win any more spade tricks. By holding up with a double stopper at trick one, you sever the opponents' communication.

Look what happens if you win the first spade trick: When you lead hearts, West will win with the king and lead another spade to drive out your last stopper. When East wins with the ace of hearts, he can cash enough spade tricks to set you.

The most common hold-up plays are with an ace, or with a king after the ace has been played. However, holding up with a card that is not high may lead to success — or to disaster.

Note the following two hands:

#6   North
                                          ♠ 8 7 6
                                          ♡ 7 4
                                          ◇ A Q 10 9 5 2
Contract: three notrump   ♣ K 3

Opening Lead: four of spades   South
                                          ♠ K 10 9
                                          ♡ A K 3 2
                                          ◇ J 6
                                          ♣ A J 8 5

Here you must establish the diamond suit before you can bring home nine tricks. On the first trick East plays the queen of spades and *you must win it with your king.* Do not hold up here because you will lose the first five tricks if West has led from a five-card spade suit headed by the ace-jack. If you win the first trick with the king of spades and West has led from a four- or six-card spade suit, you will make your contract even if the diamond finesse fails: Either the defense will be limited to three spade tricks, or East will have no more spades. If West has led from a five-card spade suit, you must depend on a successful diamond finesse to make your bid.

#7   North
                                          ♠ 8 7 6
                                          ♡ 7 4
                                          ◇ A Q 10 9 5 2
Contract: three notrump   ♣ K 3

Opening Lead: four of spades   South
                                          ♠ K J 9
                                          ♡ A K 3 2
                                          ◇ J 6
                                          ♣ A J 8 5

The only difference between this hand and the last is your spade holding; you have the K J 9 instead of K 10 9. But this time, when East plays the queen of spades on the first trick, it is correct to hold up your king because the remaining king-jack is an ironclad stopper. By allowing East to win the first trick with the queen of spades, you can make your bid even if the diamond finesse fails and West started with a five-card spade suit headed by the ace-ten; while if you win the first trick with the king, you will need a successful diamond finesse.

Suppose the four hands are:

North
♠ 8 7 6
♡ 7 4
◊ A Q 10 9 5 2
♣ K 3

West
♠ A 10 5 4 2
♡ 10 8 6
◊ 7 3
♣ Q 9 4

East
♠ Q 3
♡ Q J 9 5
◊ K 8 4
♣ 10 7 6 2

South
♠ K J 9
♡ A K 3 2
◊ J 6
♣ A J 8 5

As the cards lie, winning the first trick with the king of spades is fatal. When East wins with his king of diamonds, he will return a spade through your jack-nine.

But if you allow East to win the first trick with the queen of spades, you break up the opponents' communication. There is no way they can win more than two spade tricks.

Hold-Up Plays at Trump Contracts

Hold-up plays at trump contracts are less common, but can be just as effective when there is a need to block the opponents' communication.

For example:

#8

Contract: four hearts

Opening Lead: queen of clubs

North
♠ A Q J 2
♡ J 9 5
◊ 8 7 4 2
♣ 6 3

South
♠ K 8 7
♡ A Q 10 6 3 2
◊ K 5
♣ A 10

On the queen-of-clubs opening lead, East plays the seven and you should duck; let West win the first trick. You have four possible losers: one heart, two diamonds, and one club. Your contract is in jeopardy if West has the king of hearts and the ace of diamonds. Assuming this is the case, you can still win ten tricks by drawing trumps and then discarding one of your diamonds on the fourth round of spades — unless East is able to get the lead and play through your king of diamonds before you discard your loser. So the purpose of ducking the first trick is to deprive East of an entry.

Suppose the four hands are:

North
♠ A Q J 2
♡ J 9 5
◇ 8 7 4 2
♣ 6 3

West
♠ 10 5
♡ K 7 4
◇ A 6 3
♣ Q J 9 8 2

East
♠ 9 6 4 3
♡ 8
◇ Q J 10 9
♣ K 7 5 4

South
♠ K 8 7
♡ A Q 10 6 3 2
◇ K 5
♣ A 10

After winning the second club trick, cross to dummy with a spade and take the heart finesse. Even though it loses, your contract is safe because East cannot get the lead.

If you mistakenly won the first club trick, the king of clubs would provide East with an entry. When West wins with the king of hearts, he can put East on lead with the king of clubs to lead a diamond through your king.

In the next deal, both the bidding and the plays to the first trick offer clues as to the location of the high cards.

#9

Contract: four spades

Opening Lead: four of clubs

North
♠ A K 9 4 3
♡ K 9 7
◇ K 6
♣ 5 3 2

South
♠ Q J 10 8 5
♡ 6 3
◇ Q J 10 9
♣ A J

West	North	East	South
		1 ♣	1 ♠
Pass	4 ♠	All Pass	

It is clear that you must lose a diamond and a club, so the only chance to make your contract is to hold your heart losers to one. The opening bid marks East with the two red aces, so the only hope is to discard two of dummy's hearts on your long diamonds before the opponents can win two heart tricks. On the first trick East plays the king of clubs, so you should assume that West has the queen (third hand plays the *lowest* card of a sequence, so East would play the queen from king-queen). Although you cannot always depend on your opponents' plays, you should duck the first trick to make sure that West can never get the lead with the queen of clubs to play through your king of hearts.

Here is the full deal:

<pre>
                        North
                        ♠ A K 9 4 3
                        ♡ K 9 7
                        ◊ K 6
                        ♣ 5 3 2
        West   East
        ♠ 7   ♠ 6 2
        ♡ J 5 4 2   ♡ A Q 10 8
        ◊ 8 5 3 2   ◊ A 7 4
        ♣ Q 10 6 4   ♣ K 9 8 7
                        South
                        ♠ Q J 10 8 5
                        ♡ 6 3
                        ◊ Q J 10 9
                        ♣ A J
</pre>

After you play the jack of clubs at trick one, East returns a club to your ace. You then draw trumps and lead the king of diamonds to East's ace. Note that East cannot beat the contract no matter what he does; he is powerless. Suppose he leads another club. You simply ruff and run your diamond suit to discard two hearts from dummy.

This contract can be set only if West has a brainstorm and leads a heart originally. But note that if you mistakenly won the first trick with the ace of clubs, West would get a second chance to lead a heart when he regained the lead with the queen of clubs.

The purpose of holding up on the next deal is not truly to block the opponents' communication, but rather to gain a trick by preserving your options.

#10   North
                         ♠ A 10
                         ♡ 8
                         ◊ 10 6 4 3
Contract: four hearts   ♣ K Q 7 6 5 2

Opening Lead: king of spades   South
                         ♠ 8 4 3
                         ♡ A K Q J 5 3
                         ◊ A K 5
                         ♣ 9

You have four losers: two spades, one diamond, and one club. If you win the first trick with the ace of spades, the contract can always be set: You no longer have an entry to dummy to get a discard on a high club; and a trump lead from the enemy will prevent you from ruffing a spade.

Assume you let West win the first trick with the king of spades. If he leads another spade at trick two, you can make your bid by winning with the ace, coming to your hand with a high diamond and ruffing your last spade in dummy. If West leads anything else at trick two, the ace of spades remains as an entry to dummy, so you can drive out the ace of clubs and eventually discard one of your losers on a high club.

Second Hand High

There are ways other than hold-up plays to block the opponents' suit.
For example:

#11

Contract: three notrump

Opening Lead: eight of spades

North
♠ Q 10 3
♡ A J
♢ K Q J 10 7 3
♣ A 2

South
♠ K 6 2
♡ Q 7 3
♢ 8 5 4
♣ K J 8 7

West	North	East	South
	1 ◇	1 ♠	1 NT
Pass	3 NT	All Pass	

Since his partner bid the suit, West leads the eight of spades against three notrump. The bidding and the lead make it clear that East's spades include the A J 9. You must establish the diamond suit before you can win nine tricks and will succeed unless the opponents can run the spade suit when they get the lead with the ace of diamonds. The key play is to rise with dummy's queen of spades at trick one.
Look at the four hands to see why.

North
♠ Q 10 3
♡ A J
♢ K Q J 10 7 3
♣ A 2

West
♠ 8 4
♡ 9 8 6 5 4
♢ A 6 2
♣ 6 5 4

East
♠ A J 9 7 5
♡ K 10 2
♢ 9
♣ Q 10 9 3

South
♠ K 6 2
♡ Q 7 3
♢ 8 5 4
♣ K J 8 7

Playing the queen of spades in dummy on the first trick makes it impossible for East to establish the suit. If he wins with the ace, he cannot lead spades again without giving you an extra spade trick with the ten. If he does not cover queen of spades with the ace, you still have the guarded king behind his ace.

If you play the ten or three of spades from dummy, you also can make the contract if you guess which opponent has the ace of diamonds. If West has it, you must allow the opponents to win the first trick. If East has it, you must take the first trick with your king and develop diamonds. But why guess when you don't have to?

Obviously, playing the queen of spades is best because you can make your bid no matter who has the ace of diamonds.

The Danger Hand

If you find yourself in a position where one defender can beat your contract if he gets the lead while the other defender cannot, the obvious plan is to try to develop the required number of tricks without allowing the dangerous opponent to get the lead.

For example:

#12	North
	♠ J 9 3
	♡ 8 4
	◇ A Q
Contract: three notrump	♣ A Q 10 7 4 2
Opening Lead: six of hearts	South
	♠ A Q 10
	♡ K J 9
	◇ K J 10 6
	♣ J 8 3

East plays the ten of hearts on the first trick and you win with the jack. East would have played the ace or queen of hearts if he had either one, so West must have both of those cards. If East gets the lead and plays a heart through your king, you can expect West to win enough hearts to set you. So East is the danger hand and you must try to collect your nine tricks without allowing him to get the lead.

You have seven winners (one spade, one heart, four diamonds, and one club). You can win the two extra tricks you need in spades or clubs if the finesse you decide to take works. Since the spade finesse is into the safe hand, you should most certainly try it first. Only if the spade finesse fails should you tackle the club suit — and then you should not finesse!

Suppose the four hands are:

North
♠ J 9 3
♡ 8 4
◊ A Q
♣ A Q 10 7 4 2

West   East
♠ 8 4 2   ♠ K 7 6 5
♡ A Q 7 6 3   ♡ 10 5 2
◊ 7 5 2   ◊ 9 8 4 3
♣ 6 5   ♣ K 9

South
♠ A Q 10
♡ K J 9
◊ K J 10 6
♣ J 8 3

As you can see, if you take the club finesse first you will be set. At trick two, you should lead a diamond to dummy's ace and finesse for the king of spades. Since this finesse works, take your nine tricks and go home.

If the spade finesse fails and West exits safely by leading anything other than a heart, then you will have to turn to the club suit. The best play is the *ace* of clubs in case East has a singleton king; if the king doesn't fall, you will still make your bid if West has the king. This line of play fails only if West has the king of spades and East has the guarded king of clubs.

A notrump contract is a race. The declarer tries to win enough tricks to make his bid before the defenders can win enough tricks to set him. So you must pay attention to the timing in many hands, or you will lose the race.

For example:

#13   North
                                           ♠ K Q 9
                                           ♡ 6 3
                                           ◊ A J 4 2
Contract: three notrump   ♣ J 6 5 2

Opening Lead: ten of diamonds   South
                                           ♠ A 6 4
                                           ♡ A Q
                                           ◊ Q 5 3
                                           ♣ K Q 10 8 7

You have five winners (three spades, one heart, and one diamond) and can put this contract on ice by winning the first trick with the ace of diamonds and driving out the ace of clubs while you still have stoppers in all suits. If you mistakenly play a low diamond at trick one, you needlessly risk your contract.

Suppose the four hands are:

North
♠ K Q 9
♡ 6 3
◇ A J 4 2
♣ J 6 5 2

West
♠ J 3
♡ K 7 5 2
◇ 10 9 8 7
♣ A 4 3

East
♠ 10 8 7 5 2
♡ J 10 9 8 4
◇ K 6
♣ 9

South
♠ A 6 4
♡ A Q
◇ Q 5 3
♣ K Q 10 8 7

If you try the diamond finesse, East may win with the king and switch to the jack of hearts. West will capture the queen of hearts with his king and lead another heart to drive out the ace. Since you have no more heart stoppers and the ace of clubs is still missing, the opponents can win four hearts, one diamond, and one club to set you two tricks.

Granted, it is unlucky to find both kings wrong. But good players are not as unlucky as bad players; good players depend on luck only when they need it. The contract is a lock if you win the first trick with the ace of diamonds.

#14

North
♠ A Q 9
♡ A 8 7 6 4 3
◇ Q 10
♣ 5 2

Contract: four spades

Opening Lead: king of diamonds

South
♠ K J 10 8 4 3
♡ J 5
◇ 7
♣ K J 9 6

West	North	East	South
1 ◇	1 ♡	2 ◇	2 ♠
3 ◇	3 ♠	Pass	4 ♠
All Pass			

You must lose one heart and one diamond, so your objective is to limit your club losers to one. If the hearts divide 3-2, you can establish the suit and discard three clubs from your hand. Since you must lose a trick before you can ruff any hearts, you should lose the trick to West if possible so East cannot get the lead to play a club.

After winning the first trick with the king of diamonds, suppose West leads the ace of diamonds. Before reading further, how would you play?

North
♠ A Q 9
♡ A 8 7 6 4 3
◇ Q 10
♣ 5 2

West
♠ 7 5
♡ 9 2
◇ A K J 6 2
♣ A Q 4 3

East
♠ 6 2
♡ K Q 10
◇ 9 8 5 4 3
♣ 10 8 7

South
♠ K J 10 8 4 3
♡ J 5
◇ 7
♣ K J 9 6

The correct play is to discard a heart on the second diamond lead, and, as the cards lie, this is the only way the contract can be made. West can do no better than lead a trump at trick three, so you win with the nine in dummy. Now cash the ace of hearts, ruff a low heart in your hand, lead a spade to return to dummy, and ruff a third round of hearts in your hand. The three remaining hearts are now good, so lead to dummy's high spade and discard three clubs.

If you mistakenly ruff the ace of diamonds at trick two, you will have to concede a heart trick to East before you can ruff any hearts; East then will lead a club and set the contract.

Note that the only defense to beat the contract is for West to lead a spade at trick *two*. Although you could still discard a heart on the queen of diamonds, a second spade lead would leave dummy an entry short — you could no longer establish the heart suit.

#15

Contract: three notrump

Opening Lead: four of hearts

North
♠ K 5 4
♡ Q 7
◇ 9 8 4 3
♣ A K 6 2

South
♠ A 9
♡ K 6 3
◇ A K 7 6 5
♣ 9 8 4

The first important play is the queen of hearts in dummy. When it wins the first trick, West is marked with the ace of hearts. Your guarded king of hearts is now a stopper if West gets the lead. But if East gets the lead, he can play through your king of hearts and the opponents will run the suit.

The queen of hearts gives you seven tricks, and you must tackle the diamond suit to develop two more. If diamonds divide 2-2, or if West has three diamonds, it is easy to establish the suit without giving East the lead. If East has the Q J 10 of diamonds you cannot stop him from getting the lead. It is when West has a singleton diamond honor that you can do something about it; and you should take this possibility into consideration when you play.

Look at the four hands to see how you must maneuver:

```
                      North
                      ♠ K 5 4
                      ♡ Q 7
                      ◊ 9 8 4 3
                      ♣ A K 6 2
West                                        East
♠ 8 7 3 2                                   ♠ Q J 10 6
♡ A J 9 4 2                                 ♡ 10 8 5
◊ 10                                        ◊ Q J 2
♣ Q 10 5                                    ♣ J 7 3
                      South
                      ♠ A 9
                      ♡ K 6 3
                      ◊ A K 7 6 5
                      ♣ 9 8 4
```

After winning the opening lead with the queen of hearts, lead a diamond from dummy. East must play the two of diamonds (if he plays the queen or jack, you will be able to run the suit without losing a trick), you play any low diamond from your hand, and West wins the trick. Whatever West returns, you now have four diamond tricks, enough to make your bid. If you mistakenly play the ace or king of diamonds at trick two, East will eventually get the lead to play through your king of hearts and beat the contract. Unless diamonds divide 4-0, all you need is to find the two of diamonds onside.

Also note that if you did not play the queen of hearts on the first trick, there would be no way to prevent the defenders from running four heart tricks no matter which one gets the lead.

The next hand is very similar to the last one, but this time East captures dummy's queen of hearts with the ace and the struggle develops to keep West out of the lead.

#16   North
                            ♠ A Q 9
                            ♡ Q 3
                            ◊ 9 8 6 5 4

Contract: three notrump   ♣ A J 7

Opening Lead: four of hearts   South
                            ♠ K 8 5
                            ♡ K 8 6
                            ◊ A K 7 2
                            ♣ 10 9 2

East overtakes the queen of hearts with the ace and returns the ten of hearts. You hold up your king of hearts and win the third heart when it is led. It is probable that West started with five hearts and East with three, in which case East has no more hearts and it is safe to give him the lead. This time West is the danger hand.

Just like the last hand, you have seven winners and must establish two extra diamond tricks to make your contract. If diamonds are 2-2 or if East has three, there is no problem. If West has three diamonds, you can keep him out of the lead only if East has the singleton queen, so you must allow for it.

Here are the four hands:

North
♠ A Q 9
♡ Q 3
◊ 9 8 6 5 4
♣ A J 7

West
♠ 10 4 2
♡ J 9 7 4 2
◊ J 10 3
♣ K Q

East
♠ J 7 6 3
♡ A 10 5
◊ Q
♣ 8 6 5 4 3

South
♠ K 8 5
♡ K 8 6
◊ A K 7 2
♣ 10 9 2

After winning with the king of hearts at trick three, play a spade to get into the dummy. Now lead a diamond and duck when East contributes the queen. Since East has no more hearts, you will get the lead right back to run the remaining diamonds and make your bid. If East did not play the queen of diamonds, you would of course cash the ace and king, hoping for the best.

This concludes Chapter 2, about blocking the opponents' communication. In Chapter 3, you will learn how to solve your own communication problems.

Quiz for Chapter Two

1.
North
♠ A 8 4
♡ 10 6 2
◇ 10 9 3
♣ K J 10 7

South
♠ 9 7 6
♡ A 8 5
◇ A Q J 8 4
♣ A Q

West	North	East	South
			1 NT
Pass	2 NT	Pass	3 NT
All Pass			

West leads the three of spades.

2.
North
♠ A K 3
♡ A Q 10 8
◇ A 3 2
♣ 7 6 4

South
♠ 7
♡ J 2
◇ K Q 10 9 6 5 4
♣ K 8 3

West	North	East	South
			3 ◇
Pass	5 ◇	All Pass	

West leads the queen of spades. Diamonds divide 2-1.

3.
North
♠ 7 5 4
♡ K Q 4
◇ K J 10 9 2
♣ 8 6

South
♠ K 3 2
♡ A J 6
◇ A 8 7
♣ A K 5 3

West	North	East	South
			1 ♣
1 ♠	2 ◇	Pass	3 NT
All Pass			

West leads the queen of spades and East plays the six.

4.
North
♠ 10 6 5 2
♡ Q J 10 8
◇ 7 4
♣ A K 7

South
♠ A 7
♡ K 9 4
◇ A Q 5 2
♣ Q J 6 3

West	North	East	South
			1 NT
Pass	2 ♣	Pass	2 ◇
Pass	3 NT	All Pass	

West leads the four of spades, dummy plays the two, and East the nine.

5.   North   6.   North
            ♠ A Q J 8 2   ♠ J 9 4
            ♡ K 7   ♡ A 2
            ◇ 7 5 2   ◇ A J 10 9 8 7
            ♣ 6 5 4   ♣ 6 5

            South   South
            ♠ 10 9   ♠ A K Q 10 7 6 2
            ♡ A Q 10 4 3   ♡ 4
            ◇ K J 10   ◇ 5 3
            ♣ A K Q   ♣ K 3 2

West	North	East	South
			1 ♡
Pass	1 ♠	Pass	2 NT
Pass	3 NT	All Pass	

West	North	East	South
			1 ♠
2 ♡	3 ◇	3 ♡	4 ♠
5 ♡	5 ♠	All Pass	

West leads the six of diamonds and East plays the nine.

West leads the king of hearts.

7.   North   8.   North
            ♠ 8 7 3   ♠ J 9 3
            ♡ 5 2   ♡ A Q 10 8
            ◇ A 9 6   ◇ A Q 5
            ♣ A K 10 5 4   ♣ J 9 2

            South   South
            ♠ A 10 2   ♠ A 6 2
            ♡ K J 8   ♡ J 9 3
            ◇ K Q J 10   ◇ K 8 4
            ♣ 8 7 3   ♣ A Q 10 7

West	North	East	South
			1 ◇
1 ♡	2 ♣	Pass	2 NT
Pass	3 NT	All Pass	

West	North	East	South
			1 ♣
Pass	1 ♡	1 ♠	1NT
Pass	3 NT	All Pass	

West leads the seven of hearts and East plays the nine.

West leads the ten of spades, dummy plays the jack, and East the queen.

Answers to Quiz for Chapter Two

1.
	North	
	♠ A 8 4	
	♡ 10 6 2	
	◇ 10 9 3	
	♣ K J 10 7	

West		East
♠ Q J 5 3		♠ K 10 2
♡ 7 4 3		♡ K Q J 9
◇ K 6 2		◇ 7 5
♣ 9 5 2		♣ 8 6 4 3

	South	
	♠ 9 7 6	
	♡ A 8 5	
	◇ A Q J 8 4	
	♣ A Q	

West	North	East	South
			1 NT
Pass	2 NT	Pass	3 NT
All Pass			

West leads the three of spades.

The key play is to win the first trick with the ace of spades. Since West has only four spades, the contract is safe even though the diamond finesse fails. Note that you will be set (whether you hold up or not) if West has a five-card spade suit and the king of diamonds. The trouble with the hold-up play is that East may switch to a heart at trick two; then you may be set even if spades divide 4-3. In the hand as shown, East can tell by his partner's lead that he has a four-card spade suit, so he certainly should switch to the king of hearts. (Observe that if you hold up a heart lead from East, he can beat you by switching back to spades.)

Do not hold up in one suit when you fear another suit being led, especially when the leader of the first suit is the only one who might regain the lead.

2.
	North	
	♠ A K 3	
	♡ A Q 10 8	
	◇ A 3 2	
	♣ 7 6 4	

West		East
♠ Q J 10 9 6		♠ 8 5 4 2
♡ 9 7 4 3		♡ K 6 5
◇ 8		◇ J 7
♣ A 5 2		♣ Q J 10 9

	South	
	♠ 7	
	♡ J 2	
	◇ K Q 10 9 6 5 4	
	♣ K 8 3	

West	North	East	South
			3 ◇
Pass	5 ◇	All Pass	

West leads the queen of spades. Diamonds divide 2-1.

The sure way to win eleven tricks (even with the king of hearts and ace of clubs offside) is to establish the heart suit so you can discard one or more clubs. But you must do this without letting East gain the lead to play a club through your king.

After winning the first spade trick and cashing the king and queen of diamonds, play a heart to the ace, discard your last heart on dummy's high spade, and lead the queen of hearts to take a ruffing finesse. If East covers the queen of hearts with his king, ruff it, lead a diamond to dummy's ace, and discard a losing club on the ten of hearts. If East does not cover the queen of hearts, discard a club.

If West happens to have the king of hearts and captures your queen, the contract is still safe. As long as East cannot get the lead to play through your king of clubs, you will lose at most one more trick. Either West will cash his ace of clubs, or you will discard a losing club on the ten of hearts.

3.

	North		
	♠ 7 5 4		
	♡ K Q 4		
	◇ K J 10 9 2		
	♣ 8 6		
West		**East**	
♠ A Q J 10 9		♠ 8 6	
♡ 10 9 8 2		♡ 7 5 3	
◇ 6		◇ Q 5 4 3	
♣ Q 10 4		♣ J 9 7 2	
	South		
	♠ K 3 2		
	♡ A J 6		
	◇ A 8 7		
	♣ A K 5 3		

West	North	East	South
			1 ♣
1 ♠	2 ◇	Pass	3 NT
All Pass			

West leads the queen of spades and East plays the six.

The bidding indicated the probability of this spade division. If you win the first trick with the king of spades, you have eight winners and your contract depends on guessing the location of the queen of diamonds. If you lose the lead to *either* opponent, West can run four spade tricks.

If you hold up the king of spades at trick one, the contract is safe even if you lose a trick to the queen of diamonds. If West continues spades at trick two, it will be safe to lose the lead to East as he has no more spades. So you should finesse through *West* for the queen of diamonds. Although the finesse fails, you will have ten tricks when you regain the lead.

If West leads a heart (or a club) at trick two, you should finesse through *East* for the queen of diamonds. It is safe to lose the lead to West because you still have the guarded king of spades. To protect yourself against East having more than three diamonds, *you should not cash the king of diamonds* before you finesse. The best play is to get into dummy with a high heart, lead the jack of diamonds, and let it ride. Since East has the queen of diamonds, a second finesse will net you five diamond tricks; you will make your bid with an overtrick. Note that you have nine tricks even if the diamond finesse fails.

4.

	North		
	♠ 10 6 5 2		
	♡ Q J 10 8		
	◇ 7 4		
	♣ A K 7		
West		**East**	
♠ K Q 8 4 3		♠ J 9	
♡ A 6 2		♡ 7 5 3	
◇ 8 6 3		◇ K J 10 9	
♣ 10 5		♣ 9 8 4 2	
	South		
	♠ A 7		
	♡ K 9 4		
	◇ A Q 5 2		
	♣ Q J 6 3		

West	North	East	South
			1 NT
Pass	2 ♣	Pass	2 ◇
Pass	3 NT	All Pass	

West leads the four of spades, dummy plays the two, and East the nine.

You must drive out the ace of hearts and regain the lead before you can win nine tricks. The best play is to win the first trick with the ace of spades.

If you allow East to win the first spade trick with the nine, he will continue the suit. Although it is unlucky to find West with a five-card spade suit and the ace of hearts, you will be set if you duck the first spade lead. The key here is the ten of spades in dummy, which will cause the suit to block if you win the first trick with the ace. This way, you can survive a 5-2 spade break no matter who has the ace of hearts unless West led the four from either the four-three doubleton or the K Q J 4 3 — both very unlikely. Note also that you will succeed whether you win the first or second spade trick if the spades divide 4-3; the opponents can win only three spades and the ace of hearts.

5.

	North		
	♠ A Q J 8 2		
	♡ K 7		
	◇ 7 5 2		
	♣ 6 5 4		
West		East	
♠ 7 6		♠ K 5 4 3	
♡ 9 5		♡ J 8 6 2	
◇ A Q 8 6 3		◇ 9 4	
♣ J 10 9 2		♣ 8 7 3	
	South		
	♠ 10 9		
	♡ A Q 10 4 3		
	◇ K J 10		
	♣ A K Q		

West	North	East	South
			1 ♡
Pass	1 ♠	Pass	2 NT
Pass	3 NT	All Pass	

West leads the six of diamonds and East plays the nine.

Since East would play the ace or queen of diamonds at trick one if he had either card, this diamond layout is predictable. You must keep East from getting the lead if possible, as a diamond play from him would be fatal.

You have eight winners after winning the first trick with the jack (or ten) of diamonds (one spade, three hearts, one diamond, and three clubs) and, as the cards lie, you will be set if you cash three top hearts or take a spade finesse. The surest way to win nine tricks without allowing East to get the lead is to cash the king of hearts and then to finesse the ten of hearts. Since the finesse works, you can run the heart suit and come to ten tricks. If West happens to have the jack of hearts, the contract is still safe; as soon as you regain the lead, you will be able to run nine tricks.

6.

	North		
	♠ J 9 4		
	♡ A 2		
	◇ A J 10 9 8 7		
	♣ 6 5		
West		East	
♠ 5		♠ 8 3	
♡ K Q J 10 7 3		♡ 9 8 6 5	
◇ 6 2		◇ K Q 4	
♣ A 10 9 8		♣ Q J 7 4	
	South		
	♠ A K Q 10 7 6 2		
	♡ 4		
	◇ 5 3		
	♣ K 3 2		

West	North	East	South
			1 ♠
2 ♡	3 ◇	3 ♡	4 ♠
5 ♡	5 ♠	All Pass	

West leads the king of hearts.

With plenty of entries to dummy, your plan should be to establish the diamond suit to discard losing clubs. However, you must give up a trick before you can ruff diamonds, and if East gets the lead to play a club through your king, you will be set.

The sure way to keep East off lead is to *duck the first heart trick*. If West leads anything other than the ace of clubs at trick two, you will not lose another trick. Suppose he leads a second heart and you discard a diamond. By cashing the ace of diamonds and ruffing twice in your hand, you can establish three good diamond tricks to discard your three losing clubs. The jack and nine of spades will serve as the needed entries to dummy.

Note that if diamonds divide 4-1, you can still make your bid (assuming the same defense) as long as spades divide 2-1 and you have saved the two of spades — then the four of spades can be used as a third entry to dummy.

7.   North
                         ♠ 8 7 3
                         ♡ 5 2
                         ◇ A 9 6
                         ♣ A K 10 5 4

West   East
♠ K 9 6   ♠ Q J 5 4
♡ A Q 10 7 3   ♡ 9 6 4
◇ 8 5 4   ◇ 7 3 2
♣ Q 6   ♣ J 9 2

                         South
                         ♠ A 10 2
                         ♡ K J 8
                         ◇ K Q J 10
                         ♣ 8 7 3

West	North	East	South
			1 ◇
1 ♡	2 ♣	Pass	2 NT
Pass	3 NT	All Pass	

West leads the seven of hearts and East plays the nine.

After winning the first trick with the jack of hearts, you have eight winners and must tackle the club suit to get a ninth. Since you still have the king and another heart, it will be okay to give up the lead to West, but not to East. The best play is to lead clubs twice *from your hand*. Suppose you lead a club at trick two, West plays low and you win with the king in dummy (you should duck if West plays the queen). Next, return to your hand with a diamond and lead a second club. West must play the queen and you let him win this trick. Since it is possible to concede a club trick to West — the safe hand — the contract is secure.

Note that if West plays any club but the queen on the second round, you should win with the ace. Assuming East follows suit, you will then play a third round: If West has the third club, you will make your bid; if East has it, a heart lead through your king will set you.

8.   North
                         ♠ J 9 3
                         ♡ A Q 10 8
                         ◇ A Q 5
                         ♣ J 9 2

West   East
♠ 10 4   ♠ K Q 8 7 5
♡ 7 5 4   ♡ K 6 2
◇ J 9 3 2   ◇ 10 7 6
♣ K 6 5 4   ♣ 8 3

                         South
                         ♠ A 6 2
                         ♡ J 9 3
                         ◇ K 8 4
                         ♣ A Q 10 7

West	North	East	South
			1 ♣
Pass	1 ♡	1 ♠	1NT
Pass	3 NT	All Pass	

West leads the ten of spades, dummy plays the jack, and East the queen.

The bidding and the opening lead indicate that East has both the king and queen of spades. With the kings of hearts and clubs both offside, you will be set if you win the first trick with the ace of spades. West will eventually get the lead with the king of clubs and play another spade. Suppose you make the right play and let East win the first trick with the queen of spades. If he leads another spade, you can win a trick with the nine, so let's assume he leads a club (no other lead is better). *Do not finesse!* Win with the ace of clubs and take the heart finesse. This way, the contract is easily made even if the king of clubs and king of hearts are both offside. The opponents can win only those two kings; you will wind up with ten tricks.

3
Communication Problems

♣　　◇　　♡　　♠　　♣　　◇　　♡　　♠

Have you ever played a hand halfway through and then looked longingly at one or more good tricks in dummy that you cannot reach because you squandered an entry earlier? This is the subject we will be dealing with now: *entries* — recognizing them, saving them, and even creating them.

Ducking

The topic of the first seven illustrations will be "ducking." You give up a trick along the way to save an entry to the hand in which you plan to win long cards.

Here is the first example:

#1

Contract: three notrump

Opening Lead: jack of hearts

North
- ♠ 10 2
- ♡ 6 3
- ◇ A 9 5
- ♣ A 7 6 5 4 2

South
- ♠ A Q 6 5
- ♡ A K Q
- ◇ K 7 3 2
- ♣ 10 3

The first step is to count your winners. You have seven: one spade, three hearts, two diamonds, and one club. You can develop three extra tricks in clubs if the suit divides 3-2, and establishing that suit offers the best chance to make your bid.

The key play is to lead a club at trick two and *duck* in dummy. If you win with the ace, it will be impossible to win more than one club trick because you do not have sufficient entries.

Assuming either defender wins the club trick and returns a heart (no defense is better), next lead a club to dummy's ace. If both opponents follow suit, play a third club to establish the suit. With the ace of diamonds as an entry to the three remaining clubs, you will win at least ten tricks.

If an opponent shows out when you play the ace of clubs (clubs divide 4-1), you cannot win more than one club trick. But there is still a chance to win the two extra tricks you need if you are very lucky. You must find the king of spades onside and the diamonds dividing 3-3.

You should not depend on a favorable break when you do not need it.
For example:

#2	North
	♠ 7 5 3
	♡ 7
	◊ A J 6 4 2
Contract: three notrump	♣ 8 6 5 4
Opening Lead: queen of hearts	South
	♠ A K 4
	♡ A K 6 3
	◊ K 8 7
	♣ A 10 2

You have seven winners (two spades, two hearts, two diamonds, and one club), so you need two additional diamond tricks to make your bid. There is no problem if diamonds divide 3-2, so you should be thinking about 4-1 splits. If East has four diamonds including the queen, you will be set. But if West has four diamonds, you can make your bid by conceding a diamond trick before playing the ace or jack in dummy.

Here is the complete deal:

```
                       North
                       ♠ 7 5 3
                       ♡ 7
                       ◊ A J 6 4 2
                       ♣ 8 6 5 4
     West                                    East
     ♠ J 9 2                                 ♠ Q 10 8 6
     ♡ Q J 10 8                              ♡ 9 5 4 2
     ◊ Q 10 9 3                              ◊ 5
     ♣ J 7                                   ♣ K Q 9 3
                       South
                       ♠ A K 4
                       ♡ A K 6 3
                       ◊ K 8 7
                       ♣ A 10 2
```

Win the first heart trick (for fear of a club switch), cash the king of diamonds, and lead a second diamond toward the dummy. When West follows suit, the contract is secure (whether West began with two, three, or four diamonds) if you play a *low* diamond in dummy. Since West has four diamonds, East will show out and you have a marked finesse against West's queen; you can win three more diamond tricks when you regain the lead. Note that if you play dummy's jack on the second diamond lead, you will be limited to three tricks in the suit because you will have squandered an entry.

Here is another type of ducking play to increase your chance for success.

#3   North
                                                ♠ A Q 10 6 4
                                                ♡ 5 4 3
                                                ◇ 8 3 2
Contract: one notrump   ♣ 9 7

Opening Lead: four of diamonds   South
                                                ♠ J 7
                                                ♡ A 10 9
                                                ◇ A 7 6
                                                ♣ A 8 5 4 3

East plays the king of diamonds on the first trick and you win with your ace (there is no advantage to holding up). At trick two you should lead the jack of spades, which West covers with the king. If you win this trick with the ace of spades, you will win five tricks if the suit divides 3-3, but only three tricks against any other division.

If you counted your tricks, you should know that you need four spade tricks, not five. Therefore, the correct play is to allow West to win with the king of spades. Then you will be able to win four spade tricks when the suit divides 3-3 or 4-2.

Suppose the four hands are:

                                North
                                ♠ A Q 10 6 4
                                ♡ 5 4 3
                                ◇ 8 3 2
                                ♣ 9 7
West   East
♠ K 2   ♠ 9 8 5 3
♡ Q 8 2   ♡ K J 7 6
◇ Q 10 5 4   ◇ K J 9
♣ K J 6 2   ♣ Q 10
                                South
                                ♠ J 7
                                ♡ A 10 9
                                ◇ A 7 6
                                ♣ A 8 5 4 3

As you can see, if you cover West's king of spades with the ace, you will be limited to three spade tricks. While if you let West win with the king of spades, you save a crucial entry to dummy and will be able to win four spade tricks when you regain the lead.

There is a ducking play to save an entry in the next hand, but it is not so obvious.

#4   North
                                                            ♠ A 7 4
                                                            ♡ 10 8 5
                                                            ◇ 9 2
Contract: three notrump   ♣ K Q J 3 2

Opening Lead: five of spades   South
                                                            ♠ K Q 8
                                                            ♡ A K 2
                                                            ◇ A J 6 4 3
                                                            ♣ 7 5

You have six winners and need *three* club tricks to make your bid. If you win the spade in your hand and play a club to dummy's jack (or king or queen), the defender with the ace will hold up. Unless clubs divide 3-3 or West has a doubleton ace, you cannot win more than two club tricks. The key play, to insure three club tricks against any 4-2 break, is to play a *low* club from dummy the first time you lead the suit.

Suppose the full deal is:

                            North
                            ♠ A 7 4
                            ♡ 10 8 5
                            ◇ 9 2
                            ♣ K Q J 3 2
        West   East
        ♠ J 9 6 5 2   ♠ 10 3
        ♡ Q 9 7 3   ♡ J 6 4
        ◇ K 10   ◇ Q 8 7 5
        ♣ 8 4   ♣ A 10 9 6
                            South
                            ♠ K Q 8
                            ♡ A K 2
                            ◇ A J 6 4 3
                            ♣ 7 5

After winning the first spade trick in your hand, lead a club and play low in dummy. Suppose the opponents lead another spade (no defense is better). Win it in your hand and play club honors until the ace is driven out. You will eventually lead to dummy's ace of spades to win the remaining club tricks.

Here is another entry problem that requires a duck and some luck — or, if you prefer, "a lucky duck."

#5

Contract: three notrump

Opening Lead: queen of spades

North
♠ 9 3
♡ 7 5 3
♢ A Q 8 6 4 2
♣ 7 6

South
♠ A K
♡ A 8 6 2
♢ 7 3
♣ A Q 5 4 2

You have five winners and the best chance to get four more tricks is to find West with a doubleton or tripleton king of diamonds. At trick two lead a diamond and duck in dummy, allowing either opponent to win the trick. Presumably the opponents will lead another spade. Win it and lead a diamond, intending to finesse the queen if West follows with a lower diamond.

The full deal:

North
♠ 9 3
♡ 7 5 3
♢ A Q 8 6 4 2
♣ 7 6

West
♠ Q J 10 7 5
♡ 9 4
♢ K 10 5
♣ K J 9

East
♠ 8 6 4 2
♡ K Q J 10
♢ J 9
♣ 10 8 3

South
♠ A K
♡ A 8 6 2
♢ 7 3
♣ A Q 5 4 2

The way the cards lie, you can win nine tricks. All you have to do is play as described above and pray that you get lucky. If you do not find the fortunate diamond division, you may be set three tricks, or more.

Note: When your hand and the dummy have seven cards in a suit, the missing six cards will divide 3-3 about 36 percent of the time and 4-2 about 48 percent of the time. Therefore, if you can survive a 3-3 or 4-2 break, your chances are about 84 percent (36 plus 48) — the odds are better than 5-to-1 in your favor. So you should never play for a suit to divide 3-3 unless you are confident you cannot make your contract versus a 4-2 break.

You have already seen a couple of hands where you could make your bid against a 4-2 break if you played skillfully, and several more are coming — including the next deal.

#6   North
                                              ♠ A K 7 4 2
                                              ♡ K 4 2
                                              ◇ A 10
Contract: six hearts   ♣ 6 5 4

Opening Lead: king of diamonds   South
                                              ♠ 5 3
                                              ♡ A Q J 10 9 8 6
                                              ◇ 7
                                              ♣ A 10 2

You have two losing club tricks and must look to the spade suit for discards. With any lead but a diamond the contract is easily made against a 4-2 spade break because you would have two side entries to dummy. With the diamond lead you must improvise.

Here is the full deal to show you that spades do divide 4-2. How would you play the hand?

```
                         North
                         ♠ A K 7 4 2
                         ♡ K 4 2
                         ◇ A 10
                         ♣ 6 5 4
         West                              East
         ♠ J 9                             ♠ Q 10 8 6
         ♡ 7 3                             ♡ 5
         ◇ K Q J 9 6                       ◇ 8 5 4 3 2
         ♣ K 8 7 3                         ♣ Q J 9
                         South
                         ♠ 5 3
                         ♡ A Q J 10 9 8 6
                         ◇ 7
                         ♣ A 10 2
```

After winning the opening lead with the ace of diamonds and playing two high hearts from your hand, lead a spade and *duck* in dummy. This key play saves an entry to dummy and will be your only losing trick. Suppose the defender who wins the spade trick returns a diamond. You ruff, lead a spade to the ace, discard one club on the king of spades, and ruff the fourth round of spades in your hand. Dummy's fifth spade is now good and the king of hearts provides the entry you need to discard your other losing club.

In the next deal there are two suits you must contend with to make your contract against 4-2 breaks.

#7

Contract: six hearts

Opening Lead: ten of hearts

North
♠ K 5 4
♡ K J
◇ 10 6
♣ A K 8 7 3 2

South
♠ A 8 6 3
♡ A Q 5 4 2
◇ A Q 7
♣ 5

You have four possible losers: two spades and two diamonds. You can make your bid by establishing the club suit for discards provided neither clubs nor hearts divides worse than 4-2. This is a difficult hand; even an expert would find it a challenge. So look at the four hands and try to figure out the winning line of play before reading the analysis.

North
♠ K 5 4
♡ K J
◇ 10 6
♣ A K 8 7 3 2

West
♠ Q 7 2
♡ 10 9 8 7
◇ K J 9 4
♣ J 6

East
♠ J 10 9
♡ 6 3
◇ 8 5 3 2
♣ Q 10 9 4

South
♠ A 8 6 3
♡ A Q 5 4 2
◇ A Q 7
♣ 5

Win the first heart trick in dummy and lead a *low* club at trick two. If you play anything but a low club at trick two, the contract cannot be made. Suppose East wins the club trick and leads a diamond. You win with the ace, play a heart to get the lead in dummy, and ruff a low club in your hand. Dummy's clubs are now good and you still have the ace and queen of hearts to draw West's two trumps. So cash your two high trumps, discarding a spade and a diamond from dummy. The king of spades is the entry you need to reach dummy, and your four losers can be discarded on the good clubs.

An opening spade lead followed by a second spade lead when you concede the club trick will remove the crucial entry to dummy and beat the contract. But with the heart lead, you can control your destiny.

Overtaking

Sometimes the value of an entry is greater than the value of a trick. You must overtake one winner with another, apparently wasting a trick, to gain an entry.

For example:

#8	North
	♠ A 5 2
	♡ 6 5
	◊ J 7 4
Contract: three notrump	♣ A 9 8 3 2
Opening Lead: queen of hearts	South
	♠ K Q 4
	♡ A K 7
	◊ 10 8 5 3 2
	♣ K Q

The best way to play a suit is governed by how many tricks you need. If you need five club tricks to make your bid, you should cash the king and queen, go to dummy with the ace of spades, and cash the ace of clubs. You will have your five club tricks if the suit divides 3-3 or if someone has a doubleton jack-ten. Otherwise you will be limited to three club tricks because you have no more entries to dummy.

Here, though, you have three spade tricks and two heart tricks, so you need only *four* club tricks to make your bid. The best play is to cash one high club in your hand and *overtake* the second club honor with dummy's ace. This way, you give yourself the *extra* chance that either defender has 10 x x x or J x x x.

Suppose the four hands are:

```
                        North
                        ♠ A 5 2
                        ♡ 6 5
                        ◊ J 7 4
                        ♣ A 9 8 3 2
      West                                      East
      ♠ 8 7 3                                   ♠ J 10 9 6
      ♡ Q J 10 9                                ♡ 8 4 3 2
      ◊ A 6                                     ◊ K Q 9
      ♣ J 7 6 5                                 ♣ 10 4
                        South
                        ♠ K Q 4
                        ♡ A K 7
                        ◊ 10 8 5 3 2
                        ♣ K Q
```

With the clubs divided as shown, it is necessary to overtake the second club honor with the ace to make the contract. When the ten of clubs drops, lead the nine to drive out the jack. When you regain the lead, play a spade to dummy's ace and cash the remaining two good club tricks. If the clubs divide 3-3, your overtaking play would still provide four club tricks at the expense of an insignificant overtrick.

#9

Contract: three notrump

Opening Lead: ten of clubs

North
♠ A Q 7 6
♡ 9 8 2
◇ J 10 3
♣ 5 4 3

South
♠ K 9
♡ A K Q
◇ K 9 8 7 4
♣ Q J 6

The play begins with East winning with the king of clubs, cashing the ace of clubs, and leading a third club to which West follows suit. You now have seven winners (three spades, three hearts, and one club) and must establish the diamond suit to develop the two needed tricks. The only good chance is to find East with the queen and finesse him out of it. If East has three or more diamonds, you will need two entries to dummy so you can finesse twice.

Suppose the four hands are:

North
♠ A Q 7 6
♡ 9 8 2
◇ J 10 3
♣ 5 4 3

West
♠ 5 4 2
♡ 10 5 4 3
◇ A 2
♣ 10 9 8 7

East
♠ J 10 8 3
♡ J 7 6
◇ Q 6 5
♣ A K 2

South
♠ K 9
♡ A K Q
◇ K 9 8 7 4
♣ Q J 6

At trick four, after the three rounds of clubs have been played, lead the nine of spades to dummy's queen so you can take the first diamond finesse. When you lead the jack of diamonds, East plays low and West wins with the ace. After cashing his thirteenth club, West exits with a heart. Next lead your king of spades and *overtake with the ace*. With the lead in dummy, play the ten of diamonds to repeat the finesse and win the rest of the tricks. It wastes a trick to overtake the king of spades with the ace, but you get it back with interest.

#10   North
                                             ♠ 9 8 4 3 2
                                             ♡ A Q 5
                                             ◇ K
Contract: four spades   ♣ 10 9 7 6

Opening Lead: ten of diamonds   South
                                             ♠ K Q J 10 7 6
                                             ♡ 3
                                             ◇ A 8 4
                                             ♣ J 4 2

    You have four losers (three clubs and one spade) and are lucky the opponents led a diamond instead of taking their three club tricks. If West has the king of hearts, you can now make your contract by finessing the queen and discarding one of your club losers on the ace of hearts. However, you must do this before you relinquish the lead or the opponents may cash their club tricks.

    Suppose the four hands are:

                              North
                              ♠ 9 8 4 3 2
                              ♡ A Q 5
                              ◇ K
                              ♣ 10 9 7 6
West   East
♠ 5   ♠ A
♡ K 10 8 6   ♡ J 9 7 4 2
◇ 10 9 7 2   ◇ Q J 6 5 3
♣ A Q 5 3   ♣ K 8
                              South
                              ♠ K Q J 10 7 6
                              ♡ 3
                              ◇ A 8 4
                              ♣ J 4 2

    The key play is to *overtake dummy's king of diamonds with your ace* and take the heart finesse. Since the finesse works, discard a club on the ace of hearts and make your bid. It's true that if the finesse fails, the opponents can set you two tricks; but the amount you lose for going down an extra trick is trivial compared with what you gain if the finesse succeeds.

    Note that if you win the first trick in dummy with the king of diamonds, there is no quick entry to your hand; the opponents cannot be prevented from taking their three club tricks.

Saving and Creating Entries

As was stated earlier, you should save entries to the hand in which you plan to win long cards. It may be an entry to your own hand that must be saved.

For example:

#11	North
	♠ A 10 4
	♡ K 8 6 5
	◊ A 9 7 3
Contract: one notrump	♣ A 2
Opening Lead: two of hearts	South
	♠ 9 7 6
	♡ A 7
	◊ 8 6 5 2
	♣ Q J 10 9

You have five winners: one spade, two hearts, one diamond, and one club. The two extra tricks you need can be won in clubs if you save the ace of hearts as an entry. Simply win the first trick with dummy's king of hearts, cash the ace of clubs, and lead another club to drive out the king. You now have seven tricks. Any declarer who fails to play the king of hearts on the first trick has misplayed the hand badly. But if he is lucky, he may still make his bid due to some fortunate distribution or bad defense. Sometimes fortune smiles on those who play before they think.

A low spot-card can provide an extra entry, but it may be wasted if the suit is not played carefully.

#12	North
	♠ 8 3 2
	♡ Q 5
	◊ K Q 5 3
Contract: three notrump	♣ 7 6 4 2
Opening Lead: five of clubs	South
	♠ A Q J 10
	♡ J 10 6
	◊ A J 8 4
	♣ K Q

East wins the first trick with the ace of clubs and returns the ten of clubs. The only realistic chance to make your bid is to win four spade tricks. East must have the king of spades, or there is no hope; so assume he does. If East has four spades (or more), you will need *three* entries to dummy so you can take three spade finesses. Proper handling of the diamond suit will provide three entries if the missing diamonds divide 3-2.

Suppose this is the complete deal:

North
♠ 8 3 2
♡ Q 5
◇ K Q 5 3
♣ 7 6 4 2

West   East
♠ 6 4   ♠ K 9 7 5
♡ A 7 4   ♡ K 9 8 3 2
◇ 10 9 2   ◇ 7 6
♣ J 9 8 5 3   ♣ A 10

South
♠ A Q J 10
♡ J 10 6
◇ A J 8 4
♣ K Q

After winning the second club trick, cash the ace of diamonds, lead the *eight* of diamonds to the queen, and take the first spade finesse. Since both opponents followed suit in diamonds (there is only one more diamond missing), lead the *jack* of diamonds and overtake with the king to take the second spade finesse. The only diamonds left are the four in your hand and the five in the dummy, so this provides an entry for the third spade finesse.

Note that if an opponent showed out on the first or second lead of diamonds, you could not afford to overtake the jack of diamonds with the king. Then you would be limited to *two* entries to dummy and must hope that East has no more than three spades.

Sometimes you have to play a suit in a very strange way to solve your communication problems, as you shall see in the next two hands:

#13   North
                                     ♠ K Q J 9
                                     ♡ 10
                                     ◇ 8 7 5 3 2
Contract: three notrump   ♣ 10 6 5

Opening Lead: queen of hearts   South
                                     ♠ A
                                     ♡ A K 5
                                     ◇ Q J 6
                                     ♣ A K J 4 3 2

Since you have no quick entry to dummy, you can count only five winners: one spade, two hearts, and two clubs. You must win *four* extra tricks in clubs unless you can create an entry to dummy's spade suit. The best line of play is to win the opening lead, cash the ace of spades, and *lead the jack of clubs*. This scheme insures the contract against anything but a 4-0 club break.

Suppose the four hands are:

                                North
                                ♠ K Q J 9
                                ♡ 10
                                ◇ 8 7 5 3 2
                                ♣ 10 6 5

West   East
♠ 7 4 3 2   ♠ 10 8 6 5
♡ Q J 9 8 5   ♡ 7 6 3 2
◇ A 10 4   ◇ K 9
♣ 7   ♣ Q 9 8

                                South
                                ♠ A
                                ♡ A K 5
                                ◇ Q J 6
                                ♣ A K J 4 3 2

When you lead the jack of clubs, East cannot beat you whether he wins with his queen or not. If he does not take the queen, you can run six club tricks; if he takes the queen, the ten of clubs becomes an entry to those lovely spades.

All other lines of play are inferior. If you cash the ace and king of clubs early and the queen does not drop, you will be limited to eight tricks (one spade, two hearts, and five clubs). Since you have no entry to dummy, the spade suit is lost.

If you cash the ace of spades and then lead a low club toward dummy's ten, you will fail unless West has the queen of clubs.

If you cash the ace of spades, one high club, and then lead the jack of clubs or a low club, the defender who wins with the queen can beat you by returning a heart. Even if clubs divide 2-2, you will lack the communication to win more than eight tricks.

#14   North
                                    ♠ J 2
                                    ♡ 7
                                    ◇ A K 10 7 6 4 2
Contract: six hearts   ♣ 9 8 3

Opening Lead: queen of clubs   South
                                    ♠ A Q 8
                                    ♡ A K Q J 10 3
                                    ◇ —
                                    ♣ A K 5 4

You have three losers: one spade and two clubs. If only you could get to dummy and discard your two losing clubs on the ace and king of diamonds! There just happens to be a way. Can you figure it out before reading further?

Here are the four hands:

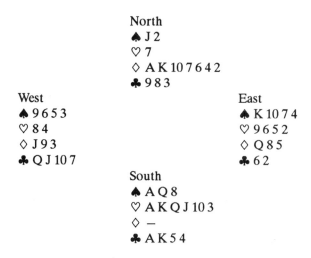

North
♠ J 2
♡ 7
◇ A K 10 7 6 4 2
♣ 9 8 3

West
♠ 9 6 5 3
♡ 8 4
◇ J 9 3
♣ Q J 10 7

East
♠ K 10 7 4
♡ 9 6 5 2
◇ Q 8 5
♣ 6 2

South
♠ A Q 8
♡ A K Q J 10 3
◇ —
♣ A K 5 4

Win the first trick with the king of clubs and *lead the queen of spades at trick two*. If East wins with the king of spades, you can get to the dummy with the jack of spades. If East ducks the queen of spades, you can get to dummy by ruffing the third round of spades with the seven of hearts. Of course, a 6-2 spade split may set you, but the odds are very much against that.

Unblocking

Another way to solve communication problems is "unblocking" – deliberately playing an unusually high card from one hand to create an entry to the opposite hand.

#15

Contract: one notrump

Opening Lead: jack of spades

North
♠ A 9 2
♡ 7 5 4
◇ 10 9 7 5
♣ 8 6 3

South
♠ Q 7
♡ A 6 3 2
◇ A K Q J
♣ J 7 5

You have six winners and the favorable opening lead gives you the seventh on a silver platter. When you play a low spade from dummy, East wins with the king and decision time is here. You must unblock, playing the queen of spades under the king! West's opening lead marks him with the ten of spades, so you can finesse dummy's nine and win the needed two spade tricks. If you fail to unblock, you can be held to one spade trick.

The full deal:

North
♠ A 9 2
♡ 7 5 4
♢ 10 9 7 5
♣ 8 6 3

West
♠ J 10 8 6 3
♡ K 9
♢ 8 2
♣ K 10 4 2

East
♠ K 5 4
♡ Q J 10 8
♢ 6 4 3
♣ A Q 9

South
♠ Q 7
♡ A 6 3 2
♢ A K Q J
♣ J 7 5

In general it pays to win a trick as cheaply as possible, but to save an entry you must sometimes be extravagant.

#16

Contract: three notrump

Opening Lead: five of spades

North
♠ Q 10 4
♡ K Q 10 9 2
♢ 7 4 3
♣ 10 5

South
♠ A J 7
♡ J 5
♢ A K 8 2
♣ A Q 6 3

On the first trick you call for the four of spades from dummy and East plays the nine. The moment of truth has arrived: You must win with the *ace* of spades even though you could take the trick with the jack. Here is the complete deal:

North
♠ Q 10 4
♡ K Q 10 9 2
◇ 7 4 3
♣ 10 5

West
♠ K 8 6 5 2
♡ 7 4 3
◇ 6 5
♣ K J 7

East
♠ 9 3
♡ A 8 6
◇ Q J 10 9
♣ 9 8 4 2

South
♠ A J 7
♡ J 5
◇ A K 8 2
♣ A Q 6 3

Counting two spade tricks, you have five winners and need four heart tricks to make three notrump. When you lead hearts East will hold up his ace once or twice, so you will need a side entry to dummy. Now consider the play of the ace of spades at trick one. With the queen-ten in dummy and the jack-seven in your hand (and double stoppers in all other suits), you can eventually get to dummy to cash your heart tricks. Do not fail to see that if you win the first trick with any card but the ace, you cannot reach dummy to enjoy your heart winners.

In the next deal West leads the five of hearts, you play the six from dummy, and East contributes the four. Which heart should you play from your hand?

#17

Contract: three notrump

Opening Lead: five of hearts

North
♠ Q J 5 3 2
♡ J 7 6
◇ 9 6 3
♣ 10 5

South
♠ A K
♡ A K 9 2
◇ A 10 7
♣ A 8 6 4

The key play is to win the first trick with the ace or king of hearts. Then the jack of hearts is an entry to dummy if West has the queen; and the plays at trick one make it fairly conclusive that he does. After winning the first trick with the ace or king of hearts, cash the ace and king of spades, and lead a low heart toward the jack.

Before explaining further, let's look at the four hands:

North
♠ Q J 5 3 2
♡ J 7 6
◇ 9 6 3
♣ 10 5

West
♠ 7 6
♡ Q 10 8 5 3
◇ K J 4
♣ 7 2

East
♠ 10 9 8 4
♡ 4
◇ Q 8 5 2
♣ K Q J 9 3

South
♠ A K
♡ A K 9 2
◇ A 10 7
♣ A 8 6 4

Observe that you will be able to get the lead in dummy with the jack of hearts whether West goes up with his queen or not. This will enable you to win five spades, three hearts, one diamond, and one club.

It is interesting to note that you will win exactly three heart tricks whether you win the first trick with the six, nine, king, or ace. But if you win with the six or nine, the jack of hearts will not provide an entry to dummy; you will be limited to two spade winners and your contract will be set two tricks.

Here is a rather spectacular unblocking play to gain an entry, but it is the only way to make the contract.

#18

Contract: three notrump

Opening Lead: five of spades

North
♠ J 9 8
♡ Q J 10 5
◇ 10 8 4
♣ Q J 9

South
♠ K 6 2
♡ 7 4
◇ A Q J 9 5 2
♣ A K

On the first trick, you play the eight of spades from dummy and East wins the ace. You should anticipate that East will return a spade to knock out your one spade stopper and, if you lose the lead again, you figure to be set two or three tricks. The only good chance to win nine tricks is to find East with the king of diamonds, but you must get to dummy so you can finesse him out of it. Now get back to trick one when East played the ace of spades. The jack of spades can be established as an entry to dummy if you unblock: *Play the king of spades under the ace.*

Here is the full deal to show you that this is the only road to success.

North
♠ J 9 8
♡ Q J 10 5
◊ 10 8 4
♣ Q J 9

West
♠ Q 10 7 5 3
♡ A 9 6
◊ 6
♣ 7 5 3 2

East
♠ A 4
♡ K 8 3 2
◊ K 7 3
♣ 10 8 6 4

South
♠ K 6 2
♡ 7 4
◊ A Q J 9 5 2
♣ A K

Jettison Plays

The dictionary's definition of "jettison" is: To cast off as superfluous or encumbering; to discard. In bridge terminology a "jettison play" is a *discard* that is made for the purpose of unblocking. Usually the card jettisoned is an honor.

Here are four examples:

#19

North
♠ K 4 2
♡ Q J 10
◊ A K 6 2
♣ 9 6 5

Contract: six spades

Opening Lead: queen of diamonds

South
♠ A Q J 10 9 6 5
♡ A
◊ 3
♣ A 8 7 4

You have three losing clubs and will be set unless you can discard two of them on dummy's high cards. Since the diamond suit offers only one discard, you must utilize dummy's hearts to make your bid. The problem is that you can get to dummy only one more time: with the king of spades.

Do not despair, there is a solution. After winning the first trick with the ace of diamonds, lead the king of diamonds and *jettison your ace of hearts*. Now lead the queen of hearts. If East plays the king, ruff it. If East plays low, discard a club. Either way, you will have twelve tricks by way of seven spades, two hearts, two diamonds, and one club.

#20

North
♠ J 10 9 4 2
♡ A 6 3
◇ J 8 5

Contract: seven hearts

♣ A K

Opening Lead: king of diamonds

South
♠ A K Q
♡ K Q J 9 8 7
◇ A 7 6 3
♣ —

Seven notrump is a much better contract, but here you are in seven hearts.

If hearts divide 2-2, the contract is easily made. But when you win the opening lead with the ace of diamonds and cash the king and queen of hearts, West shows out on the second heart lead (East has one more heart).

Since you have three losing diamonds and can get rid of only two of them on the ace and king of clubs, you must do some discarding on dummy's spade suit or you will be set. If you lead a heart to dummy's ace immediately to draw East's last trump, you have no more entries to dummy and the spade suit is lost. If you cash three high spades before you play the third round of hearts, East will trump unless he was dealt at least three spades. Suppose East has a singleton spade, as is shown in the diagram. Can you make this grand slam?

North
♠ J 10 9 4 2
♡ A 6 3
◇ J 8 5
♣ A K

West
♠ 8 6 5 3
♡ 4
◇ K Q 10
♣ Q 7 5 4 2

East
♠ 7
♡ 10 5 2
◇ 9 4 2
♣ J 10 9 8 6 3

South
♠ A K Q
♡ K Q J 9 8 7
◇ A 7 6 3
♣ —

At trick four, after winning the opening lead and cashing the king and queen of hearts, cash *one* high spade. Then lead a heart to dummy's ace (drawing East's last trump) and *jettison your two remaining high spades on the ace and king of clubs.* Since your hand is now void of spades, you can discard your three losing diamonds on the jack-ten-nine of spades.

#21   North
                                           ♠ 9 5 2
                                           ♡ 7 3
                                           ◊ A K Q 4 2
Contract: six spades   ♣ J 8 4

Opening Lead: three of diamonds   South
                                           ♠ A K Q J 10
                                           ♡ A
                                           ◊ 10 9 8 6
                                           ♣ A 7 2

Since you have only seven winners in the other three suits, you must win five diamond tricks to make this slam. The three-of-diamonds opening lead appears to be a singleton. Assuming it is, how do you play to win five diamond tricks?

Here is the full deal:

```
                    North
                    ♠ 9 5 2
                    ♡ 7 3
                    ◊ A K Q 4 2
                    ♣ J 8 4
West                                East
♠ 7 4 3                             ♠ 8 6
♡ K J 8 6 4                         ♡ Q 10 9 5 2
◊ 3                                 ◊ J 7 5
♣ 9 6 5 3                           ♣ K Q 10
                    South
                    ♠ A K Q J 10
                    ♡ A
                    ◊ 10 9 8 6
                    ♣ A 7 2
```

The problem is that the diamond suit is blocked. When you win the fourth round of diamonds the lead will be in your hand, and there is no entry to dummy to win the fifth diamond. So you will lose two club tricks and be set.

The solution to the problem is to unblock the diamond suit by discarding one of the diamonds in your hand. Win the first trick with the queen of diamonds, draw the missing trumps, cash the ace of hearts, and lead a diamond to dummy's king. The remaining diamonds in the dummy are the ace-four-two, you have the ten-nine, and East has the lone jack. Now lead the low heart from dummy and *jettison the nine or ten of diamonds*. This will be your only losing trick. When you regain the lead, you can run the diamond suit and discard your two losing clubs.

The last hand in this section is a "par hand," from when I was Tournament Director for the National Inter-Collegiate Bridge Championship many years ago. It is the grand-daddy unblocking play of them all. The contract is seven notrump and the opening lead is the jack of spades. See if you can make the contract "double dummy"—looking at all four hands.

#22

North
♠ A Q
♡ K Q J
◇ 3
♣ J 9 7 6 5 4 2

West
♠ J 10 2
♡ 10 8 7 4
◇ J 7 5 2
♣ 8 3

East
♠ 9 8 7 6 5 4 3
♡ 9 6 5 3 2
◇ —
♣ 10

South
♠ K
♡ A
◇ A K Q 10 9 8 6 4
♣ A K Q

The spade lead is devastating as it takes away your only entry to dummy. Since it is impossible to win more than three diamond tricks without losing a trick, you must find a way to keep the lead in dummy so you can run the club suit. This requires four jettison plays. Win the first trick with the ace of spades and cash the queen of spades to jettison the ace of hearts. Next cash the king, queen, and jack of hearts and jettison the ace, king, and queen of clubs. The lead is still in dummy and you can now run the club suit and make the grand slam. Note that if the ten of clubs did not fall under the jack, the contract could still be made if the diamond suit ran.

Incidentally, the college students had to make this contract "single dummy" – looking at the North and South hands only.

Quiz for Chapter Three

1.

North
♠ Q 5
♡ Q J 10
◊ K Q 10 9 2
♣ 8 7 4

South
♠ A 9 8 3
♡ A 7 4
◊ J 6
♣ A K 5 2

West	North	East	South
			1 NT
Pass	3 NT	All Pass	

West leads the six of hearts and East plays the three.

2.

North
♠ 8 5
♡ 9 7 2
◊ J 6 4 3
♣ K 10 9 2

South
♠ A K J 10 9 7
♡ A K 8
◊ A K Q
♣ A

West	North	East	South
			2 ♠
Pass	2 NT	Pass	6 ♠
All Pass			

West leads the queen of hearts.

3.

North
♠ 9 5 3
♡ 9 5 4
◊ A K Q 4 2
♣ 8 6

South
♠ A K Q
♡ K 10 2
◊ 9 6 5 3
♣ K J 7

West	North	East	South
			1 NT
Pass	3 NT	All Pass	

West leads the seven of hearts and East plays the queen.

4.

North
♠ 10 9 6
♡ 9 7 5
◊ A K Q 4 2
♣ Q 8

South
♠ A K Q J 2
♡ K 8 3
◊ 9 7 6 5
♣ J

West	North	East	South
			1 ♠
2 ♣	2 ◊	Pass	3 ◊
Pass	3 ♠	Pass	4 ♠
All Pass			

West leads first the king of clubs and then the ace of clubs.

5.

North
♠ A K 7
♡ 8 7 2
♢ 5 4 3
♣ 10 9 6 4

South
♠ 8 5 3 2
♡ A K J
♢ A K 7 6
♣ A Q

West	North	East	South
			2 NT
Pass	3 NT	All Pass	

West leads the four of hearts.

6.

North
♠ 7 6 4
♡ 4 2
♢ A J 9 8 7
♣ 10 9 3

South
♠ A K 3 2
♡ A Q 6
♢ K 10
♣ A J 8 5

West	North	East	South
			2 NT
Pass	3 NT	All Pass	

West leads the seven of hearts and East plays the nine.

7.

North
♠ 6 4
♡ Q 7 5
♢ K Q 8 4 3
♣ A 10 2

South
♠ A J 10
♡ A K J 8 6 2
♢ 10
♣ K Q 5

West	North	East	South
			1 ♡
Pass	2 ♢	Pass	3 ♡
Pass	4 ♡	Pass	4 NT
Pass	5 ♢	Pass	6 ♡
All Pass			

West leads the nine of diamonds.

8.

North
♠ 7 3 2
♡ Q J 10
♢ 8 6 5 4
♣ A K Q

South
♠ A K Q J 10 8
♡ A K
♢ K 10 9 3
♣ 7

West	North	East	South
			2 ♠
Pass	3 ♠	Pass	4 NT
Pass	5 ♢	Pass	6 ♠
All Pass			

West leads the jack of clubs.

Answers to Quiz for Chapter Three

1.

```
              North
              ♠ Q 5
              ♡ Q J 10
              ◇ K Q 10 9 2
              ♣ 8 7 4
West                      East
♠ 6 4 2                   ♠ K J 10 7
♡ K 9 8 6 2               ♡ 5 3
◇ 7 3                     ◇ A 8 5 4
♣ Q J 9                   ♣ 10 6 3
              South
              ♠ A 9 8 3
              ♡ A 7 4
              ◇ J 6
              ♣ A K 5 2
```

West	North	East	South
			1 NT
Pass	3 NT	All Pass	

West leads the six of hearts, and East plays the three.

You have five winners (one spade, two hearts, and two clubs), so you need four diamond tricks to make three notrump. To ensure you can get to dummy to run the diamond suit, you must win the first trick with the *ace* of hearts. Assuming you have done this, lead diamonds until the ace is driven out. With the spades and clubs securely stopped, you will have plenty of time to regain the lead, drive out the king of hearts, and eventually get to dummy with the remaining heart honor.

If you mistakenly win the first heart trick in dummy, East will duck your first diamond lead and win the second. With no entry to dummy, you can kiss the diamond suit (and your contract) goodbye.

2.

```
              North
              ♠ 8 5
              ♡ 9 7 2
              ◇ J 6 4 3
              ♣ K 10 9 2
West                      East
♠ Q 4 2                   ♠ 6 3
♡ Q J 10                  ♡ 6 5 4 3
◇ 9 5 2                   ◇ 10 8 7
♣ 8 7 6 3                 ♣ Q J 5 4
              South
              ♠ A K J 10 9 7
              ♡ A K 8
              ◇ A K Q
              ♣ A
```

West	North	East	South
			2 ♠
Pass	2 NT	Pass	6 ♠
All Pass			

West leads the queen of hearts.

Your only possible losers are one heart and one spade. You could make your bid by discarding your heart loser on the king of clubs if there were an entry to dummy, or if the queen of spades drops under your ace or king. As you can see in the diagram, neither of these things happens. But you can also make your bid if either defender has three spades to the queen as long as you take advantage of the eight of spades in dummy.

After winning the first heart trick, cash the ace of clubs and lead the jack (or ten or nine) of spades. If West wins with the queen of spades, you will eventually lead to dummy's eight of spades and discard your losing heart on the king of clubs. If West does not take his queen of spades, you can cash the ace and king, eliminating your spade loser.

Note that this line also succeeds if a defender has four spades to the queen and is not smart enough to duck when you lead the jack.

3.

	North		
	♠ 9 5 3		
	♡ 9 5 4		
	◇ A K Q 4 2		
	♣ 8 6		
West		East	
♠ 8 7 2		♠ J 10 6 4	
♡ A J 8 7 6		♡ Q 3	
◇ 10		◇ J 8 7	
♣ A 9 5 3		♣ Q 10 4 2	
	South		
	♠ A K Q		
	♡ K 10 2		
	◇ 9 6 5 3		
	♣ K J 7		

West	North	East	South
			1 NT
Pass	3 NT	All Pass	

West leads the seven of hearts and East plays the queen.

Unless the diamonds divide 4-0, you have nine tricks: three spades, one heart, and five diamonds. However, there is a trap. If the diamonds divide 3-1 (the most likely division), you must unblock by playing the five, six, and nine of diamonds under the queen, king, and ace. With the four-two left in dummy and the three in your hand, you can win two more diamond tricks.

If you carelessly play the three of diamonds on any of the first three leads, you will wind up with the four-two in dummy and the nine, six, or five in your hand. With no side entry to dummy, you will be limited to four diamond tricks.

4.

	North		
	♠ 10 9 6		
	♡ 9 7 5		
	◇ A K Q 4 2		
	♣ Q 8		
West		East	
♠ 8 7		♠ 5 4 3	
♡ A 6 4 2		♡ Q J 10	
◇ 10		◇ J 8 3	
♣ A K 9 5 3 2		♣ 10 7 6 4	
	South		
	♠ A K Q J 2		
	♡ K 8 3		
	◇ 9 7 6 5		
	♣ J		

West	North	East	South
			1 ♠
2 ♣	2 ◇	Pass	3 ◇
Pass	3 ♠	Pass	4 ♠
All Pass			

West leads first the king of clubs and then the ace of clubs.

You have four losers: three hearts and one club. Unless the ace of hearts is onside (unlikely from the bidding), the only chance is to discard one of your losing hearts on dummy's fifth diamond. If diamonds divide 2-2, there is no problem, and if they divide 4-0, there is no chance. It is the 3-1 split you must contend with; and the trouble is that, with no side entries after trumps have been drawn, you must maneuver to win the *fourth* diamond trick in dummy.

Unlike the last deal, you have no diamond in your hand that is lower than dummy's fourth-highest diamond, so you must find a different way to unblock. If you ruff the second club lead, draw trumps, and cash the ace, king, and queen of diamonds, you will wind up with the four-two in dummy and a higher diamond in your hand (five, six, seven, or nine). You will have to win the fourth diamond trick in your hand and will be unable to get to dummy to cash the fifth diamond.

The solution is to get rid of one of the diamonds in your hand. The only way this can be done is to *jettison a diamond on the second club lead*. With only three diamonds in your hand, the suit will not block. West can win only one more trick with his ace of hearts. If West does not take his ace, you will discard two hearts on the diamond suit.

5.

	North	
	♠ A K 7	
	♡ 8 7 2	
	◇ 5 4 3	
	♣ 10 9 6 4	

West	East
♠ 9	♠ Q J 10 6 4
♡ Q 10 6 4 3	♡ 9 5
◇ Q 10 9 2	◇ J 8
♣ K J 5	♣ 8 7 3 2

	South	
	♠ 8 5 3 2	
	♡ A K J	
	◇ A K 7 6	
	♣ A Q	

West	North	East	South
			2 NT
Pass	3 NT	All Pass	

West leads the four of hearts.

With the heart lead, you have eight winners (two spades, three hearts, two diamonds, and one club) and several obvious chances for a ninth: Spades divide 3-3, diamonds divide 3-3, or the club finesse works. As you can see in the diagram, none of these chances works; nor should any of them be tried. There is a way to win a ninth trick in clubs, and it does not matter how the East-West cards are divided. After winning the first heart trick, cash the ace of clubs and lead the queen of clubs to drive out the king. When you regain the lead, play a spade to dummy and lead the ten of clubs, which loses to the jack. The nine of clubs is now a good trick and the high spade still in dummy will serve as an entry.

Note that you will be set if you try the club finesse because you must waste one of dummy's entries.

6.

	North	
	♠ 7 6 4	
	♡ 4 2	
	◇ A J 9 8 7	
	♣ 10 9 3	

West	East
♠ 10 9	♠ Q J 8 5
♡ K J 8 7 5	♡ 10 9 3
◇ 6 3 2	◇ Q 5 4
♣ Q 4 2	♣ K 7 6

	South	
	♠ A K 3 2	
	♡ A Q 6	
	◇ K 10	
	♣ A J 8 5	

West	North	East	South
			2 NT
Pass	3 NT	All Pass	

West leads the seven of hearts and East plays the nine.

You have seven winners (two spades, two hearts, two diamonds, and one club). Prospects for winning two extra diamond tricks are poor because you have no side entry to dummy. A better chance is to take a double finesse in clubs, using the diamond suit to provide the two needed entries to dummy.

After winning the first trick with the queen of hearts, lead the *ten* of diamonds and overtake with the *jack* in dummy. If East wins this with the queen, you can make your bid when you regain the lead by overtaking the king of diamonds with the ace and running four diamond tricks.

Assuming the jack of diamonds is allowed to win the trick, you now have the two entries you need to take two club finesses. So lead the ten of clubs and let it ride; in this case West will win with the queen. Upon regaining the lead, enter dummy by overtaking the king of diamonds with the ace and, assuming the queen of diamonds does not drop, repeat the club finesse. This gives you the three club tricks you need to make your bid. You will be set only if West has both the king and queen of clubs and if the queen of diamonds does not show up on the first or second round.

7.

	North	
	♠ 6 4	
	♡ Q 7 5	
	◇ K Q 8 4 3	
	♣ A 10 2	

West		East
♠ K 8 7 5 3		♠ Q 9 2
♡ 10 9 4		♡ 3
◇ 9		◇ A J 7 6 5 2
♣ J 9 7 6		♣ 8 4 3

	South	
	♠ A J 10	
	♡ A K J 8 6 2	
	◇ 10	
	♣ K Q 5	

West	North	East	South
			1 ♡
Pass	2 ◇	Pass	3 ♡
Pass	4 ♡	Pass	4 NT
Pass	5 ◇	Pass	6 ♡
All Pass			

West leads the nine of diamonds.

The contract is optimistic, but you must give it a whirl—the only chance is to discard two spades on the diamond suit. The nine-of-diamonds lead is predictably a singleton; why else would West lead your partner's bid suit?

The key play is a *low* diamond from dummy on the first trick (if you play the king or queen, you cannot get two discards), which East wins with the jack. Suppose East returns a low diamond, hoping to promote a trump trick for his partner (this would be the winning defense if West had ♡ J 9 4, instead of ♡ 10 9 4). Here, though, you ruff with a high trump.

The dummy is left with ◇ K Q 8 and East with ◇ A 7 6 5. You have the two entries to dummy you need to get your discards (the ace of clubs and the queen of hearts), but you must draw West's trumps before leading any more diamonds. So play three rounds of hearts with the lead winding up in the dummy. The rest is easy: Just lead diamonds—when East plays the ace, ruff; when he plays low, discard the jack and ten of spades.

8.

	North	
	♠ 7 3 2	
	♡ Q J 10	
	◇ 8 6 5 4	
	♣ A K Q	

West		East
♠ 5 4		♠ 9 6
♡ 7 6 5 2		♡ 9 8 4 3
◇ A Q		◇ J 7 2
♣ J 10 9 8 3		♣ 6 5 4 2

	South	
	♠ A K Q J 10 8	
	♡ A K	
	◇ K 10 9 3	
	♣ 7	

West	North	East	South
			2 ♠
Pass	3 ♠	Pass	4 NT
Pass	5 ◇	Pass	6 ♠
All Pass			

West leads the jack of clubs.

With any lead but a club, you could draw trumps, cash the ace and king of hearts, lead a club to dummy, and discard three of your four losing diamonds on the two high clubs and one high heart. But the club opening lead uses up your only entry to dummy, so you are in dummy for the last time. You might discard two diamonds on the top clubs and then lead a diamond toward your king; but that is just a 50-50 chance. The odds are much better with a neat jettison play.

Win the first three tricks with the ace, king, and queen of clubs and *jettison the ace and king of hearts*. Now you can discard three losing diamonds on the queen, jack, and ten of hearts. Only with extraordinary distribution, such as a 6-2 heart split, will this line of play fail.

4

Trump Entries; Timing; and Ruffing Losers in the Dummy

♣   ◇   ♡   ♠   ♣   ◇   ♡   ♠

Using the Trump Suit for Entries

One of the most important sources of entries (not covered in Chapter 3) is in the trump suit itself, so entries must be taken into consideration when you are deciding when and how to draw trumps.

Here are several illustrations.

#1	North
	♠ A 7
	♡ 8 4 2
	◇ Q 10 7 6 5
Contract: six spades	♣ A J 9
Opening Lead: king of clubs	South
	♠ K Q J 9 5 4 2
	♡ A K Q 3
	◇ 8
	♣ 10

The king of clubs is a very fortunate opening lead and now the contract is unbeatable (unless you encounter very weird distribution). Win the first trick with the ace of clubs and, *before drawing any trumps*, lead the jack of clubs (or the nine) to discard your losing diamond. Suppose West wins this trick with the queen of clubs and leads a diamond, which you ruff. After cashing one high trump in your hand, lead to dummy's ace of spades and discard your other loser (the three of hearts) on the good nine of clubs. With a different opening lead, the success of the slam is likely to depend on a 3-3 heart division.

In the next deal an entry is more important than a trick. You give away one trick and get back two in return.

#2   **North**
                                                ♠ 7 6 3 2
                                                ♡ 10 8 5
                                                ◇ K Q 4 3

Contract: six clubs   ♣ 9 7

Opening Lead: queen of spades   **South**
                                                ♠ A K 9
                                                ♡ A K 4
                                                ◇ A
                                                ♣ A K Q J 8 5

You have two major-suit losers and no trump losers. However, if you give away a trump trick, you can *create an entry* to dummy and discard the two major-suit losers on the diamond suit.

After winning the opening lead, cash the ace of diamonds, and lead the five of clubs to dummy's seven. You can expect the defender with the ten of clubs to win this trick, but when you regain the lead you will play the eight of clubs to the nine so you can discard your two losers on dummy's high diamonds.

Before reading the explanation, how would you play the following hand?

#3   **North**
                                                ♠ 6 5 3
                                                ♡ 10 9 8
                                                ◇ A 8 6 4 2

Contract: four hearts   ♣ Q 10

Opening Lead: king of spades   **South**
                                                ♠ A 9 4
                                                ♡ A K Q J 7 5 3
                                                ◇ 9
                                                ♣ J 7

You have four losers: two spades and two clubs. The only hope to win ten tricks is to find the missing diamonds divided 4-3, so you can establish dummy's fifth diamond to discard one of your losers. You need four entries — three to ruff diamonds and one to win a trick with the fifth diamond — and they are the ace of diamonds and the ten, nine, and eight of hearts.

Suppose the four hands are:

North
♠ 6 5 3
♡ 10 9 8
♢ A 8 6 4 2
♣ Q 10

West   East
♠ K Q 10 2   ♠ J 8 7
♡ 6 4   ♡ 2
♢ J 7 3   ♢ K Q 10 5
♣ A 9 8 5   ♣ K 6 4 3 2

South
♠ A 9 4
♡ A K Q J 7 5 3
♢ 9
♣ J 7

After winning the first trick with the ace of spades, lead a diamond to dummy's ace and ruff a diamond in your hand *with the ace, king, queen, or jack.* The next four plays should be: Lead a low heart to dummy's eight, ruff a third round of diamonds with a high trump, lead another low heart to dummy's nine, and ruff a fourth round of diamonds with a high trump. The ten of hearts is still in dummy and will provide the entry so you can discard one of your losers on the fifth diamond.

Note that if you ruff any of dummy's diamonds with a low heart, you waste an entry and will be set. Also observe that an original heart lead would take away one of your entries prematurely and beat the contract.

#4   North
                                              ♠ Q J 3
                                              ♡ 7 4 3
                                              ♢ 8 6 5
Contract: four spades   ♣ Q J 10 9

Opening Lead: five of spades   South
                                              ♠ A K 10 9 8 7 2
                                              ♡ K 5 2
                                              ♢ A Q 3
                                              ♣ —

You have five possible losers: three hearts and two diamonds. You might think you need to find both the ace of hearts and king of diamonds onside to make your bid; but if the missing spades divide 2-1, it doesn't matter how the missing honor cards are distributed. You can establish two good club tricks in dummy and discard two of your losers. However, you must play carefully and preserve the three entries to dummy that you need.

Suppose the hands are:

North
♠ Q J 3
♡ 7 4 3
◇ 8 6 5
♣ Q J 10 9

West
♠ 5 4
♡ A 8 6
◇ K 10 9 7
♣ A 6 4 2

East
♠ 6
♡ Q J 10 9
◇ J 4 2
♣ K 8 7 5 3

South
♠ A K 10 9 8 7 2
♡ K 5 2
◇ A Q 3
♣ —

Win the opening spade lead in dummy with the jack and play the seven from your hand; you must save the two of spades as it will be needed for the crucial third entry to dummy. At trick two lead the queen of clubs from dummy to take a "ruffing finesse." If East plays the king of clubs, you will ruff; but he plays low and you discard the three of diamonds, allowing West to win with the ace of clubs. West can do no better than to lead another spade, which you win with dummy's queen and unblock in your hand by playing the eight. Now lead the jack of clubs, intending to ruff if East plays his ace, or to discard if he plays low. Although it makes no difference, let's assume East covers and you ruff with the nine of spades. All that is left to be done is to lead the carefully preserved two of spades to dummy's three and discard two of your losers on the ten and nine of clubs.

Entries to dummy may be needed to take finesses, as well as to discard losers. For example:

#5

North
♠ 10 9 8
♡ 8 5 4 2
◇ 6 3 2

Contract: four spades

♣ J 7 5

Opening Lead: king of clubs

South
♠ A Q J 7 6 4
♡ A Q J
◇ A K
♣ 10 9

You have two inevitable club losers, so you cannot afford to lose both a spade trick and a heart trick. You need entries to the dummy to take finesses. There are no entries for a spade finesse, but you can use the spade suit to provide the two entries you need to finesse twice for the king of hearts.

Suppose these are the four hands:

North
♠ 10 9 8
♡ 8 5 4 2
◇ 6 3 2
♣ J 7 5

West
♠ 2
♡ 10 6 3
◇ Q J 7 5 4
♣ A K 8 3

East
♠ K 5 3
♡ K 9 7
◇ 10 9 8
♣ Q 6 4 2

South
♠ A Q J 7 6 4
♡ A Q J
◇ A K
♣ 10 9

Assuming the opponents win the first two club tricks and lead a third club, *ruff with the queen or jack of spades.* You must save your low spades so you can get the lead in dummy twice for heart finesses. Your first spade lead must be a low card to dummy's eight. East wins this trick with his king of spades and does the best he can by leading a diamond, which you win in your hand. All that remains to be done is to use dummy's nine and ten of spades as entries to take two heart finesses. You must find the king of hearts onside to make your bid, but there is no better line of play.

Another way in which trumps can serve as entries to the dummy is by ruffing losers — and also by ruffing *winners.*

For example:

#6

Contract: six spades

Opening Lead: queen of clubs

North
♠ 4 3 2
♡ A J 10 7 5 2
◇ A 10 7 4
♣ —

South
♠ A K Q J 10 8
♡ —
◇ 8 6 3 2
♣ A K 5

You have three losing diamonds and the best chance to make your bid is to discard at least two of them on the heart suit. You will have to reach the dummy several times to establish the heart suit, so you must not waste any entries. How many entries to dummy do you see? What are they?

Here are the four hands:

North
♠ 4 3 2
♡ A J 10 7 5 2
♦ A 10 7 4
♣ —

West
♠ 9 6 5
♡ 6 4 3
♦ K 9
♣ Q J 10 9 8

East
♠ 7
♡ K Q 9 8
♦ Q J 5
♣ 7 6 4 3 2

South
♠ A K Q J 10 8
♡ —
♦ 8 6 3 2
♣ A K 5

You can get to dummy four times by ruffing three clubs and leading to the ace of diamonds. To start, ruff the opening lead, cash the ace of hearts to discard one diamond, and ruff a heart in your hand. Your next four plays will be: Ruff the king of clubs in dummy, ruff the third round of hearts in your hand, ruff the ace of clubs in dummy, and ruff the fourth round of hearts in your hand. The last two hearts in dummy are now good tricks.

The time has finally come to draw the missing trumps. Since the spades divide 3-1, draw three rounds and discard dummy's low diamonds. So far you have won ten tricks and can win three more with dummy's ace of diamonds and two good heart tricks; so the slam is made with an overtrick.

Note that an opening spade or diamond lead would beat the contract because it uses up one of your entries. Also note that if you had three low clubs, you would play this hand correctly without even thinking. The fact that you have to ruff your ace and king of clubs creates the problem: "Sorry I went down partner, my hand was too strong."

A trump entry to dummy may depend on how the trump suit divides. For example:

#7

Contract: four hearts

Opening Lead: jack of clubs

North
♠ J 4
♡ Q 6 3
♦ A K Q 7 3
♣ A 4 2

South
♠ Q 5
♡ A K J 10 9
♦ 8 4
♣ 7 6 5 3

You have two losing spades and three losing clubs. The best chance to make your bid is to discard *two* of the losers on the diamond suit. If trumps divide 3-2, you can win ten tricks if diamonds divide no worse than 4-2. If trumps do not divide 3-2, you will have to rely on a 3-3 diamond break. So the first move is to find out how the trump suit splits.

Win the opening lead with the ace of clubs and cash two rounds of hearts leaving the queen in dummy and the ace or king in your hand.

1. If both opponents follow suit (hearts divide 3-2), cash *two* high diamonds. Assuming both opponents follow, ruff a *low* diamond in your hand. The queen of hearts will draw the last trump and is the entry you need to get to dummy to discard two of your losers on the remaining two good diamonds.

2. If an opponent shows out on first or second trump lead, draw all of the missing trumps and hope for a 3-3 diamond split.

If this were the full deal, the first plan would succeed:

```
                          North
                          ♠ J 4
                          ♡ Q 6 3
                          ◊ A K Q 7 3
                          ♣ A 4 2
        West                                East
        ♠ A 10 9 7 3                        ♠ K 8 6 2
        ♡ 8 2                               ♡ 7 5 4
        ◊ J 9 6 5                           ◊ 10 2
        ♣ J 10                              ♣ K Q 9 8
                          South
                          ♠ Q 5
                          ♡ A K J 10 9
                          ◊ 8 4
                          ♣ 7 6 5 3
```

The Timing: First Things First

Timing refers to the order in which you play your tricks, and this technique applies to practically every deal. So the following six hands could just as well be placed under other headings in this book, but they do illustrate that the best chance to fulfill your contract requires making good plays at exactly the right time. So here goes!

One of the most common ways to eliminate a loser is to discard it on a winning card in another suit. However, if you do not play the tricks in the right sequence, you may lose the trick before you can discard it.

For example:

#8

Contract: four spades

Opening Lead: queen of diamonds

North
♠ J 9 7 2
♡ K Q 4
◇ A 9 5
♣ 10 8 6

South
♠ Q 10 8 6 5 3
♡ 6 2
◇ K 7 4
♣ A K

You have four losers (two spades, one heart, and one diamond) and have only one good chance to make your bid: You must find West with the ace of hearts so you can establish the king or queen to discard your losing diamond.

Here is the full deal:

North
♠ J 9 7 2
♡ K Q 4
◇ A 9 5
♣ 10 8 6

West
♠ 4
♡ A 9 8 5
◇ Q J 10 6
♣ 7 5 3 2

East
♠ A K
♡ J 10 7 3
◇ 8 3 2
♣ Q J 9 4

South
♠ Q 10 8 6 5 3
♡ 6 2
◇ K 7 4
♣ A K

The right line of play is to win the first trick in your hand with the king of diamonds and lead a heart. If West plays low (it only makes your task easier if he plays the ace), win with the king (or queen) in dummy, return to your hand with a club, and lead another heart. If West ducks the second heart lead, you will not lose a heart trick; if he rises with the ace, you will have time to discard your losing diamond on the queen of hearts.

Note that if you carelessly play a trump at trick two or three, you lose the timing. East will win the trick and lead a diamond, enabling West to set you by cashing a diamond trick when he gets the lead with the ace of hearts.

#9   North
                                          ♠ K 6 3 2
                                          ♡ A Q 7
                                          ◇ 8 5 4
Contract: four spades   ♣ Q 10 6

Opening Lead: two of hearts   South
                                          ♠ A Q J 9 8 7
                                          ♡ 6 4
                                          ◇ A K 7
                                          ♣ J 3

You have four potential losers (one heart, one diamond, and two clubs). You can discard your diamond loser on a high club if you can drive out the ace and king of clubs before the opponents can drive out your ace and king of diamonds. The key play is to win the first trick with the *ace* of hearts.

Suppose the four hands are:

	North	
	♠ K 6 3 2	
	♡ A Q 7	
	◇ 8 5 4	
	♣ Q 10 6	
West		East
♠ 10 5		♠ 4
♡ 10 8 3 2		♡ K J 9 5
◇ Q 6 2		◇ J 10 9 3
♣ A 9 5 4		♣ K 8 7 2
	South	
	♠ A Q J 9 8 7	
	♡ 6 4	
	◇ A K 7	
	♣ J 3	

If you win with the ace of hearts at trick one, the contract is 100 percent safe. You have time to draw trumps and establish a club trick in dummy to discard your losing diamond.

Note that the heart finesse is an unnecessary risk, and you will be set as the cards lie if you do finesse. East has a routine switch to the jack of diamonds at trick two and the timing is now in the enemy's favor; they can dislodge the ace and king of diamonds and cash a diamond trick before you can obtain a discard in clubs.

In the last hand the key to success was to shun the finesse. This will *not* be the way to make the next hand.

#10   North
            ♠ A K J 8
            ♡ Q 7 4 2
            ◇ 3
Contract: six hearts   ♣ J 9 6 5

Opening Lead: king of clubs   South
            ♠ 7
            ♡ K J 10 9 8
            ◇ A K Q 4
            ♣ A 3 2

Since the ace of trumps is a sure loser, you cannot afford to concede a club trick. It will be necessary to discard *two* clubs on the spade suit *before* you relinquish the lead, so the only chance to make your bid is to finesse the jack of spades at trick two. If you are lucky and the finesse succeeds (and spades divide no worse than 5-3), you will be able to discard your two club losers on the ace and king of spades. If the finesse fails, you will probably be set two tricks (or three if they get a club ruff). The amount you win if you fulfill your contract, compared to the amount you lose if you go down an extra trick or two, makes the spade finesse a bargain.

Before reading the explanation, how would you play the following hand?

#11   North
            ♠ J 10 9 6
            ♡ J 3
            ◇ A K 2
Contract: four spades   ♣ 10 8 7 2

Opening Lead: ten of hearts   South
            ♠ A Q 8 7 3
            ♡ A 6
            ◇ 9 5 4
            ♣ K Q J

If you chose to win with the ace of hearts and cash the ace of spades, you played well. If you won with the ace of hearts and led a diamond to dummy so you could try the spade finesse, you failed the test.

Suppose the four hands are:

North
♠ J 10 9 6
♡ J 3
◇ A K 2
♣ 10 8 7 2

West
♠ K 5 2
♡ 10 9 8 4
◇ 8 7 6 3
♣ A 5

East
♠ 4
♡ K Q 7 5 2
◇ Q J 10
♣ 9 6 4 3

South
♠ A Q 8 7 3
♡ A 6
◇ 9 5 4
♣ K Q J

You have four losers, one in each suit. You can discard your diamond loser on dummy's ten of clubs if you draw the trumps and drive out the ace of clubs before the opponents can establish their diamond trick.

Now let's return to trick two. If you play a diamond to get the lead in dummy and take a losing spade finesse, the opponents will cash their heart trick and drive out your other high diamond. When they regain the lead with the ace of clubs, they will cash the setting trick in diamonds. Playing this way, your contract hinges on the spade finesse.

If you properly play the ace and another spade at tricks two and three (shunning the finesse) while you still have two diamond stoppers, you will have time to establish the club suit and discard your losing diamond; the trump suit will provide an entry to the ten of clubs.

At a notrump contract it is often necessary to give up the lead twice before you can develop the required number of tricks. If this is the case and you have only one more stopper in the enemy suit, try to drive out the entry in the hand of the defender who holds the long suit first.

For example:

#12

Contract: three notrump

Opening Lead: four of diamonds

North
♠ A Q J 9
♡ 5 2
◇ 8 6 3
♣ Q J 10 4

South
♠ 10 6 3
♡ A J 10
◇ A Q 7
♣ A 9 5 2

East plays the jack of diamonds on the first trick and you capture it with your queen. This gives you five winners, so you must develop tricks in both clubs and spades to make your bid. There is no problem if either the king of spades or the king of clubs is onside, but a good declarer would consider what will happen if both finesses fail.

Suppose this is the full deal:

North
♠ A Q J 9
♡ 5 2
◇ 8 6 3
♣ Q J 10 4

West
♠ 7 4
♡ Q 9 6 3
◇ K 10 5 4 2
♣ K 8

East
♠ K 8 5 2
♡ K 8 7 4
◇ J 9
♣ 7 6 3

South
♠ 10 6 3
♡ A J 10
◇ A Q 7
♣ A 9 5 2

West obviously has the length in diamonds, so you must knock out his entry first. If you mistakenly take the losing spade finesse at trick two, you will be set routinely. East will return a diamond to drive out your ace, and when you eventually take the club finesse West will win with the king and cash enough diamonds to defeat you.

Let's go back to the beginning and play the hand correctly. It would be nice to try the club finesse first but you have no entry to dummy, so cash your ace and lead another club to West's king. The contract is now secure against any defense. Suppose West leads the king of diamonds and you win with the ace (it is immaterial whether you hold up or not). Now take the losing spade finesse. Even if East has another diamond to lead, you cannot be set because the suit will be divided 4-3. You will regain the lead in time to take your nine tricks.

In the next deal a bid from an opponent is a helpful clue.

#13

Contract: six hearts

Opening Lead: queen of clubs

North
♠ 6 3
♡ K J 10 5
◇ Q 4 3
♣ A K 6 2

South
♠ A 10 5
♡ A Q 9 8 6 4 2
◇ K 7 2
♣ —

West overcalls your one-heart opening bid with one spade, and you reach a contract of six hearts. The problem is what to discard on the ace and king of clubs. If you discard two spades, you are left with two diamond losers; if you discard two diamonds, you are left with a losing spade and a losing diamond. The solution is to postpone your discarding. With this clue, can you see the winning line of play?

Here are the four hands:

                                     North
                                     ♠ 6 3
                                     ♡ K J 10 5
                                     ◇ Q 4 3
                                     ♣ A K 6 2

West   East
♠ K J 9 7 4   ♠ Q 8 2
♡ 7   ♡ 3
◇ A J 9   ◇ 10 8 6 5
♣ Q J 10 3   ♣ 9 8 7 5 4

                                     South
                                     ♠ A 10 5
                                     ♡ A Q 9 8 6 4 2
                                     ◇ K 7 2
                                     ♣ —

You can still make the bid if you play *one* high club and discard a diamond, but let's say you play a low club from dummy on the first trick and ruff in your hand. After drawing the missing trumps, the key play is to lead a low diamond from your hand. If West wins with the ace, you have no more diamond losers and can make your bid by discarding the two spades on the ace and king of clubs. If West plays a low diamond, you can make your bid by winning with the queen and discarding your two remaining diamonds on the ace and king of clubs.[1]

Note that the slam can be made if East has the ace of diamonds by leading the first diamond from dummy; but West bid, so it is logical to play him for the ace. Also observe that a spade lead will beat the contract; but what would you lead with the West hand?

Ruffing Losers in the Dummy

One reason for not drawing the enemy trumps right away is because dummy's trumps are needed to ruff losers from your hand. In such cases it is usually right not to draw any trumps.

For example:

---

1. This play, postponing your discard until you force a defender to commit himself to one play or another, is called "Morton's Fork Coup."

#14   North
                              ♠ A 8
                              ♡ 8 6 4 2
                              ♢ 7 2

Contract: four spades   ♣ Q 9 5 4 3

Opening Lead: jack of hearts   South
                              ♠ K Q J 10 9 4
                              ♡ A Q
                              ♢ A Q 6
                              ♣ 8 2

Thanks to the heart lead you have only four losers: two diamonds and two clubs. Your goal is to hold your diamond losers to one. It is tempting to lead a spade to dummy at trick two and try the diamond finesse, but this line of play puts the contract in jeopardy. If the diamond finesse fails, a trump lead from West will remove dummy's last trump and prevent you from ruffing a diamond.

The only way to be sure not to lose more than one diamond trick is to give up on the diamond finesse. Suppose you play the ace and another diamond at tricks two and three. Since the dummy still has two trumps, a trump lead from the opponents will do no harm; you will still have a trump in dummy to ruff your third diamond.

It is true you can win eleven tricks if you try the diamond finesse and it works; but the bid is *four* spades, not five.

Sometimes the possibility of ruffing a loser in dummy is obscure because the dummy has three cards in the suit.

For example:

#15   North
                              ♠ Q 9 4
                              ♡ 9 7 2
                              ♢ A 8 7

Contract: three spades   ♣ 8 7 5 3

Opening Lead: king of diamonds   South
                              ♠ K J 10 8 2
                              ♡ A K 5 4
                              ♢ 10 3
                              ♣ A 2

In your hand you have five losers: one spade, two hearts, one diamond, and one club. To make your bid you must hold your heart losers to one. If the suit divides 3-3, you can win a trick with the fourth heart in your hand; but you can also survive a 4-2 break by trumping the fourth round with a high trump in dummy.

Win the first trick with the ace of diamonds, cash the ace of clubs and the ace and king of hearts, and lead a third round of hearts before touching trumps. (Even one spade lead could be fatal; the opponents might be able to eliminate all of dummy's trumps before you can ruff a heart.) When you regain the lead, you will trump the fourth heart in dummy with the nine or queen of spades. The contract is safe unless one of your top tricks is ruffed, and the odds are better than 5-to-1 against that.

In the next deal the plan is the same as the last: to trump a heart loser in dummy. However, the trump suit has been changed so that you will not be able to ruff the fourth round of hearts with a high trump. This alters the way you should play the heart suit and when and how you should draw trumps.

#16	North
	♠ 7 4 3
	♡ 9 7 2
	◇ A 8 7
Contract: three spades	♣ 8 7 5 3
Opening Lead: king of diamonds	South
	♠ A K 8 6 5
	♡ A K 5 4
	◇ 10 3
	♣ A 2

Let's assume that spades divide 3-2 (otherwise the contract is hopeless), so you have the same five losers as in the last hand: one spade, two hearts, one diamond, and one club. Your goal is to hold your heart losers to one against a 4-2 split by ruffing the fourth round of hearts in dummy.

The best play is to win the ace of diamonds, cash one high spade (although this play is optional), and give up a heart trick to the enemy; do not play the ace or king of hearts. When you regain the lead, cash the remaining high spade, then the ace and king of hearts and, if the hearts do not divide 3-3, ruff your losing heart with dummy's remaining trump.

Here is the full deal to show you that other lines of play are inferior:

North
♠ 7 4 3
♡ 9 7 2
◇ A 8 7
♣ 8 7 5 3

West
♠ Q 10 9
♡ Q J 10 3
◇ K Q J
♣ 9 6 4

East
♠ J 2
♡ 8 6
◇ 9 6 5 4 2
♣ K Q J 10

South
♠ A K 8 6 5
♡ A K 5 4
◇ 10 3
♣ A 2

Note that if you play the ace, king, and another heart before you draw trumps, West can lead a fourth heart and promote a second spade trick for the defense. If you cash both the ace and king of spades before conceding a heart trick, West can prevent the heart ruff by cashing his high trump. Only the recommended line of play succeeds.

Here is one more look at ruffing a loser from your hand when the dummy has three cards in the suit:

#17

Contract: four spades

Opening Lead: ten of hearts

North
♠ 9 6
♡ 7 6 5 4
◇ 5 4 2
♣ Q 9 7 3

South
♠ A K Q J 3 2
♡ A J
◇ A K 8 7
♣ 4

You have four losers (one heart, two diamonds, and one club) and must limit your diamond losers to one if you are going to make your bid. If diamonds divide 3-3, you will always succeed; if the suit divides 5-1, you will always fail. If diamonds divide 4-2, you can hold the diamond losers to one if the player with four diamonds has the ten of spades.

Look at the four hands to see how it is done:

North
♠ 9 6
♡ 7 6 5 4
◇ 5 4 2
♣ Q 9 7 3

West
♠ 10 7 5
♡ 10 9 3
◇ Q 10 9 6
♣ A 8 2

East
♠ 8 4
♡ K Q 8 2
◇ J 3
♣ K J 10 6 5

South
♠ A K Q J 3 2
♡ A J
◇ A K 8 7
♣ 4

After winning East's queen of hearts with the ace, play the ace, king, and another diamond. Since West has four diamonds and the ten of spades, you can avoid losing your fourth diamond by ruffing it with the nine of spades. With a little bit of skill and a little bit of luck, the contract is made.

It is sometimes possible to ruff losers from your hand when the dummy has more cards in the suit than you, but first you must do some discarding.

For example:

#18   North
                                          ♠ J 5
                                          ♡ A 10 6 5 3 2
                                          ◊ 9 8 7 4
Contract: six spades   ♣ 4

Opening Lead: queen of diamonds   South
                                          ♠ A K Q 10 9 3
                                          ♡ 4
                                          ◊ A K 6
                                          ♣ K Q J

You must lose a trick to the ace of clubs, so the only hope to make your bid is to ruff your losing diamond in dummy.

Here is the full deal:

                          North
                          ♠ J 5
                          ♡ A 10 6 5 3 2
                          ◊ 9 8 7 4
                          ♣ 4
        West   East
        ♠ 8 7 4 2   ♠ 6
        ♡ K 9   ♡ Q J 8 7
        ◊ Q J 3   ◊ 10 5 2
        ♣ 10 6 5 2   ♣ A 9 8 7 3
                          South
                          ♠ A K Q 10 9 3
                          ♡ 4
                          ◊ A K 6
                          ♣ K Q J

Win the opening diamond lead and play a club, which East will win with his ace. Let's assume that East returns a diamond (although it doesn't matter), and you win the trick. Now cash your two high clubs, discarding two diamonds from dummy, and ruff your last diamond with the jack of spades. As the cards lie, the contract cannot be beaten if you play this way. Even a trump opening lead wouldn't matter, as East could not lead a second trump when he wins with the ace of clubs.

#19

North
♠ 10 8 3
♡ 7 6 5 2
◇ 6 4

Contract: four spades

♣ A Q J 10

Opening Lead: three of hearts

South
♠ A K 7 6 4
♡ K
◇ K Q J 10 9
♣ 8 2

West	North	East	South
		1 ♡	1 ♠
Pass	2 ♠	Pass	4 ♠
All Pass			

If the missing spades divide 3-2, you have one losing trick in each suit. Assuming a 3-2 trump split, it appears that the contract hinges on the club finesse (which figures to lose because of East's opening bid). But you do not need a winning club finesse to make your bid; if all goes well, you can ruff your losing club in the dummy.

Look at the four hands as you read the analysis.

North
♠ 10 8 3
♡ 7 6 5 2
◇ 6 4
♣ A Q J 10

West
♠ J 9
♡ Q 4 3
◇ 8 7 3 2
♣ 9 7 5 4

East
♠ Q 5 2
♡ A J 10 9 8
◇ A 5
♣ K 6 3

South
♠ A K 7 6 4
♡ K
◇ K Q J 10 9
♣ 8 2

East wins the opening heart lead with the ace and plays another heart, which you ruff. Now cash one high trump (optional) and lead a diamond; East wins with his ace and continues with another heart. You ruff and cash your second high trump. When both opponents follow suit, the contract is cold. You will lead your good diamonds and discard the queen-jack-ten of clubs from the dummy. East may ruff one of the diamonds in the interim, but he cannot stop you from ruffing your club loser in dummy. It takes an opening club lead to beat the contract.

Quiz for Chapter Four

1.

North
♠ Q 8 7 6
♡ 10 3
◇ A 9 8
♣ J 6 5 2

South
♠ K J 10 9 4 2
♡ A Q J
◇ 7 6 3
♣ A

West	North	East	South
			1 ♠
Pass	2 ♠	Pass	4 ♠
All Pass			

West leads the king of clubs.

2.

North
♠ A 4
♡ A J 7 5 2
◇ A 8 6 2
♣ A 6

South
♠ Q J 10 9 8 2
♡ 9
◇ 4 3
♣ K 8 7 5

West	North	East	South
	1 ♡	Pass	1 ♠
Pass	2 ◇	Pass	2 ♠
Pass	3 ♠	Pass	4 ♠
All Pass			

West leads the queen of diamonds.

3.

North
♠ Q 7 6 3
♡ 10 9 4
◇ –
♣ A K J 6 5 2

South
♠ A K J 10 9 8
♡ K J 6 5 3
◇ A 2
♣ –

West	North	East	South
			1 ♠
Pass	2 ♣	Pass	2 ♡
Pass	3 ♠	Pass	6 ♠
All Pass			

West leads the queen of diamonds.

4.

North
♠ A K 5
♡ 7 4 2
◇ A Q
♣ A 9 8 6 3

South
♠ Q J 10 8 6 4
♡ A 10 3
◇ J 2
♣ 7 5

West	North	East	South
	1 NT	Pass	4 ♠
All Pass			

West leads the five of diamonds.

5.

North
♠ K Q
♡ K Q 8 5
◇ J 9 7 6 4 3
♣ 2

South
♠ A J 10 9 8 7
♡ A
◇ 10 2
♣ K 6 5 3

West	North	East	South
			1 ♠
Pass	2 ◇	Pass	2 ♠
Pass	3 ♠	Pass	4 ♠
All Pass			

West leads the jack of hearts.

6.

North
♠ J 6 3
♡ 5 2
◇ K 8 4
♣ A Q 9 8 7

South
♠ K Q 5
♡ A Q 8
◇ A 9 6 3
♣ J 10 2

West	North	East	South
			1 NT
Pass	3 NT	All Pass	

West leads the six of hearts and East plays the ten.

7.

North
♠ Q 10 4
♡ Q 8 3
◇ Q 9 5
♣ A K 6 2

South
♠ A 8 6
♡ A K J 10 9 5 2
◇ K 4
♣ 4

West	North	East	South
	1 ♣	Pass	1 ♡
1 ♠	Pass	Pass	4 NT
Pass	5 ◇	Pass	6 ♡
All Pass			

West leads the ten of clubs.

8.

North
♠ 3
♡ 9 8 5
◇ J 10 7 6 2
♣ 10 8 5 4

South
♠ K Q J 10 9
♡ A K 7 6 2
◇ A Q
♣ 3

West	North	East	South
			1 ♠
1 NT	Pass	Pass	3 ♡
Pass	4 ♡	All Pass	

West leads first the king of clubs and then the ace of clubs.

Answers to Quiz for Chapter Four

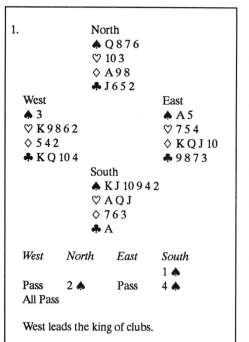

1.

North
♠ Q 8 7 6
♡ 10 3
♢ A 9 8
♣ J 6 5 2

West
♠ 3
♡ K 9 8 6 2
♢ 5 4 2
♣ K Q 10 4

East
♠ A 5
♡ 7 5 4
♢ K Q J 10
♣ 9 8 7 3

South
♠ K J 10 9 4 2
♡ A Q J
♢ 7 6 3
♣ A

West	North	East	South
			1 ♠
Pass	2 ♠	Pass	4 ♠
All Pass			

West leads the king of clubs.

You have four losers (one spade, one heart, and two diamonds) but should make your bid even though the king of hearts is offside. Win the first trick with the ace of clubs and lead any heart from your hand. Let's say you select the jack of hearts. West wins with the king and leads a diamond (his best defense). Win with the ace and cash two high hearts, discarding a diamond from dummy. This eliminates one of your diamond losers and the contract is made. This is by far the best line of play, although it is likely to fail if hearts divide worse than 5-3.

Note that if you lead a spade at trick two, you lose the timing. East will win with the ace of spades and switch to the king of diamonds to drive out your ace. Since the heart finesse fails, the opponents can cash two diamond tricks and set you.

2.

North
♠ A 4
♡ A J 7 5 2
♢ A 8 6 2
♣ A 6

West
♠ 5 3
♡ 8 6 4
♢ Q J 10
♣ Q 10 9 3 2

East
♠ K 7 6
♡ K Q 10 3
♢ K 9 7 5
♣ J 4

South
♠ Q J 10 9 8 2
♡ 9
♢ 4 3
♣ K 8 7 5

West	North	East	South
	1 ♡	Pass	1 ♠
Pass	2 ♢	Pass	2 ♠
Pass	3 ♠	Pass	4 ♠
All Pass			

West leads the queen of diamonds.

You have four losers (one spade, one diamond, and two clubs) and can make your bid by ruffing *one* of your club losers in dummy. Win the diamond opening lead with the ace, cash two high clubs and — to guard against East having a doubleton — ruff the third club with the *ace* of spades. The contract is now safe.

Note that if you ruffed with the *four* of spades, East could overruff and return a spade. Then you would be unable to ruff any club losers and wind up down one. If the bid were five spades, it would be necessary to ruff two clubs in dummy; only then should you risk ruffing the third round of clubs with the four of spades.

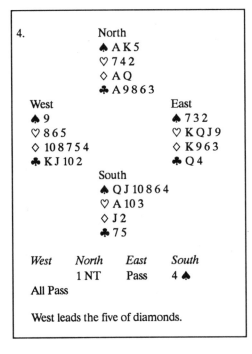

3.

North
- ♠ Q 7 6 3
- ♡ 10 9 4
- ◇ —
- ♣ A K J 6 5 2

West
- ♠ 5 4
- ♡ A Q 2
- ◇ Q J 9 8 6
- ♣ 10 8 7

East
- ♠ 2
- ♡ 8 7
- ◇ K 10 7 5 4 3
- ♣ Q 9 4 3

South
- ♠ A K J 10 9 8
- ♡ K J 6 5 3
- ◇ A 2
- ♣ —

West	North	East	South
			1 ♠
Pass	2 ♣	Pass	2 ♡
Pass	3 ♠	Pass	6 ♠
All Pass			

West leads the queen of diamonds.

To make this slam, you must limit your heart losers to one trick. It will not be necessary to risk a heart finesse if the club suit can be established to discard four of your five hearts. The trump suit provides the entries you need and you must be careful not to waste any of them.

Ruff the opening diamond lead and cash the ace and king of clubs, discarding two hearts from your hand. Now ruff a club, cash one high spade, lead over to dummy's queen to draw the last missing trump, and ruff a fourth round of clubs in your hand. The two remaining clubs are good tricks and you can get to dummy to discard two more hearts by ruffing your ace of diamonds.

If the club suit does not divide satisfactorily, or if the trumps are 3-0, you will find this out in time to be able to try the heart finesse.

4.

North
- ♠ A K 5
- ♡ 7 4 2
- ◇ A Q
- ♣ A 9 8 6 3

West
- ♠ 9
- ♡ 8 6 5
- ◇ 10 8 7 5 4
- ♣ K J 10 2

East
- ♠ 7 3 2
- ♡ K Q J 9
- ◇ K 9 6 3
- ♣ Q 4

South
- ♠ Q J 10 8 6 4
- ♡ A 10 3
- ◇ J 2
- ♣ 7 5

West	North	East	South
	1 NT	Pass	4 ♠
All Pass			

West leads the five of diamonds.

With four possible losers (two hearts, one diamond, and one club), the best chance to make your bid is to establish the club suit for a discard. This line of play will succeed unless spades divide 4-0 or clubs divide worse than 4-2. If you make the mistake of finessing the queen of diamonds at trick one, you lose the timing if the finesse fails. East will lead a heart and the opponents will collect four tricks before you can establish the clubs.

Since establishing the club suit offers a much better chance than a finesse, win the first trick with the ace of diamonds. Do *not* cash the ace of clubs and do *not* draw trumps as you will need the entries to dummy. At trick two, concede a club trick to the opponents. Suppose they cash the king of diamonds and lead a heart, which you win with the ace. Now cash the queen of spades (optional), lead a club to the ace, and ruff a club with a high trump. (If clubs divided 3-3, you would be able to discard two losing hearts and make an overtrick.) Since clubs divide 4-2, cross to dummy with a spade and ruff another club. Finally, lead a spade to dummy to draw the last trump, and discard one of your losing hearts on the good club.

5.

```
                North
                ♠ K Q
                ♡ K Q 8 5
                ◇ J 9 7 6 4 3
                ♣ 2
West                          East
♠ 4 2                         ♠ 6 5 3
♡ J 10 9 6 4                  ♡ 7 3 2
◇ K 5                         ◇ A Q 8
♣ A Q 9 7                     ♣ J 10 8 4
                South
                ♠ A J 10 9 8 7
                ♡ A
                ◇ 10 2
                ♣ K 6 5 3
```

West	North	East	South
			1 ♠
Pass	2 ◇	Pass	2 ♠
Pass	3 ♠	Pass	4 ♠
All Pass			

West leads the jack of hearts.

You have two losing diamonds and four losing clubs. The best chance to make your bid is to discard two losers on the king and queen of hearts, and to ruff a club in dummy. Win the opening heart lead with the ace and *lead a club from your hand.* The opponents can win two diamond tricks if they choose, but that is all they will get. Regardless of how they defend, they cannot stop you from ruffing a club and discarding two losers on the high hearts.

If you chose to lead a spade to dummy at trick two—so that you can lead a club toward your king—you can be set with the ace of clubs offside if West returns a trump. With no trumps left in dummy, you can no longer ruff a club.

6.

```
                North
                ♠ J 6 3
                ♡ 5 2
                ◇ K 8 4
                ♣ A Q 9 8 7
West                          East
♠ A 10 7                      ♠ 9 8 4 2
♡ K J 9 6 4                   ♡ 10 7 3
◇ 7 2                         ◇ Q J 10 5
♣ 5 4 3                       ♣ K 6
                South
                ♠ K Q 5
                ♡ A Q 8
                ◇ A 9 6 3
                ♣ J 10 2
```

West	North	East	South
			1 NT
Pass	3 NT	All Pass	

West leads the six of hearts and East plays the ten.

With the heart lead, you have five winners: two hearts, two diamonds, and one club. The layout that puts your contract in jeopardy is the one you see: East has the king of clubs and West the ace of spades. To guard against this, you must knock out the entry of the defender with the long suit first: *Play a spade before trying the club finesse.* Let's assume you lead the king of spades. If West wins with the ace and leads a heart, hold up till the third round and take the club finesse. Since East has no more hearts, the king of clubs will be the last trick for the defense. If West ducks your king of spades lead, you have nine sure tricks by abandoning spades and taking the club finesse.

Note that if you try the club finesse first, East will win with the king and return a heart. The timing is now in the opponents' favor; West will get the lead with the ace of spades and run enough heart tricks to set you before you can score a ninth trick.

7.

	North	
	♠ Q 10 4	
	♡ Q 8 3	
	◇ Q 9 5	
	♣ A K 6 2	

West		East
♠ K J 9 5 3 2		♠ 7
♡ 6		♡ 7 4
◇ A J 7		◇ 10 8 6 3 2
♣ 10 9 8		♣ Q J 7 5 3

	South	
	♠ A 8 6	
	♡ A K J 10 9 5 2	
	◇ K 4	
	♣ 4	

West	North	East	South
	1 ♣	Pass	1 ♡
1 ♠	Pass	Pass	4 NT
Pass	5 ◇	Pass	6 ♡
All Pass			

West leads the ten of clubs.

8.

	North	
	♠ 3	
	♡ 9 8 5	
	◇ J 10 7 6 2	
	♣ 10 8 5 4	

West		East
♠ A 5 2		♠ 8 7 6 4
♡ Q J 4		♡ 10 3
◇ K 9 8		◇ 5 4 3
♣ A K J 6		♣ Q 9 7 2

	South	
	♠ K Q J 10 9	
	♡ A K 7 6 2	
	◇ A Q	
	♣ 3	

West	North	East	South
			1 ♠
1 NT	Pass	Pass	3 ♡
Pass	4 ♡	All Pass	

West leads first the king of clubs and then the ace of clubs.

With so few high cards missing, it is hard to imagine that West could have bid without the ace of diamonds and the king of spades. This is important information, as the winning line of play depends on guessing the location of these cards.

After winning the opening club lead, draw two rounds of trumps (optional, but good technique) and *lead the four of diamonds*. If West plays low, win with the queen of diamonds and discard your king of diamonds on dummy's high club; your only losing trick will be the king of spades. If West goes up with his ace of diamonds, your two spade losers can be discarded on dummy's high club and queen of diamonds; the ace of diamonds will be your only loser. Whether West takes the ace of diamonds or not, he will win only one trick—another example of "Morton's Fork Coup."

Note that if East has the ace of diamonds, the contract also can be made; but then the first diamond lead must be a low one from dummy. The bidding helped you to guess right in this case.

If trumps divide 3-2 (otherwise the contract is hopeless), you have four losers, one in each suit. There is nothing you can do about the spade, heart, and club losers, but the diamond loser can be eliminated—without taking a finesse. You should play to *ruff the queen of diamonds in dummy*.

After ruffing the second club lead, cash one high trump (optional) and play the *nine* of spades—West may not take his ace. Assume West does win with the ace of spades and lead a third round of clubs for you to ruff. Now cash your other high trump and run the spade suit to discard four diamonds from dummy. West can take his high trump by ruffing the fourth or fifth round of spades if he chooses, but it is the only trick he will get. Eventually you will be able to ruff the queen of diamonds in the dummy.

5
Trump Control Problems

♣   ◇   ♡   ♠   ♣   ◇   ♡   ♠

The fate of many contracts is determined by the way declarer handles the trump suit. The problem may be how to draw trumps, when to draw trumps, whether or not to ruff, to establish a side suit, to prevent a winner from being ruffed, or to avoid an overruff or trump promotion. Here are twenty-three hands on the subject.

When to Draw the High Trump(s)

When you have drawn all the trumps except one or two high ones, the usual strategy is to go about your business establishing and winning tricks in the other suits; it is not necessary or advisable to draw the opponent's high trump(s).

Here is a fundamental example:

#1	North
	♠ 7 6 3
	♡ 8 5 4 2
	◇ A K 9
Contract: four spades	♣ Q J 10
Opening Lead: king of hearts	South
	♠ A K 8 5 4
	♡ 7
	◇ Q 10
	♣ K 9 4 3 2

You must lose one heart and one club, so you need a 3-2 spade break to make your bid. Suppose the defenders lead two rounds of hearts and you ruff the second. Next you cash the ace and king of spades, both opponents following suit. Your contract is now safe if you drive out the ace of clubs; you still have two trumps left and cannot be prevented from winning ten tricks.

Suppose these are the four hands:

<pre>
                            North
                            ♠ 7 6 3
                            ♡ 8 5 4 2
                            ◇ A K 9
                            ♣ Q J 10
        West   East
        ♠ Q 10 2   ♠ J 9
        ♡ K Q J 6   ♡ A 10 9 3
        ◇ 7 5 4 3   ◇ J 8 6 2
        ♣ A 8   ♣ 7 6 5
                            South
                            ♠ A K 8 5 4
                            ♡ 7
                            ◇ Q 10
                            ♣ K 9 4 3 2
</pre>

Note that if you lead a third round of spades (after cashing the ace and king), you will lose control of the trump suit; West will win with the queen and lead another heart. Whether you ruff this trick with your last trump or not, the opponents will be able to win a second heart trick and set the contract.

An exception to the rule that you should not draw the high trump (or trumps) occurs when you have a long suit in dummy that you would like to run unmolested.
For example:

<pre>
#2   North
                            ♠ 9 3
                            ♡ A 8 7
                            ◇ A K J 7 5
Contract: four spades   ♣ 6 4 2

Opening Lead: queen of hearts   South
                            ♠ A K 7 6 4 2
                            ♡ 3
                            ◇ Q 9 2
                            ♣ K J 5
</pre>

The best plan to make your bid is to draw *all* of the missing trumps, *including the high trumps,* and then to discard two clubs on the diamond suit. After winning the first trick with the ace of hearts, suppose you cash the ace and king of spades and East shows out on the second lead.
This is a likely layout:

North
♠ 9 3
♡ A 8 7
◇ A K J 7 5
♣ 6 4 2

North
♠ Q 10 8 5
♡ Q J 10 4
◇ 8 6
♣ A 7 3

East
♠ J
♡ K 9 6 5 2
◇ 10 4 3
♣ Q 10 9 8

South
♠ A K 7 6 4 2
♡ 3
◇ Q 9 2
♣ K J 5

As the cards lie, you can make your bid if you drive out the two high trumps before trying to run the diamond suit. At trick four, lead a spade, which West wins with the ten. No lead from West can set you, so let's say he plays another heart, which you ruff. Now lead a fourth spade to drive out his queen. You still have one trump left and cannot be stopped from regaining the lead and running five diamond tricks to make your contract.

Note that if you try to run the diamond suit before driving out the high trumps, West can ruff the third round of diamonds. Since you have no further entry to dummy, you must lose at least two club tricks.

Keeping Trump Control

When your objective is to keep trump control, the general rule is to hoard the trumps in the *long hand*. This is especially true when you have only seven trumps between your hand and dummy.

For example:

#3

Contract: four spades

Opening Lead: king of hearts

North
♠ A Q 10
♡ 10 8 2
◇ A Q 10
♣ J 9 5 4

South
♠ K J 8 6
♡ 5
◇ K J 9 5 3
♣ A 6 3

You have ten cashable tricks, but you must draw the enemy trumps before you can win them all. There is no problem if they are divided 3-3, but if they are 4-2 — as you should expect them to be — you must save all four spades in your hand .

Suppose the full deal is:

North
♠ A Q 10
♡ 10 8 2
◊ A Q 10
♣ J 9 5 4

West
♠ 9 7 5 2
♡ A K 4 3
◊ 6 4
♣ 8 7 2

East
♠ 4 3
♡ Q J 9 7 6
◊ 8 7 2
♣ K Q 10

South
♠ K J 8 6
♡ 5
◊ K J 9 5 3
♣ A 6 3

After winning the first heart trick, West leads the ace of hearts and you discard one of your losing clubs — a "loser on a loser." (If you mistakenly ruff, West will have more trumps than you and can set your contract no matter how you proceed.) At trick three, West leads a third heart and you discard your other club loser. (There is no way the enemy can force you to trump in your hand — if a fourth heart is led, you can ruff in dummy.) Regardless of what they lead next, you will be able to draw the trumps and make your bid as long as spades divide no worse than 4-2.

The next hand is an oddity. The best play to make your contract is to discard a *winner*.

#4

Contract: four spades

Opening Lead: king of diamonds

North
♠ 10 5 2
♡ A K 8 3
◊ 10 7 4
♣ 6 4 3

South
♠ A K Q J
♡ 10 7
◊ 9 2
♣ A K Q J 10

West overcalls your one-club opening bid with one diamond, and you wind up in a good contract of four spades (though five clubs is safer). West leads the king, ace, and queen of diamonds, and you look around for a loser to discard, but you do not have one. So what do you do? You discard a winner of course!
Suppose the four hands are:

North
♠ 10 5 2
♡ A K 8 3
◇ 10 7 4
♣ 6 4 3

West
♠ 9 8 6 4
♡ 5 2
◇ A K Q 8 3
♣ 7 5

East
♠ 7 3
♡ Q J 9 6 4
◇ J 6 5
♣ 9 8 2

South
♠ A K Q J
♡ 10 7
◇ 9 2
♣ A K Q J 10

Once you discard on the third diamond, the rest is easy. If West leads a fourth diamond, you will trump with dummy's ten of spades. If West leads anything else, you simply win that trick, draw four rounds of trumps, and claim the rest. Incidentally, since it does not matter which winner you discard, you might as well give your partner a thrill and discard the ace of clubs. Show-off!

You may have analyzed that you can trump the third round of diamonds and still make the contract. This is true, as you could against many other distributions; but you must *guess the opposing distributions* and *play skillfully*. The recommended play avoids any guesswork.

Here is another way to guard against losing trump control to the opponents.

#5

Contract: four hearts

Opening Lead: queen of spades

North
♠ 8 3 2
♡ 6 4
◇ J 2
♣ A Q 9 8 7 5

South
♠ A
♡ A K J 9 3
◇ K Q 10 9 5 4
♣ 6

Although you have only seven trumps, four hearts is a good contract. Outside the trump suit, you have only one losing trick. So you must play as safely as possible to lose no more than two heart tricks. After winning the opening spade lead with the ace, the best way to play the heart suit is to cash the ace and king. *Do not lead another heart until the bitter end.*

Suppose the four hands are:

                                    North
                                    ♠ 8 3 2
                                    ♡ 6 4
                                    ◇ J 2
                                    ♣ A Q 9 8 7 5
        West   East
        ♠ Q J 9 5   ♠ K 10 7 6 4
        ♡ Q 10 8 2   ♡ 7 5
        ◇ A 7 6   ◇ 8 3
        ♣ 10 3   ♣ K J 4 2
                                    South
                                    ♠ A
                                    ♡ A K J 9 3
                                    ◇ K Q 10 9 5 4
                                    ♣ 6

After cashing the ace and king of hearts, lead a diamond to force out the ace. Ruff the spade return and lead diamonds at every opportunity; you will lose only two heart tricks and one diamond trick. This line of play is foolproof as long as both opponents follow to the second trump lead.

If you play the ace, king, and another heart (hoping for a 3-3 split), or try the heart finesse, you will lose trump control and be set if the opponents lead spades at every opportunity. If you don't believe me, try it.

In the next hand you have eight trumps, but the suit still requires delicate handling.

#6   North
                                    ♠ J 7
                                    ♡ 8 6 3 2
                                    ◇ K 7 4
Contract: four hearts   ♣ J 9 5 4

Opening Lead: queen of diamonds   South
                                    ♠ A K 6 5 3 2
                                    ♡ A 9 7 4
                                    ◇ 5
                                    ♣ A K

A 4-4 trump fit is often better than 5-3 or 6-2, and it is certainly true here. A four-spade contract has virtually no chance; but four hearts can be made with normal breaks in the major suits.

Whether you play the king of diamonds on the first trick or not, the defenders will win it and lead a diamond at trick two. Before reading further, how would you play this hand?

                              North
                              ♠ J 7
                              ♡ 8 6 3 2
                              ◊ K 7 4
                              ♣ J 9 5 4
        West   East
        ♠ Q 10 8   ♠ 9 4
        ♡ K Q 10   ♡ J 5
        ◊ Q J 10 9   ◊ A 8 6 3 2
        ♣ 6 3 2   ♣ Q 10 8 7
                              South
                              ♠ A K 6 5 3 2
                              ♡ A 9 7 4
                              ◊ 5
                              ♣ A K

You should ruff the second diamond trick and lead a *low* heart. Suppose West wins this trick and leads another diamond (no other defense is better). You trump it, and cash the ace and king of spades. When both opponents follow suit, cash the ace of hearts and then ruff the third round of spades in dummy. The rest of your spades are now good, so lead a club to your hand and keep leading spades until West takes his heart trick. Since you still have a trump in dummy and the high club in your hand, the contract is safe. Your only losers are two hearts and one diamond.

The success of this contract depends on how you handle the trump suit. If your first heart play is the ace, or if you try to ruff a spade before you draw two rounds of trumps, you will be set.

When you have a losing trump trick, or a possible losing trump trick, it may be important to give up that trick while there is still a trump in the dummy.

For example:

#7   North
                              ♠ 8 5 4
                              ♡ —
                              ◊ A K 9 7 4
Contract: six spades   ♣ K Q J 10 2

Opening Lead: queen of hearts South
                              ♠ A K 6 3 2
                              ♡ K 9 7 5 4
                              ◊ 8 6
                              ♣ A

The six-spade contract is a good one, essentially requiring a 3-2 spade break. After ruffing the first trick in dummy, lead a spade and *duck it*; let the opponents win the first spade trick. Since you still have a trump in dummy, you can ruff if the opponents lead a second heart. No matter what they return, you can win the trick and play the ace and king of spades to draw the rest of the trumps. Your losing hearts can be discarded on dummy's good clubs.

Other lines of play might succeed on a lucky day, but these require favorable distribution in addition to a 3-2 trump break. Save your luck for when you really need it.

Note that conceding the first spade trick is correct even if you hold ♠ A K Q x x – to guard against a 4-1 trump split.

How would you play the next hand?

#8	North
	♠ K 10
	♡ A
	◇ A Q 7 5 3
Contract: six spades	♣ A K Q J 2
Opening Lead: king of hearts	North
	♠ A J 9 7 6 2
	♡ 9 4 2
	◇ 4 2
	♣ 10 5

In your hand you have two losing hearts and one losing diamond, but they all can be discarded on dummy's club suit. You can make your slam whether you lose a trick to the queen of spades or not, provided the opponent who wins with the queen of spades cannot cash a heart trick. Once again, the best solution is to leave a trump in the dummy.

After winning the first trick with the ace of hearts, *lead the ten of spades and let it ride*.

1. If West wins with the queen of spades, he cannot win a heart trick because the dummy still has a trump. Whatever West returns, you will be able to draw the rest of the trumps and discard your losers on the club suit.

2. If East has the queen of spades, the ten will win the second trick; then you will cash the king of spades. If East started with two or three spades, you can draw trumps and win all thirteen tricks.

If East started with four spades (you will know this if West shows out when you cash the king of spades), the contract is safe if East has at least two clubs. Just run the club suit. You will overruff if East chooses to ruff, and discard a loser if he chooses to discard.

Establishing a Side Suit

When you have a two-suited hand (at least 5-4), ruffing once or twice in the dummy is a common way to establish the side suit.

For example:

#9	North
	♠ Q 6 5 4
	♡ J 5
	◊ 9 2
Contract: four hearts	♣ Q 10 8 7 3
Opening Lead: jack of spades	South
	♠ 7
	♡ A K Q 10 2
	◊ A K Q 6 4
	♣ 9 5

Since you are going to lose one spade and two clubs, you must avoid any losers in the red suits. Suppose the play begins with the opponents winning the first spade trick and leading another spade, which you ruff. If you draw trumps right away, or immediately try to cash three high diamonds, you will fail unless diamonds divide 3-3.

The best play, which will succeed as long as both red suits divide no worse than 4-2, is first to cash *two* high diamonds and then to ruff a low diamond with the jack of hearts. Now the remaining diamonds in your hand will be good, so you can draw trumps and claim ten tricks.

#10	North
	♠ A 5 4 3
	♡ 7
	◊ 9 3
Contract: six spades	♣ A Q 8 7 4 2
Opening Lead: nine of clubs	South
	♠ K Q J 10
	♡ A K 10 8 5 2
	◊ A
	♣ 6 3

It is very likely that West's nine-of-clubs opening lead is a singleton, so you rise with the ace of clubs and turn your thoughts to making your slam by establishing the heart suit.

This time let's look at the four hands while we play.

                                North
                                ♠ A 5 4 3
                                ♡ 7
                                ◇ 9 3
                                ♣ A Q 8 7 4 2

West   East
♠ 7 6   ♠ 9 8 2
♡ Q J 9 4   ♡ 6 3
◇ K J 8 6 5 2   ◇ Q 10 7 4
♣ 9   ♣ K J 10 5

                                South
                                ♠ K Q J 10
                                ♡ A K 10 8 5 2
                                ◇ A
                                ♣ 6 3

After winning with the ace of clubs, lead a heart to your ace and ruff a heart in dummy with a low spade. In order to establish the heart suit, you must ruff one more in dummy. Get back to your hand with a trump and ruff another low heart with the *ace* of spades. The remaining hearts in your hand are now good, so draw the missing trumps and claim twelve tricks. The contract is safe as long as hearts divide no worse than 4-2 and spades no worse than 4-1 — better than an 80-percent chance.

Now let's look at a 6-5 two-suiter:

#11   North
                                            ♠ 6 4
                                            ♡ 5 3
                                            ◇ 9 8 6 2
Contract: four hearts   ♣ J 10 8 7 5

Opening Lead: king of diamonds   South
                                            ♠ A K Q 5 3
                                            ♡ A 10 8 7 4 2
                                            ◇ —
                                            ♣ A 6

You have one club loser and at least two heart losers, so hearts must divide 3-2 to have any chance. The challenge is to avoid a spade loser if possible. If spades are 3-3, there is no problem. You can win ten tricks by ruffing the opening lead and playing the ace and another heart. But you can also succeed versus a 4-2 spade split if the defender with the doubleton spade has three hearts.

Suppose the full deal is:

North
♠ 6 4
♡ 5 3
◇ 9 8 6 2
♣ J 10 8 7 5

West
♠ J 9 8 7
♡ J 6
◇ A K 10 4
♣ K 9 2

East
♠ 10 2
♡ K Q 9
◇ Q J 7 5 3
♣ Q 4 3

South
♠ A K Q 5 3
♡ A 10 8 7 4 2
◇ —
♣ A 6

After ruffing the opening lead, cash two high spades and ruff a low spade in dummy. Whether East overruffs or not, you will play the ace and another heart as soon as you can to make your contract.

Note that you would be set if the defender with the doubleton spade also had a doubleton heart—you would lose three heart tricks—but you would also be set with any other line of play. The recommended play gives you an extra chance.

Here is another kind of extra chance to set up your side suit without losing a trick.

#12

Contract: four spades

Opening Lead: king of diamonds

North
♠ 7 5 4
♡ A 2
◇ 8 6 5 2
♣ Q 9 6 4

South
♠ A K Q J 2
♡ K Q 8 7 3
◇ 4 3
♣ 7

With three inevitable minor-suit losers, you must avoid losing a heart trick. There is no problem if hearts divide 3-3; but can you figure out a distribution of the cards that allows you to make your bid versus a 4-2 heart break?

Here is the kind of layout to hope for:

```
                        North
                        ♠ 7 5 4
                        ♡ A 2
                        ◇ 8 6 5 2
                        ♣ Q 9 6 4
        West                              East
        ♠ 9 6 3                           ♠ 10 8
        ♡ J 10 5 4                        ♡ 9 6
        ◇ A K Q                           ◇ J 10 9 7
        ♣ 10 8 5                          ♣ A K J 3 2
                        South
                        ♠ A K Q J 2
                        ♡ K Q 8 7 3
                        ◇ 4 3
                        ♣ 7
```

The lucky break that gives you the extra chance is to find either defender with a doubleton heart and a doubleton spade, in which case you can make your bid by ruffing the third round of hearts in dummy. Let's assume West leads three rounds of diamonds and you ruff the third. Cash two spade tricks and, when both opponents follow suit, cash two (or three) high hearts and lead a low heart to ruff with dummy's last trump. Since East has no more spades, he cannot overruff. All that is left to be done is to ruff another diamond in your hand, draw the last trump, and cash your remaining heart winners.

Note that if either defender shows out on the second spade lead—the suit divides 4-1—this plan will not work. You would then have to draw all of the trumps and hope for a 3-3 heart break.

Another way of establishing a side suit is the ruffing finesse.
For example:

#13   North
                                ♠ 9 8 4
                                ♡ —
                                ◇ K 10 5 3
Contract: four spades   ♣ Q 8 7 6 3 2

Opening Lead: queen of spades   South
                                ♠ A K 7 6 2
                                ♡ Q J 10 9 8
                                ◇ A 4
                                ♣ 5

With one losing club and hopefully only one losing spade, you must hold your heart losers to one or you will surely be set. What you need to make your contract is a 3-2 spade split and to find West with at least one of the heart honors.

Suppose the full deal is:

```
                          North
                          ♠ 9 8 4
                          ♡ —
                          ◊ K 10 5 3
                          ♣ Q 8 7 6 3 2
         West                              East
         ♠ Q J 10                          ♠ 5 3
         ♡ K 7 5 3                          ♡ A 6 4 2
         ◊ Q 6 2                            ◊ J 9 8 7
         ♣ K 9 4                            ♣ A J 10
                          South
                          ♠ A K 7 6 2
                          ♡ Q J 10 9 8
                          ◊ A 4
                          ♣ 5
```

After winning the first trick with a high spade, lead any heart to execute a ruffing finesse. If West covers with the king, you will ruff in dummy; but assuming he plays a low heart, you discard a club from dummy, and East wins with the ace. East returns a trump (no defense is better), you win in your hand, and lead another heart. If West covers with the king, you will ruff with dummy's last trump; while if he plays low, you will discard from dummy, and continue leading hearts until he does cover. This limits your losers to one heart, one spade, and one club, so the contract is made.

Protecting Winners from Being Ruffed

If you are aware that the opponents may trump one of your winning tricks, you can sometimes take preventive measures.

For example:

#14

Contract: six hearts

Opening Lead: four of clubs

```
North
♠ A 9 8
♡ A Q J 3
◊ 5
♣ A Q 10 9 7

South
♠ 7
♡ 10 9 8 6 4
◊ A K 4 2
♣ K J 3
```

On the surface it appears that you may lose only one trick to the king of hearts, but you are in danger of a club ruff. Suppose the four hands are:

North
♠ A 9 8
♡ A Q J 3
◇ 5
♣ A Q 10 9 7

West
♠ Q 10 6 5 2
♡ 7 5
◇ Q J 8 7 3
♣ 4

East
♠ K J 4 3
♡ K 2
◇ 10 9 6
♣ 8 6 5 2

South
♠ 7
♡ 10 9 8 6 4
◇ A K 4 2
♣ K J 3

If you win the first club trick and take a heart finesse, East will return a club for West to trump. So you must not risk the heart finesse. Play the ace and another heart, and the contract is safe no matter what distribution you encounter.

#15

Contract: four hearts

Opening Lead: ten of diamonds

North
♠ A Q 4
♡ K 10 2
◇ 9 7 3 2
♣ K J 8

South
♠ K
♡ Q J 9 8 7 3
◇ K Q 5
♣ Q 5 2

East wins the first trick with the ace of diamonds and returns the four of diamonds. You win the second trick with the king of diamonds as West follows suit with the eight. Since the nine of diamonds is in sight, it is almost certain that West has no more diamonds (he would not lead the ten from 10 8 x). Since you have three top losers, you must prevent the diamond ruff to make the contract.

Suppose the full deal is:

North
♠ A Q 4
♡ K 10 2
◊ 9 7 3 2
♣ K J 8

West
♠ 10 9 7 3 2
♡ 6 5 4
◊ 10 8
♣ A 7 6

East
♠ J 8 6 5
♡ A
◊ A J 6 4
♣ 10 9 4 3

South
♠ K
♡ Q J 9 8 7 3
◊ K Q 5
♣ Q 5 2

If you lead a heart at trick three, East will win with the ace of hearts and give his partner the diamond ruff. To prevent this you must get rid of the diamond in your hand before touching trumps. This is easily done: Overtake your king of spades with dummy's ace, and discard your remaining diamond on the queen of spades. Now when East wins the ace of hearts and leads a diamond, you can ruff in your hand with a high trump and draw the rest of the trumps.

This deal is not as obvious as the last two, but the theme is the same: to prevent a winner from being ruffed.

#16

Contract: four spades

Opening Lead: eight of clubs

North
♠ 5 3 2
♡ A 7 4
◊ A 9 2
♣ 10 6 5 4

South
♠ A K Q J 10
♡ K 8
◊ K 7
♣ K 7 3 2

East wins the first trick with the ace of clubs and returns the queen of clubs. The only clubs still missing are the jack and nine. Although it is possible that West has led from jack-nine-eight, it is much more likely that he has led a singleton. If you play the king and it is ruffed, you will be set if you lose two more club tricks to East.

The sure way to make your contract is to let East win with the queen of clubs at trick two; do not play your king. Look at the four hands to see how this works.

```
                              North
                              ♠ 5 3 2
                              ♡ A 7 4
                              ◇ A 9 2
                              ♣ 10 6 5 4
      West                                          East
      ♠ 9 7 4                                       ♠ 8 6
      ♡ Q 10 9 5                                    ♡ J 6 3 2
      ◇ Q J 6 5 3                                   ◇ 10 8 4
      ♣ 8                                           ♣ A Q J 9
                              South
                              ♠ A K Q J 10
                              ♡ K 8
                              ◇ K 7
                              ♣ K 7 3 2
```

After East wins with the queen of clubs at trick two, suppose he leads another club. If he leads the *nine*, let it ride around to dummy's ten; if he leads the *jack*, cover with the king. In either case West will ruff, but you will be left with the high club and will win the rest of the tricks.

Note that winning or ducking the second club makes no difference if West has led the eight from jack-nine-eight; you will win eleven tricks regardless.

Here is a case where you must ruff your own winning trick, or else the opponents will ruff it.

#17   North
                                              ♠ 8 3
                                              ♡ 9 8
                                              ◇ Q 10 7 6 4
Contract: four hearts   ♣ Q 7 5 2

Opening Lead: king of diamonds   South
                                              ♠ A K Q 4
                                              ♡ K Q J 10 7 6 2
                                              ◇ —
                                              ♣ 9 6

You have three inevitable losers — the ace of hearts and two clubs. So to make your bid you must not lose any spade tricks. You begin by ruffing the opening lead, cashing two high spades, and ruffing the four of spades in the dummy. Both opponents follow to the three spade leads. You may think your troubles are over, but you are in danger of an enemy ruff.

Suppose the complete deal is:

North
♠ 8 3
♡ 9 8
◇ Q 10 7 6 4
♣ Q 7 5 2

West
♠ 9 7 2
♡ 5 4
◇ A K J 8
♣ A 10 4 3

East
♠ J 10 6 5
♡ A 3
◇ 9 5 3 2
♣ K J 8

South
♠ A K Q 4
♡ K Q J 10 7 6 2
◇ —
♣ 9 6

To insure your contract, you must continue as follows: Return the lead to your hand by ruffing a diamond and *ruff your high spade in dummy with the nine of hearts*. If you mistakenly try to draw trumps while you still have a high spade in your hand, East can win with the ace of hearts and lead his remaining spade for West to ruff. Since you still have two club losers, the contract is lost.

Another good way to prevent a winner from being ruffed is to lead *toward* it (instead of leading the high card itself). If second hand ruffs, you can play low and save your high card.

For example:

#18

Contract: four hearts

Opening Lead: king of clubs

North
♠ A 8 6 3
♡ 7 4 3
◇ 9 5 2
♣ 10 6 5

South
♠ K 2
♡ A K Q 6 5
◇ A K Q 7
♣ 8 4

West wins the first two club tricks and leads a third club, which you ruff. The seven of diamonds is a loser unless the suit divides 3-3; and you are subject to a heart loser unless that suit divides 3-2. At tricks four and five, you cash two high hearts and West shows out on the second lead, so East has a natural heart trick. The fate of the hand now depends on whether or not you lose a diamond trick. It may appear that diamonds must divide 3-3, but all you need is to find East with at least two diamonds.

Suppose the four hands are:

                          North
                          ♠ A 8 6 3
                          ♡ 7 4 3
                          ◊ 9 5 2
                          ♣ 10 6 5

West   East
♠ J 9 5 4   ♠ Q 10 7
♡ 2   ♡ J 10 9 8
◊ J 10 8 6   ◊ 4 3
♣ K Q J 3   ♣ A 9 7 2

                          South
                          ♠ K 2
                          ♡ A K Q 6 5
                          ◊ A K Q 7
                          ♣ 8 4

After discovering the bad trump break, cash two high diamonds. Your next plays should be a spade to dummy's ace and a low diamond *from dummy.*

If East ruffs the diamond lead, play the seven (East will have ruffed his partner's trick) and you will have the balance of the tricks after drawing the last trump.

If East discards on the diamond lead from dummy, win with your high diamond and lead the seven of diamonds to ruff with dummy's last trump. East will be able to win only one more trick whether he overruffs dummy or not. (If East followed suit to the diamond lead from dummy, you would of course win with your high diamond and ruff the seven in dummy if necessary.)

Note that you would be set if you led the third round of diamonds from your hand; East would ruff and you would be left with an unavoidable diamond loser.

The technique of leading toward high cards as a way to protect them from being ruffed is not always obvious to the average player. So here is another deal showing how it saves a trick.

#19   North
                                        ♠ K Q J
                                        ♡ A 8 2
                                        ◊ K 7 3
Contract: six spades   ♣ A Q 9 5

Opening Lead: queen of hearts   South
                                        ♠ A 10 9 8 7 6
                                        ♡ 3
                                        ◊ A 9 5 4 2
                                        ♣ 8

You can make the contract if you avoid two diamond losers. If diamonds divide 3-2, there is no problem. If diamonds divide 4-1 and spades 2-2, there is again no problem as you will be able to draw trumps and establish the diamond suit by ruffing the fourth round in dummy. Now suppose that when you win the first trick with the ace of hearts and cash two rounds of spades, West shows out (the suit divides 3-1). Can you see a way to make the hand if West has four diamonds and East only one?

Here are the four hands to show you that it can be done.

                              North
                              ♠ K Q J
                              ♡ A 8 2
                              ◊ K 7 3
                              ♣ A Q 9 5
        West   East
        ♠ 5   ♠ 4 3 2
        ♡ Q J 10 7 5   ♡ K 9 6 4
        ◊ Q J 10 6   ◊ 8
        ♣ 4 3 2   ♣ K J 10 7 6
                              South
                              ♠ A 10 9 8 7 6
                              ♡ 3
                              ◊ A 9 5 4 2
                              ♣ 8

After drawing two rounds of trumps, the key plays are to cash the king of diamonds and then lead a diamond *toward* your ace. If East ruffs, play a low diamond from your hand, and eventually you will establish the diamond suit by ruffing the fourth round with dummy's remaining trump. If East discards on the second diamond lead, win with the ace and concede the third diamond trick to West. When you regain the lead, you will still be able to ruff the fourth diamond in dummy and draw East's last trump.

Preventing Overruffs and Trump Promotions

If you ruff with a low trump, an opponent may gain a trick by overruffing. If you ruff with a high trump, an opponent's trump may be promoted into a trick. In many cases there is nothing you can do about it. The next four deals show cases where you can prevent the trump loser.

For example:

#20

Contract: four spades

Opening Lead: king of clubs

North
♠ K Q 5 4
♡ A J 10 9 8
◇ Q
♣ 5 3 2

South
♠ A 10 7 2
♡ 3
◇ A K J 10
♣ J 9 6 4

West	North	East	South
			1 ◇
2 ♣	2 ♡	Pass	2 ♠
Pass	4 ♠	All Pass	

West wins the first three tricks by cashing the king, ace, and queen of clubs. East follows suit to the first club lead and then discards two diamonds. West leads a fourth club and you are over a barrel: If you ruff low, East will overruff; if you ruff high, you must waste one of your trump honors, after which you are likely to lose a trump trick.

Since ruffing low offers no chance to make your bid, you ruff the fourth club lead with dummy's king of spades. Next you cash the queen of spades, on which East plays the three and West the jack. Unless West is "false-carding" (playing the jack when he has another card in the suit), East still has the nine-eight-six of spades; you should assume this and play accordingly.

Suppose the full deal is:

North
♠ K Q 5 4
♡ A J 10 9 8
◇ Q
♣ 5 3 2

West
♠ J
♡ K 4 2
◇ 8 7 6 5
♣ A K Q 10 8

East
♠ 9 8 6 3
♡ Q 7 6 5
◇ 9 4 3 2
♣ 7

South
♠ A 10 7 2
♡ 3
◇ A K J 10
♣ J 9 6 4

You can avoid a spade loser by taking a double finesse. Lead a low spade from dummy and insert the *seven* if East plays low. Note that it would do East no good to "split" his nine-eight, as you could win that trick, return to dummy, and finesse again.

#21   North
                                       ♠ 6 5
                                       ♡ 5 4 3 2
                                       ◊ A K Q
Contract: four spades   ♣ A J 8 7

Opening Lead: seven of hearts   South
                                       ♠ K Q J 10 4 3
                                       ♡ A 10 6
                                       ◊ J 8 7
                                       ♣ 2

After East opens the bidding with one heart, you reach a contract of four spades. On the surface it appears that you have only three losers (two hearts and one spade), but the opponents may win a second spade trick via a trump-promotion play if spades divide 4-1. Suppose East plays the jack of hearts on the first trick and you win with the ace. How would you play the spade suit?

The spade division shown below is the one you must guard against:

```
                       North
                       ♠ 6 5
                       ♡ 5 4 3 2
                       ◊ A K Q
                       ♣ A J 8 7
    West                                   East
    ♠ 9 8 7 2                              ♠ A
    ♡ 7                                    ♡ K Q J 9 8
    ◊ 10 9 3                               ◊ 6 5 4 2
    ♣ Q 6 5 4 3                            ♣ K 10 9
                       South
                       ♠ K Q J 10 4 3
                       ♡ A 10 6
                       ◊ J 8 7
                       ♣ 2
```

If you mistakenly lead a spade honor from your hand, East will win with the ace, cash two heart winners, and lead another heart to promote a spade trick for West. If you ruff with a low spade, West will overruff; if you ruff high, West will discard and eventually win a natural spade trick.

The correct play, which will win even if spades divide 4-1, is to *lead the first spade from dummy*. Cross to dummy with the *ace of clubs* (do not lead a diamond or West will discard the rest of his diamonds on high hearts and be able to ruff a diamond). Now lead a spade. Since you will not waste a spade honor to drive out the ace, you can ruff high when East leads the fourth round of hearts; then you will be able to draw all of West's trumps without losing a trick.

#22

Contract: four spades

Opening Lead: king of clubs

North
♠ Q 7 3 2
♡ K 9 8 4
◇ 8 5 4
♣ J 6

South
♠ A K 6 5 4
♡ A 5
◇ A K 3
♣ 10 7 4

West	North	East	South
			1 ♠
2 ♣	2 ♠	Pass	4 ♠
All Pass			

Since you have one diamond and two club losers, you will be set if you lose a trump trick. The play begins with West leading the king, ace, and queen of clubs. Since West bid the suit and East plays high-low on the first two club leads, it becomes clear that East started with a doubleton. If you ruff the third club lead low, East will overruff; if you ruff with the queen, you will lose a spade trick unless the suit divides 2-2. It is true that ruffing with the queen is better than ruffing low, but this time the winning play is *not to trump at all*. Instead, discard a diamond on the third club lead; play a loser on a loser.

Suppose the four hands are:

North
♠ Q 7 3 2
♡ K 9 8 4
◇ 8 5 4
♣ J 6

West
♠ 10
♡ 7 6
◇ Q J 9 2
♣ A K Q 8 5 3

East
♠ J 9 8
♡ Q J 10 3 2
◇ 10 7 6
♣ 9 2

South
♠ A K 6 5 4
♡ A 5
◇ A K 3
♣ 10 7 4

Note that if you ruff the third club lead in dummy, East will get a spade trick whether you ruff low or with the queen. But if you "transfer the ruff" by discarding a diamond on the third club lead, you can win the rest of the tricks. No matter what West leads at trick four, you will be able to ruff your losing diamond in dummy *after* you have drawn East's three trumps.

#23   North
                                           ♠ K 3 2
                                           ♡ 7 4
                                           ◊ J 10 9 8 5 2
Contract: six spades   ♣ J 6

Opening Lead: king of clubs   South
                                           ♠ A Q J 10 9 5
                                           ♡ A K 5 3
                                           ◊ A
                                           ♣ A 7

You have three losers: two hearts and one club. The simple solution seems to be to ruff the two heart losers in dummy, so you win the first trick with the ace of clubs, cash the ace and king of hearts, and lead a third heart to ruff in dummy. Since you must ruff two heart losers, you ruff this one with a low spade — but East overruffs. What rotten luck to go down in your contract because East had a doubleton heart. Or was it rotten luck?

Here is the full deal:

```
                          North
                          ♠ K 3 2
                          ♡ 7 4
                          ◊ J 10 9 8 5 2
                          ♣ J 6
         West                                East
         ♠ 7 4                               ♠ 8 6
         ♡ Q 10 8 6 2                        ♡ J 9
         ◊ 4 3                               ◊ K Q 7 6
         ♣ K Q 10 9                          ♣ 8 5 4 3 2
                          South
                          ♠ A Q J 10 9 5
                          ♡ A K 5 3
                          ◊ A
                          ♣ A 7
```

The best play to make this slam is to transfer the ruff; play a loser on a loser as you did in the last hand. When you lead the third round of hearts, instead of ruffing in dummy and risking the overruff, discard dummy's last club. No matter what the defenders do, you will be able to ruff your losing club with a *low* spade and your fourth heart with the *king* of spades.

Note that it would be a mistake to cash even one round of trumps. When you give up the heart trick, a second spade lead from the enemy would be fatal.

Quiz for Chapter Five

1.
North
♠ 8 4
♡ A Q 7 6 3
♢ A Q J 10 9
♣ A

South
♠ A K 7 6 5 3
♡ 9 8
♢ K
♣ 8 7 4 2

West	North	East	South
	1 ♡	Pass	1 ♠
Pass	2 ♢	Pass	3 ♠
Pass	6 ♠	All Pass	

(a) How would you play if West leads the queen of clubs? (b) How would you play if West leads the five of hearts?

2.
North
♠ 4 2
♡ A J 5 2
♢ A Q J 7
♣ K J 8

South
♠ A 7 6
♡ K 6 4 3
♢ K 3
♣ A Q 10 2

West	North	East	South
			1 NT
Pass	2 ♣	Pass	2 ♡
Pass	6 ♡	All Pass	

West leads the queen of spades.

3.
North
♠ J 8
♡ A 4 3
♢ K 6
♣ Q 10 9 6 5 3

South
♠ A 4
♡ K Q J 10 9
♢ A 8 7 4 2
♣ A

West	North	East	South
			1 ♡
Pass	2 ♣	Pass	2 ♢
Pass	2 ♡	Pass	2 ♠
Pass	3 ♡	Pass	6 ♡
All Pass			

West leads the king of spades.

4.
North
♠ 6 2
♡ A 8 3
♢ A Q
♣ A Q 10 8 5 4

South
♠ A Q 4
♡ K Q J 7 5 2
♢ K 9
♣ 3 2

West	North	East	South
	1 ♣	Pass	1 ♡
Pass	3 ♣	Pass	3 ♡
Pass	4 ♡	Pass	4 NT
Pass	5 ♠	Pass	5 NT
Pass	6 ♣	Pass	6 ♡
All Pass			

West leads the nine of clubs.

5.

North
♠ A 8 7 6 3
♡ A 7 2
♢ 4 3 2
♣ 8 5

South
♠ Q 2
♡ K Q J 10
♢ K
♣ A K 10 7 4 3

West	North	East	South
			1 ♣
Pass	1 ♠	Pass	2 ♡
Pass	3 ♡	Pass	4 ♡
All Pass			

West leads the queen of diamonds and East wins with the ace. The opponents lead diamonds at every opportunity.

6.

North
♠ K 6 5
♡ A Q 10 3
♢ A K 7 5 4
♣ 2

South
♠ A Q J 10
♡ K J 2
♢ 10 3 2
♣ A 10 7

West	North	East	South
	1 ♢	Pass	1 ♠
Pass	2 ♡	Pass	3 ♣
Pass	3 ♠	Pass	4 NT
Pass	5 ♡	Pass	6 ♠
All Pass			

West leads the four of hearts.

7.

North
♠ A 8 5
♡ 8 6 3
♢ A J 7 2
♣ A 4 3

South
♠ 10 9
♡ A K 7 4 2
♢ 6
♣ K Q 8 5 2

West	North	East	South
	1 ♢	Pass	1 ♡
Pass	1 NT	Pass	3 ♣
Pass	3 ♡	Pass	4 ♡
All Pass			

West leads the queen of spades. You win with the ace and cash the ace and king of hearts. West discards a spade on the second heart lead.

8.

North
♠ 6
♡ 10 9 8 7
♢ K 5 4 2
♣ K 8 6 3

South
♠ A K J 10 9 3
♡ —
♢ Q J 10 6
♣ A Q 2

West	North	East	South
			1 ♠
Pass	1 NT	Pass	4 ♠
All Pass			

West leads the king of hearts.

Answers to Quiz for Chapter Five

1.	North		
	♠ 8 4		
	♡ A Q 7 6 3		
	◇ A Q J 10 9		
	♣ A		
West		East	
♠ Q 10 9		♠ J 2	
♡ 5 2		♡ K J 10 4	
◇ 4 2		◇ 8 7 6 5 3	
♣ Q J 10 6 5 3		♣ K 9	
	South		
	♠ A K 7 6 5 3		
	♡ 9 8		
	◇ K		
	♣ 8 7 4 2		

West	North	East	South
	1 ♡	Pass	1 ♠
Pass	2 ◇	Pass	3 ♠
Pass	6 ♠	All Pass	

(a) How would you play if West leads the queen of clubs? (b) How would you play if West leads the five of hearts?

2.	North		
	♠ 4 2		
	♡ A J 5 2		
	◇ A Q J 7		
	♣ K J 8		
West		East	
♠ Q J 9		♠ K 10 8 5 3	
♡ 9 8		♡ Q 10 7	
◇ 10 9 5 2		◇ 8 6 4	
♣ 7 6 4 3		♣ 9 5	
	South		
	♠ A 7 6		
	♡ K 6 4 3		
	◇ K 3		
	♣ A Q 10 2		

West	North	East	South
			1 NT
Pass	2 ♣	Pass	2 ♡
Pass	6 ♡	All Pass	

West leads the queen of spades.

You have one losing heart and three losing clubs, and these all can be discarded on the diamond suit; there is no need to ruff any clubs in dummy. The fate of this hand hinges on losing no more than one trump trick, which means you need a 3-2 spade break.

With the queen of clubs lead, the best play is to concede a spade trick to the enemy at trick two. It does not matter what the opponents do: With a trump still in dummy, they will not be able to cash any club tricks. When you regain the lead, cash the ace and king of trumps, and discard your losers on the diamond suit. As the cards lie, all other lines of play fail.

It is interesting to note that with any opening lead but a club, you would draw trumps differently. For example, with the five-of-hearts lead, you should win with the ace and cash the ace and king of spades immediately. Then overtake your king of diamonds with the ace and run the diamond suit to discard your four losers, making sure the first discard is a heart. It does not matter when West decides to ruff with his high spade; with the ace of clubs still in dummy, there is no defense to beat you.

The normal way to play this heart combination is to cash the king and lead toward the ace-jack for a finesse. As you can see in this case, the queen of hearts is offside and you will be set if you finesse; East will win and cash a spade trick.

Rather than rely on a 50-50 finesse, there is a better plan, which will succeed with normal breaks in hearts and diamonds (plus a few extra chances). This swings the odds in your favor.

After winning the first trick with the ace of spades, cash the ace and king of hearts. If the queen of hearts falls, you will also cash the jack. But in this case the queen does not fall, so lead four rounds of diamonds and discard your two spade losers. As long as East has at least three diamonds, he cannot ruff in time to prevent the two spade discards. The contract is safe.

3.

	North		
	♠ J 8		
	♡ A 4 3		
	◊ K 6		
	♣ Q 10 9 6 5 3		
West		East	
♠ K Q 7 6		♠ 10 9 5 3 2	
♡ 7 2		♡ 8 6 5	
◊ Q 10 9 5		◊ J 3	
♣ 8 4 2		♣ K J 7	
	South		
	♠ A 4		
	♡ K Q J 10 9		
	◊ A 8 7 4 2		
	♣ A		

West	*North*	*East*	*South*
			1 ♡
Pass	2 ♣	Pass	2 ◊
Pass	2 ♡	Pass	2 ♠
Pass	3 ♡	Pass	6 ♡
All Pass			

West leads the king of spades.

4.

	North		
	♠ 6 2		
	♡ A 8 3		
	◊ A Q		
	♣ A Q 10 8 5 4		
West		East	
♠ K J 5 3		♠ 10 9 8 7	
♡ 10 9 4		♡ 6	
◊ J 8 7 6 2		◊ 10 5 4 3	
♣ 9		♣ K J 7 6	
	South		
	♠ A Q 4		
	♡ K Q J 7 5 2		
	◊ K 9		
	♣ 3 2		

West	*North*	*East*	*South*
	1 ♣	Pass	1 ♡
Pass	3 ♣	Pass	3 ♡
Pass	4 ♡	Pass	4 NT
Pass	5 ♠	Pass	5 NT
Pass	6 ♣	Pass	6 ♡
All Pass			

West leads the nine of clubs.

You do not have enough entries in dummy to set up the club suit, so you must establish the diamond suit by ruffing in dummy. If diamonds divide 3-3, all that is required is to ruff the third round and draw trumps. The challenge is to make your bid when the diamond suit divides 4-2. It will then be necessary to ruff *twice* in dummy. After winning the first trick with the ace of spades and before drawing any trumps, play a diamond to the king, a diamond to the ace, and lead a third diamond toward dummy. To guard against East having no more diamonds (in which case he will overruff if you ruff with a low trump), *discard a spade*. When you regain the lead, you can win the rest of the tricks by ruffing your losing spade with a low heart and the fourth round of diamonds with the ace of hearts.

Note that you can also make your bid by ruffing the third diamond with the ace of hearts, returning to your hand with a club, and discarding a spade from dummy on the fourth round of diamonds.

Suspecting that West has led a singleton, you should win the first trick with the ace of clubs. It would be foolish to take a finesse because you can make the contract without it no matter how the clubs divide (except in the unlikely event that East is void in clubs).

After winning the first trick with the ace of clubs, draw three rounds of trumps, and lead a club to the eight, which East will win with the jack. Suppose East returns a spade (no other lead is better). You win with the ace, lead the nine of diamonds to dummy's queen and play the queen of clubs. If East covers with the king, ruff; if he plays low, discard a spade. With the ace of diamonds still in dummy, you cannot be prevented from discarding your two losing spades on the good clubs.

5.

	North		
	♠ A 8 7 6 3		
	♡ A 7 2		
	◇ 4 3 2		
	♣ 8 5		

West		East
♠ K 5 4		♠ J 10 9
♡ 6 3		♡ 9 8 5 4
◇ Q J 10 8 7		◇ A 9 6 5
♣ J 9 2		♣ Q 6

	South	
	♠ Q 2	
	♡ K Q J 10	
	◇ K	
	♣ A K 10 7 4 3	

West	North	East	South
			1 ♣
Pass	1 ♠	Pass	2 ♡
Pass	3 ♡	Pass	4 ♡
All Pass			

West leads the queen of diamonds and East wins with the ace. The opponents lead diamonds at every opportunity.

The obvious plan to make this bid is to ruff a third round of clubs in dummy, draw trumps, and cash the rest of the clubs. As long as clubs divide 3-2 and hearts no worse than 4-2, you will make your bid—*provided you do not shorten your trump holding by ruffing a diamond in your hand*. To guard against the probable 4-2 heart split, you must save the four high hearts in your hand to draw the missing trumps.

When East leads a diamond at trick two, discard a spade (a loser on a loser). When the third diamond is led, discard a club. Even though you may be parting with a winning trick, you can afford another loser and saving the four trumps is more important. When the fourth diamond is led (no other defense is better), ruff it in the dummy. Now cash the ace and king of clubs, ruff a club with the *ace* of hearts, draw trumps, and claim.

6.

	North	
	♠ K 6 5	
	♡ A Q 10 3	
	◇ A K 7 5 4	
	♣ 2	

West		East
♠ 9 8 4 2		♠ 7 3
♡ 4		♡ 9 8 7 6 5
◇ Q J 9 8		◇ 6
♣ K 8 5 3		♣ Q J 9 6 4

	South	
	♠ A Q J 10	
	♡ K J 2	
	◇ 10 3 2	
	♣ A 10 7	

West	North	East	South
	1 ◇	Pass	1 ♠
Pass	2 ♡	Pass	3 ♣
Pass	3 ♠	Pass	4 NT
Pass	5 ♡	Pass	6 ♠
All Pass			

West leads the four of hearts.

Here again you are playing with only seven trumps, but six spades is an excellent contract and it is the only makable slam as the cards lie. The key to making this bid is to count your tricks accurately and then to play safely for twelve tricks. You have three losers: one diamond and two clubs. After you draw trumps, you can discard one loser on the fourth round of hearts, so it is necessary to ruff only *one* club.

Win the opening heart lead, cash the ace of clubs, ruff a club in dummy, and then draw four rounds of trumps. This gives you twelve tricks: five spades (including the ruff in dummy), four hearts, two diamonds, and one club.

If you make the mistake of leading a heart at trick four, in an attempt to get to your hand for a second club ruff, West will ruff and can beat the contract by leading a spade or diamond. You will also be set if you lead a spade to your hand at trick four and then ruff a club; you will be locked in dummy, unable to draw trumps, and the opponents can maneuver to get two ruffs.

7.   North
                ♠ A 8 5
                ♡ 8 6 3
                ◇ A J 7 2
                ♣ A 4 3
West   East
♠ Q J 6 2   ♠ K 7 4 3
♡ 5   ♡ Q J 10 9
◇ Q 5 4 3   ◇ K 10 9 8
♣ J 10 9 7   ♣ 6
                South
                ♠ 10 9
                ♡ A K 7 4 2
                ◇ 6
                ♣ K Q 8 5 2

West	North	East	South
	1 ◇	Pass	1 ♡
Pass	1 NT	Pass	3 ♣
Pass	3 ♡	Pass	4 ♡
All Pass			

West leads the queen of spades. You win with the ace and cash the ace-king of hearts. West discards a spade on the second heart lead.

With normal breaks, this game would roll home. But when West shows out on the second heart lead, the contract hinges on avoiding a club loser. This is easy if East has two, three, or four clubs, but you can also make your bid if he has a singleton club provided you do not allow him to ruff one of your honors. This is accomplished by winning with the ace *first* and leading *toward* the king and queen.

At trick four, play a club to dummy's ace, and then lead a club toward your hand. If East ruffs, play a low club and the rest of your clubs are good tricks.

If East discards when you lead the club from dummy, win the trick with the king, play a diamond to the ace, and lead another club toward your hand. Once again, if East ruffs, play low; if he discards, win with the queen. If East does not ruff, you are left with two low clubs and West with the jack. So lead a club and ruff in dummy; you will win ten tricks whether East overruffs or not.

8.   North
                ♠ 6
                ♡ 10 9 8 7
                ◇ K 5 4 2
                ♣ K 8 6 3
West   East
♠ Q 8 7 5   ♠ 4 2
♡ K Q J 5 2   ♡ A 6 4 3
◇ 9   ◇ A 8 7 3
♣ J 7 4   ♣ 10 9 5
                South
                ♠ A K J 10 9 3
                ♡ —
                ◇ Q J 10 6
                ♣ A Q 2

West	North	East	South
			1 ♠
Pass	1 NT	Pass	4 ♠
All Pass			

West leads the king of hearts.

You might not think there is any problem with trump control when you have such a powerful suit; but you have only seven trumps, and the heart lead forces you to ruff in the long hand right away. Since you can afford to lose *two* spade tricks and still make your bid, the contract is safe as long as spades divide no worse than 4-2 — provided you play the trumps correctly.

After ruffing the opening heart lead, cash the ace and king of spades, and then lead diamonds until the ace is driven out. Assume East leads another heart. Ruff it, and lead your high clubs and diamonds. West can win his two trump tricks whenever he chooses.

With the cards as shown in the diagram, you will be set in routine fashion if you take a spade finesse, or if you lead another trump after cashing the ace and king. The opponents will lead hearts at every opportunity; you will lose trump control and be unable to win any diamond tricks.

6

Choosing the Master Hand; the Crossruff; and Ruffing in the Long Hand

♣　　♢　　♡　　♠　　♣　　♢　　♡　　♠

This chapter includes some of the more exotic bridge plays, such as the "dummy reversal," the "elopement play" (trump coup en passant), the "trump coup," and the "trump endplay."

Making Dummy the Master Hand

When the dummy's trumps are as long, or longer, than the declarer's, it is sometimes better to make the dummy the "master hand." In other words, declarer ruffs dummy's losers in his own hand and then draws trumps from the dummy. It all begins when you count your tricks.

For example:

#1

Contract: six hearts

Opening Lead: ten of spades

North
♠ K 7 2
♡ A Q J 10
♢ K 9 8 6 4 3
♣ —

South
♠ A Q J
♡ K 6 5 4
♢ 7
♣ K 9 7 6 2

In your hand you have six losers: one diamond and five clubs. If you waste dummy's high trumps ruffing clubs, you will not be able to draw the opponents' trumps successfully because the trumps in your hand are too weak. Since dummy's trumps are very strong, you should make it the master hand. In other words, *count the losing tricks in dummy's hand* and see if you can hold the losers to one trick by establishing the dummy.

The dummy has six diamond losers, but the prospects of ruffing diamonds in your hand and establishing the diamond suit are promising. However, some good luck will be needed.

Suppose these are the four hands:

North
♠ K 7 2
♡ A Q J 10
♢ K 9 8 6 4 3
♣ —

West
♠ 10 9 8 4 3
♡ 8 7 2
♢ A 5
♣ Q 10 5

East
♠ 6 5
♡ 9 3
♢ Q J 10 2
♣ A J 8 4 3

South
♠ A Q J
♡ K 6 5 4
♢ 7
♣ K 9 7 6 2

The East-West cards are favorably located, so you can make the slam. Win the opening spade lead in your hand and lead a diamond toward dummy's king. Suppose West wins with the ace of diamonds and leads another spade (although you can make your bid no matter how he defends). Win with dummy's king of spades and lead a low diamond, which you ruff in your hand with a *low* heart. Next play a heart to dummy's ten, and lead another low diamond and ruff with the *king* of hearts. The king-nine-eight of diamonds are now good tricks, so draw the missing trumps and claim the rest of the tricks.

In the next deal you have four strong trumps in *each* hand, but it is still very important that you choose the right master hand.

#2   North
                                          ♠ A Q 10 9
                                          ♡ A K J 2
                                          ◊ Q 8 6 3

Contract: six spades   ♣ 7

Opening Lead: seven of diamonds   South
                                          ♠ K J 8 7
                                          ♡ 7
                                          ◊ A K J 5
                                          ♣ Q J 6 2

In your own hand you have four club losers. You must lose one club and can discard another on dummy's second high heart, so you will have to ruff two clubs in dummy to make your bid. The problem is that you must give up a club trick before you can ruff, and this subjects you to a potential diamond ruff.

Suppose the four hands are:

                                    North
                                    ♠ A Q 10 9
                                    ♡ A K J 2
                                    ◊ Q 8 6 3
                                    ♣ 7

West   East
♠ 6 5 4 2   ♠ 3
♡ 5 4 3   ♡ Q 10 9 8 6
◊ 7   ◊ 10 9 4 2
♣ K 10 9 8 3   ♣ A 5 4
                                   South
                                   ♠ K J 8 7
                                   ♡ 7
                                   ◊ A K J 5
                                   ♣ Q J 6 2

If you win the diamond opening lead and play a club, East can win with the ace and give his partner a diamond ruff. This is a foolish line of play because you can win twelve tricks without losing the lead by making dummy the master hand.

The dummy has three losing tricks: two hearts and one club. The remedy is simple: Win the opening lead and, before drawing any trumps, cash one high heart and ruff a heart in your hand. Now return to dummy with a trump and ruff the other losing heart in your hand. All that remains to be done is to lead your last spade to dummy, draw the missing trumps, and cash the rest of your winners. The only loser left in dummy is the seven of clubs. Playing this way, you win the first twelve tricks (four spades, two hearts, two heart ruffs, and four diamonds), and you even survive a 4-1 trump break.

Note that you would be set if you led even *one* round of trumps before ruffing a heart. This would leave you shy an entry to dummy.

#3

Contract: six diamonds

Opening Lead: ten of hearts

North
♠ 7 5
♡ J 8 6
◊ Q J 10 9
♣ A K 3 2

South
♠ K 10 6 2
♡ A K Q 3
◊ A K 8 7
♣ 4

Once again you have four solid trumps in each hand and must choose the right master hand to make your bid. If you use your hand as the master, you count four losing spade tricks; the only chance to hold your losers to one is to find East with the ace of spades.

In the following diagram West has the ace of spades, but the contract can be made if you establish the dummy's hand instead of your own.

North
♠ 7 5
♡ J 8 6
◊ Q J 10 9
♣ A K 3 2

West
♠ A Q
♡ 10 9 7 4 2
◊ 5
♣ J 9 8 6 5

East
♠ J 9 8 4 3
♡ 5
◊ 6 4 3 2
♣ Q 10 7

South
♠ K 10 6 2
♡ A K Q 3
◊ A K 8 7
♣ 4

The dummy has four losers: two spades and two clubs. The plan is to ruff the two club losers in your hand (you must ruff a club before leading any trumps), and then draw all of the missing trumps in dummy. Eventually, you will discard one of dummy's losing spades on your fourth heart, and the only loser left in dummy is one spade.

There are entry problems to contend with, so here is a play-by-play description: Win the opening heart lead in either hand, cash one high club, ruff a low club in your hand with the *ace* (or *king*) of diamonds, lead a low diamond to dummy's nine, and ruff the other low club with the *king* (or *ace*) of diamonds. At trick six, lead your last diamond to draw the missing trumps from dummy. Finally, cash the high club and three more heart tricks. This gives you the first twelve tricks: four diamonds, two clubs, two club ruffs, and four hearts. Note that it was vitally important to ruff the two losing clubs from dummy with the ace and king of diamonds, otherwise you would have had no entry to get back to dummy to draw the trumps.

The Dummy Reversal

"Making dummy the master hand" and the "dummy reversal" follow the same strategy (ruffing losers in declarer's hand and drawing trumps from the dummy), but in bridge terminology this technique is called a dummy reversal only when the dummy has *fewer* trumps.

Dummy reversals are rare and contradict the general rule that you should hoard the trumps in the long hand. In a vast majority of cases, if you ruff in the hand with the short trumps, you gain a trick; if you ruff in the hand with the long trumps, you do not gain a trick and increase the chance of losing trump control. So do not attempt a dummy reversal unless you determine that the normal play will fail.

The objective of a dummy reversal is to increase the number of trump tricks you can win. Suppose, in a given hand, your trumps are:

> Dummy
> K J 10
>
> Your Hand
> A Q 9 8 7

You have five tricks in this suit and it appears that you cannot win more without ruffing in dummy. But if you can ruff *three* times in your hand and use the dummy's hand to draw trumps, you can win six trump tricks.

Now let's see how it works in a full deal:

#4

	North
	♠ K J 10
	♡ K J
	◇ Q 7 4 3
Contract: six spades	♣ 9 8 5 2
Opening Lead: king of clubs	South
	♠ A Q 9 8 7
	♡ A Q 10 9 5
	◇ A 8
	♣ 7

If you count losers in your hand, you have two: one diamond and one club. If you count winners, you have eleven: five spades, five hearts, and one diamond. It looks like a hopeless contract, but it can be made by a dummy reversal if the missing trumps divide 3-2 (a 68-percent chance).

If you count losers in dummy, you have seven: three diamonds and four clubs. The scheme is to trump three clubs in your hand, draw the missing trumps from dummy, and discard the three losing diamonds on your long hearts.

Suppose these are the four hands:

North
♠ K J 10
♡ K J
◇ Q 7 4 3
♣ 9 8 5 2

West
♠ 6 5 2
♡ 8 7 3
◇ K 9 6
♣ K Q 10 4

East
♠ 4 3
♡ 6 4 2
◇ J 10 5 2
♣ A J 6 3

South
♠ A Q 9 8 7
♡ A Q 10 9 5
◇ A 8
♣ 7

West wins the first trick with the king of clubs and leads another club (this defense is helpful, although the contract can be made regardless of what he leads at trick two). You trump the club lead and play as follows: Lead a heart to dummy's jack, ruff a third club in your hand, lead a spade to dummy's ten, and ruff the fourth club in your hand with the ace of spades. You still have one more spade in your hand, so lead it and draw the missing trumps from dummy. On dummy's last trump lead you will discard the eight of diamonds, so you have the rest of the tricks.

A dummy reversal usually requires that the dummy has strong trumps in order to be able to draw the enemy trumps.

Here is an exceptional case:

#5

Contract: four hearts

Opening Lead: king of hearts

North
♠ 5 4
♡ 4 3 2
◇ A 7 6 2
♣ K J 9 8

South
♠ A J 3
♡ A 9 8 7 6
◇ 8
♣ A Q 10 4

In your own hand you count two spade losers and two heart losers, assuming a 3-2 trump break. The hope of ruffing a spade in dummy is quashed by the opening trump lead; since you must give up a spade trick before you can ruff one, the opponents probably will be able to remove all of dummy's trumps and prevent the spade ruff.

Looking from a different angle, the dummy has six losers (one spade, three diamonds, and two hearts). If you can ruff *three* diamonds in your hand, you will be left with only three losers.

Suppose the full deal is:

```
                         North
                         ♠ 5 4
                         ♡ 4 3 2
                         ◇ A 7 6 2
                         ♣ K J 9 8
West                                    East
♠ K 10 9 6 2                            ♠ Q 8 7
♡ K Q J                                 ♡ 10 5
◇ K 5 4                                 ◇ Q J 10 9 3
♣ 5 3                                   ♣ 7 6 2
                         South
                         ♠ A J 3
                         ♡ A 9 8 7 6
                         ◇ 8
                         ♣ A Q 10 4
```

Your first good play should be to *duck* the king of hearts; by holding up your ace, you can be sure that exactly two rounds will be led. Assume West leads the jack of hearts at trick two, East follows suit, and you win with your ace. The contract is now ironclad — no matter how the cards divide — by a dummy reversal.

Your next six plays should be: Lead a diamond to dummy's ace, ruff a diamond, lead a club to dummy, ruff a diamond, lead another club to dummy, and ruff the last diamond. Whether West overruffs the fourth diamond lead or not, you will lose only two more tricks (the high trump and one spade); the contract is secure.

Once again, the dummy reversal produces an extra trump trick. By ruffing three diamonds in your hand, you win four trump tricks instead of three.

The Crossruff

Now we come to another way to handle the trump suit: the crossruff. The purpose of the crossruff is to make trump tricks separately in both hands by ruffing back and forth.

Here is the first example:

```
#6                              North
                                ♠ A Q 5 3
                                ♡ K 10 8 4
                                ◇ —
Contract: four spades           ♣ A 7 6 3 2

Opening Lead: queen of clubs    South
                                ♠ K J 6 2
                                ♡ 6 3 2
                                ◇ A 10 8 5 4
                                ♣ 9
```

As usual, you start out by counting the losing tricks in one hand. In your hand you have seven losers: three hearts and four diamonds. The best chance to eliminate four losers is to ruff four diamonds in the dummy, but to do this you must get the lead back in your hand four times by ruffing clubs. The first two club ruffs in your hand and two diamond ruffs in the dummy should be with the low spades; the risk of being overruffed is much greater in the later rounds. If all goes well, you will win two minor-suit aces and *eight* spade tricks.

In most cases you will lose trump control when you crossruff; that is, you will be unable to draw the enemy trumps. If you have any winners in the side suits that you need to make your bid, you should cash them early in the play; the longer you wait, the better the chance an opponent will trump one of your winners. For example:

#7	North
	♠ K J 10 7
	♡ A K 7 3
	◇ 4
Contract: six spades	♣ A 6 5 2
Opening Lead: queen of clubs	South
	♠ A Q 9 8
	♡ 5 4 2
	◇ A Q 7 6 3
	♣ 8

In your hand you have five losers (one heart and four diamonds) and, just like the last hand, you should crossruff in the minor suits. The twelve tricks you plan to win are two hearts, one diamond, one club, and eight spades. Since you are not going to draw the trumps, *you should cash your side winners immediately.*

Suppose this is the full deal:

```
                        North
                        ♠ K J 10 7
                        ♡ A K 7 3
                        ◇ 4
                        ♣ A 6 5 2
        West                            East
        ♠ 6 5 3 2                       ♠ 4
        ♡ J 6                           ♡ Q 10 9 8
        ◇ 10 2                          ◇ K J 9 8 5
        ♣ Q J 10 9 7                    ♣ K 4 3
                        South
                        ♠ A Q 9 8
                        ♡ 5 4 2
                        ◇ A Q 7 6 3
                        ♣ 8
```

If you cash the ace and king of hearts early and then crossruff in diamonds and clubs, you will win twelve tricks. Now suppose you mistakenly crossruff a few tricks before cashing your heart tricks. On the third diamond lead, West will *discard a heart*; then you cannot win two heart tricks as West will ruff the second heart lead. Since your opponents may be able to discard while you are crossruffing, it is usually best to cash your winners before you begin to crossruff.

This deal contains another trap. After cashing the ace and king of hearts, it is important to start ruffing *diamonds* first; else your crossruff will fizzle. If a club is ruffed first, you will end up stranded in dummy, unable to get the lead back in your hand to ruff the last diamond and make your last two trumps separately.

Also, you might have been thinking that West would have done better to lead a spade on this hand. You are right. Let's look at the same hand with a spade opening lead. How would you play?

#8	North
	♠ K J 10 7
	♡ A K 7 3
	◇ 4
Contract: six spades	♣ A 6 5 2
Opening Lead: two of spades	South
	♠ A Q 9 8
	♡ 5 4 2
	◇ A Q 7 6 3
	♣ 8

You have the same five losers in your hand (one heart and four diamonds), but you can no longer ruff four diamonds in dummy because the dummy has only three trumps left. You can win a maximum of seven spade tricks and therefore must win five tricks elsewhere. Although a finesse is only a 50-50 proposition, the diamond finesse offers the best chance to get the extra trick you need. If the finesse works, you can make your bid by cashing your side winners and crossruffing the rest of the way. If the diamond finesse fails, all is lost — but you will have made a noble effort.

As stated in the last deal, before you start crossruffing, you should cash any winners in the side suits *that you need to make your bid*.

For example:

#9	North
	♠ 10 9 8
	♡ 9 8 7 5 4
	◇ A K 4 2
Contract: four spades	♣ J
Opening Lead: king of hearts	South
	♠ A K Q J 2
	♡ —
	◇ 6 5 3
	♣ A 8 7 4 3

West	North	East	South
			1 ♠
2 NT	3 ♠	Pass	4 ♠
All Pass			

West's two-notrump bid is the "unusual notrump overcall" showing two long minor suits (presumably at least five diamonds and five clubs), so you should anticipate that the suits will not divide normally; West has at most three major-suit cards and East has at most three minor-suit cards. Before reading further, how would you play the hand?

You can win eight spade tricks by crossruffing and therefore need only two side winners. The safest play is to cash the ace of clubs and *only one high diamond* before crossruffing.

Here is the full deal:

```
                        North
                        ♠ 10 9 8
                        ♡ 9 8 7 5 4
                        ◇ A K 4 2
                        ♣ J
        West                                East
        ♠ 3                                 ♠ 7 6 5 4
        ♡ K Q                               ♡ A J 10 6 3 2
        ◇ Q 10 9 8 7                        ◇ J
        ♣ K Q 10 5 2                        ♣ 9 6
                        South
                        ♠ A K Q J 2
                        ♡ —
                        ◇ 6 5 3
                        ♣ A 8 7 4 3
```

After ruffing the first heart trick, you should lead a diamond to dummy's king, a club to your ace, then crossruff clubs and hearts to win ten tricks. Although cashing exactly one high diamond is the safest way to make your contract regardless of the bidding, you were forewarned by West's bid that East has a singleton.

If you make the mistake of trying to cash the second high diamond, East will ruff it and lead a trump. You are now limited to seven spade tricks and will be set. Alternatively, if you decide not to cash any high diamonds before crossruffing, East will discard his diamond on the third club lead and you will never get a diamond trick.

Ruffing in the Long Hand

There are several situations where you can win more trump tricks by ruffing in the long hand than by drawing trumps. One of these occurs *when you have an uncertain trump suit.* For example:

#10

North
♠ —
♡ A 10 5 4
◇ A 9 6 3 2
♣ A 8 7 2

Contract: two spades

Opening Lead: queen of clubs

South
♠ Q J 9 6 5 2
♡ K 7 3
◇ 8 7 5
♣ 4

Two spades is not the best contract, but here you are; you must give it a try. You have three losers in the side suits (one heart and two diamonds), and if you lead spades you will lose more spade tricks than you can afford. If you try to draw the trumps, you will almost surely be set — probably by two tricks.

With this uncertain trump suit, you can win more trump tricks by ruffing than by drawing trumps. You have four side winners, so your goal is to win four spade tricks; this can be done if the club suit divides favorably.

Suppose the four hands are:

North
♠ —
♡ A 10 5 4
◇ A 9 6 3 2
♣ A 8 7 2

West
♠ K 10 8 7 3
♡ 6 2
◇ K J
♣ Q J 10 9

East
♠ A 4
♡ Q J 9 8
◇ Q 10 4
♣ K 6 5 3

South
♠ Q J 9 6 5 2
♡ K 7 3
◇ 8 7 5
♣ 4

Your plan is to ruff as many clubs in your hand as you can. Win with the ace of clubs, ruff a club, cash two heart winners ending in dummy, ruff another club, lead a diamond to dummy's ace, and ruff the last club. You now have won seven tricks and still have the queen-jack-nine of spades, with which you can win an eighth trick provided you do not lead trumps yourself. Just exit with a heart or a diamond and wait for another trump trick.

Ruffing in the long hand may gain an extra trick by the positional advantage of playing after your right-hand opponent. This technique is called an "elopement play," or a "trump coup en passant."

Here are two examples:

#11   North
                                       ♠ 5 4
                                       ♡ A 10 8
                                       ◊ A 6 5 2
Contract: two spades   ♣ 7 6 4 3

Opening Lead: queen of diamonds   South
                                       ♠ A K Q 6 2
                                       ♡ 7 4 3
                                       ◊ K 8
                                       ♣ J 10 9

You have five losers in the side suits (two hearts and three clubs), so it seems you must avoid a spade loser to make your bid. Your first four plays should be to win the first diamond trick with the king and cash three top spades. West shows out on the third spade lead, so you know you have a spade loser. Is all lost? No, not if East has at least one more diamond.

Suppose these are the four hands:

                           North
                           ♠ 5 4
                           ♡ A 10 8
                           ◊ A 6 5 2
                           ♣ 7 6 4 3
        West   East
        ♠ 10 3   ♠ J 9 8 7
        ♡ 9 6 5 2   ♡ K Q J
        ◊ Q J 10 7   ◊ 9 4 3
        ♣ A Q 8   ♣ K 5 2
                           North
                           ♠ A K Q 6 2
                           ♡ 7 4 3
                           ◊ K 8
                           ♣ J 10 9

Although you have six apparent losers, you can escape with eight winners if you score tricks with the two and six of spades. Lead a diamond to dummy's ace, and ruff a low diamond with the two of spades. Now play a heart to dummy's ace and lead another diamond. Whether East trumps this trick or not, you cannot be prevented from scoring your eighth trick with the six of spades.

#12   North
                                         ♠ 6 3
                                         ♡ 8 6 5 3
                                         ◇ A K Q
Contract: four spades   ♣ A 9 7 5

Opening Lead: king of clubs   South
                                         ♠ A K 8 7 4 2
                                         ♡ A
                                         ◇ 6 5 2
                                         ♣ 8 4 3

After winning the first trick with the ace of clubs, cash your ace and king of spades. West shows out on the second spade lead, so East has two natural spade tricks. Outside the trump suit, you have two club losers, so the contract seems hopeless. But you can hold your losers to three via an elopement play if East's distribution in the red suits is favorable.

Suppose the four hands are:

                          North
                          ♠ 6 3
                          ♡ 8 6 5 3
                          ◇ A K Q
                          ♣ A 9 7 5
West   East
♠ 5   ♠ Q J 10 9
♡ K J 10 4 2   ♡ Q 9 7
◇ J 9 7 4   ◇ 10 8 3
♣ K Q J   ♣ 10 6 2
                          South
                          ♠ A K 8 7 4 2
                          ♡ A
                          ◇ 6 5 2
                          ♣ 8 4 3

You have five winners in the side suits, so you need five spade tricks to make your bid. You can get the three additional spade tricks you need by leading hearts from dummy.

After discovering the bad trump break, cash your ace of hearts, lead a diamond to dummy, and ruff a heart in your hand. Next lead another diamond to dummy, ruff a second heart in your hand, and lead your last diamond to dummy. At this point, you have won nine tricks and these are the four remaining cards, with the lead in dummy:

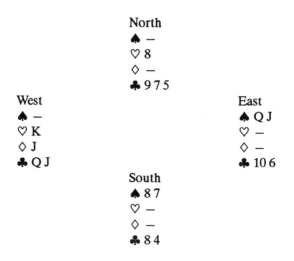

North
♠ —
♡ 8
◊ —
♣ 9 7 5

West
♠ —
♡ K
◊ J
♣ Q J

East
♠ Q J
♡ —
◊ —
♣ 10 6

South
♠ 8 7
♡ —
◊ —
♣ 8 4

If you lead dummy's last heart, you cannot be prevented from winning one more spade trick. If East discards a club, you will ruff; if East ruffs with his queen or jack, you will discard a club and eventually win a trump trick with your eight-seven.

Note that if the lead were in *any hand* but dummy, you would lose all of the tricks in the four-card ending.

Another advantage of ruffing in the long hand is to prepare for a "trump coup." The dictionary defines a coup as "a brilliant and highly successful act." So you might say that a trump coup is a brilliant and highly successful act in the trump suit. This may be a slight exaggeration because declarer's objective is merely to win an extra trump trick; but the technique is important and worth knowing.

For example:

#13

Contract: six spades

Opening Lead: jack of diamonds

North
♠ 10 3
♡ Q J 10 9 2
◊ Q 5 4
♣ A K Q

South
♠ A Q J 9 6 2
♡ K
◊ A K 7
♣ 8 5 4

The key to making six spades is to avoid a spade loser. You win the first trick with the queen of diamonds, and lead the ten of spades, which holds, then a spade to your nine as West disappointingly shows out. East is left with king-eight of spades and you with ace-queen-jack-six, but you cannot take a third finesse because dummy has no more spades.

You may still avoid the spade loser if you can execute a trump coup. First, you must be able to reduce your trump holding until you have equal length with East, without East being able to ruff one of your good tricks during the trump reduction. Second, you must be able to lead from dummy, forcing East to play before you in the end-position.

Suppose this is the full deal:

```
                    North
                    ♠ 10 3
                    ♡ Q J 10 9 2
                    ◇ Q 5 4
                    ♣ A K Q
West                                    East
♠ 5                                     ♠ K 8 7 4
♡ 8 7 6 4                               ♡ A 5 3
◇ J 10 9 8 6                            ◇ 3 2
♣ 10 3 2                                ♣ J 9 7 6
                    South
                    ♠ A Q J 9 6 2
                    ♡ K
                    ◇ A K 7
                    ♣ 8 5 4
```

At trick four, lead your king of hearts. Suppose East wins with the ace and returns a diamond to your king (no other defense is better). Your next four plays must be to lead a club to dummy, ruff a heart, lead a second club to dummy, and ruff another heart. You have now reduced your trump holding to two cards and the position is:

```
                    North
                    ♠ —
                    ♡ Q J
                    ◇ 5
                    ♣ A
West                                    East
♠ —                                     ♠ K 8
♡ 8                                     ♡ —
◇ 10 9                                  ◇ —
♣ 10                                    ♣ J 9
                    South
                    ♠ A Q
                    ♡ —
                    ◇ A
                    ♣ 8
```

Lead a club to dummy's ace and play the good queen of hearts. If East ruffs the queen of hearts, you will overruff and draw his last trump; if East discards his last club, you will discard your ace of diamonds. Either way, you have the rest of the tricks.

After reducing your trump length, it is sometimes possible to throw an opponent on lead and force him to lead into your trump tenace — a "trump endplay."

For example:

#14   North
                                   ♠ A K 9 6
                                   ♡ 6 2
                                   ◊ A 5 4 3
Contract: four hearts   ♣ A 7 2

Opening Lead: queen of diamonds   South
                                   ♠ 3 2
                                   ♡ A Q J 10 7 5
                                   ◊ 8 7
                                   ♣ 8 6 3

   You have three losers in the side suits, so you must avoid losing a heart trick to make your bid. To put it another way, you have four winners in the side suits and need six heart tricks to make your bid. [1]
   After winning with the ace of diamonds, take a heart finesse, lead a spade to dummy's ace, and take a second heart finesse, on which West discards a diamond. Before explaining further, here are the four hands:

                                   North
                                   ♠ A K 9 6
                                   ♡ 6 2
                                   ◊ A 5 4 3
                                   ♣ A 7 2
          West   East
          ♠ Q 8 5   ♠ J 10 7 4
          ♡ 4   ♡ K 9 8 3
          ◊ Q J 10 9 6   ◊ K 2
          ♣ K 9 5 4   ♣ Q J 10
                                   South
                                   ♠ 3 2
                                   ♡ A Q J 10 7 5
                                   ◊ 8 7
                                   ♣ 8 6 3

   East now holds king-nine of hearts and you have ace-queen-seven-five, but there are no more trumps in dummy to finesse. With two entries still in dummy, you can win all of your hearts by reducing your trump length. Lead a spade to dummy's king and ruff a spade in your hand. Next play a club to the ace and ruff the fourth round of spades in your hand. You have won eight tricks so far and still have the ace-queen of hearts behind East's king-nine. Just exit with a club or a diamond to give the opponents the lead, and you will eventually win two more trump tricks.

---

1. When your plan of play involves shortening the trumps in the long hand, crossruffing, or losing trump control, the method of counting winning tricks (instead of losers) may be better. However, it is not necessary to switch back and forth. You will notice that throughout I have maintained the losing-trick method for suit contracts.

How would you play the following hand?

#15   **North**
                                ♠ A 7 4
                                  ♡ 5 3
                                  ◊ J 7 3 2

Contract: four hearts   ♣ A 8 6 5

Opening Lead: queen of clubs   **South**
                                  ♠ K 6 5
                                  ♡ A K Q 10 4 2
                                  ◊ A 9 8
                                  ♣ 7

You have only three losers in the side suits, so the contract is safe unless you lose a trump trick. If you win the opening lead with the ace of clubs and cash two high trumps right away, you will lack the entries to reduce your trump holding and endplay East if he began with four hearts to the jack. This time you must consider the possibility of an endplay and begin your trump reduction *before* you find out how the trump suit divides.

The correct line of play is to win with the ace of clubs and *ruff a club in your hand at trick two*. This play has nothing to lose (unless West led a singleton, which is extremely unlikely), and it will gain a trick if it develops that East has four hearts to the jack.

Suppose this is the full deal:

                         North
                         ♠ A 7 4
                         ♡ 5 3
                         ◊ J 7 3 2
                         ♣ A 8 6 5

West   **East**
♠ Q 10 8 3   ♠ J 9 2
♡ 9   ♡ J 8 7 6
◊ 6 5 4   ◊ K Q 10
♣ Q J 10 9 2   ♣ K 4 3
                         South
                         ♠ K 6 5
                         ♡ A K Q 10 4 2
                         ◊ A 9 8
                         ♣ 7

After ruffing a club in your hand, you cash the ace and king of hearts and get the news about the trump split. East is left with jack-eight and you with queen-ten-four. The trump reduction and endplay can now be executed with ease: Cash your ace of diamonds and king of spades, lead a spade to dummy's ace, ruff a club in your hand, and play any of your losers to give up the lead. You have won eight tricks so far, and must get two more with your queen-ten of hearts.

If you did not ruff a club at trick two, you could not reduce your trump length sufficiently and would be set with good defense.

Ruffing in the long hand may also gain a trick *when the trumps are stacked behind you.* For example:

#16   North
                                             ♠ A 6
                                             ♡ 10 8 6 5
                                             ◇ A K 3 2
Contract: four spades   ♣ 9 7 4

Opening Lead: king of clubs   South
                                             ♠ K Q 10 7 4 2
                                             ♡ A
                                             ◇ 8 6 5
                                             ♣ A 6 3

Once again you need six trump tricks to make your bid and must time your plays accurately to guard against a 4-1 split. Win the first trick with the ace of clubs, cash the ace of hearts and king of spades, and lead a spade to dummy's ace. This time East shows out of spades (West started with four to the jack), but you can still make your bid if the distribution in the side suits is favorable.

Suppose the full deal is:

                                   North
                                   ♠ A 6
                                   ♡ 10 8 6 5
                                   ◇ A K 3 2
                                   ♣ 9 7 4
West   East
♠ J 9 8 3   ♠ 5
♡ K J 7 2   ♡ Q 9 4 3
◇ 10 4   ◇ Q J 9 7
♣ K Q 10   ♣ J 8 5 2
                                   South
                                   ♠ K Q 10 7 4 2
                                   ♡ A
                                   ◇ 8 6 5
                                   ♣ A 6 3

The lead is in dummy and West has ♠ J 9 behind your ♠ Q 10 7 4. Your plan is to ruff dummy's hearts with your low trumps. Note that West cannot overruff because he has as many hearts as dummy. Your next six plays should be: Ruff a heart in your hand, cash the queen of spades (optional, if you are to succeed, but as a precaution against being set two tricks if West has fewer than four hearts), lead a diamond to dummy's ace, ruff another heart in your hand, lead a diamond to dummy's king, and ruff the last heart in your hand. You have just won the first ten tricks — and the admiration of your partner.

It is true you will be set if West has fewer than four hearts (or one diamond and exactly four hearts), but at least you have a reasonable chance. If you do not play as recommended, you will be set regardless of West's distribution in the side suits.

Quiz for Chapter Six

1.

	North
	♠ K Q 9 8
	♡ 8 7 2
	◇ A 10 6 4 3
	♣ 2

	South
	♠ A J 10 2
	♡ J 9 5
	◇ 7
	♣ A Q 6 4 3

West	North	East	South
			1 ♣
Pass	1 ◇	Pass	1 ♠
Pass	3 ♠	Pass	4 ♠
All Pass			

West leads the king of hearts. The defenders cash three heart tricks and then switch to a spade.

2.

	North
	♠ K Q J 10
	♡ A K 9 8 7 2
	◇ 6 4
	♣ 3

	South
	♠ A 6 5 4
	♡ 3
	◇ A 9 8 7
	♣ A 10 5 4

West	North	East	South
			1 ◇
Pass	1 ♡	Pass	1 ♠
Pass	4 NT	Pass	5 ♠
Pass	6 ♠	All Pass	

West leads the king of clubs.

3.

	North
	♠ 6 4
	♡ A 10 3 2
	◇ Q 8 7 5
	♣ A K 4

	South
	♠ A K 7 5 3 2
	♡ 7 5 4
	◇ 2
	♣ 9 8 6

West	North	East	South
	1 ◇	Pass	1 ♠
Pass	1 NT	Pass	2 ♠
All Pass			

West leads the queen of spades and East discards the two of clubs.

4.

	North
	♠ 10 5 2
	♡ 8 6 2
	◇ A Q 4
	♣ K 6 5 3

	South
	♠ A K 6 4 3
	♡ A 7 4
	◇ K J 2
	♣ A 7

West	North	East	South
			1 ♠
Pass	2 ♠	Pass	4 ♠
All Pass			

West leads the three of hearts. You win with the ace of hearts and cash two high spades; West discards the five of hearts on the second spade lead.

5.

North
♠ A 8 7
♡ A K Q 6
◊ A
♣ A 10 8 6 3

South
♠ K Q J 10 9
♡ 9 5 3
◊ 7 6 4 2
♣ 2

West	North	East	South
	1 ♣	Pass	1 ♠
Pass	2 ♡	Pass	2 ♠
Pass	6 ♠	All Pass	

West leads the six of spades and East discards the four of clubs.

6.

North
♠ 10 9
♡ A J
◊ K Q J 7 3 2
♣ 6 5 4

South
♠ A Q J 8 6 4
♡ K Q 10 9 5
◊ A
♣ 7

West	North	East	South
			1 ♠
Pass	2 ◊	Pass	2 ♡
Pass	2 ♠	Pass	4 NT
Pass	5 ◊	Pass	6 ♠
All Pass			

West leads the king and ace of clubs. You ruff, play a heart to dummy and take two spade finesses. West discards a club on the second spade.

7.

North
♠ K J 9 8
♡ Q J 5 4 3 2
◊ A K
♣ 7

South
♠ A Q 10 6 2
♡ —
◊ 8 7 4 3
♣ A Q 10 6

West	North	East	South
	1 ♡	Pass	1 ♠
Pass	4 ♠	Pass	5 ♣
Pass	5 ◊	Pass	6 ♠
All Pass			

West leads the five of spades and East follows suit.

8.

North
♠ A K
♡ K 6 5 2
◊ A 7 4
♣ 9 8 7 3

South
♠ J 8 7 6 5 2
♡ A 4
◊ 10 9 3
♣ A K

West	North	East	South
	1 ♣	Pass	1 ♠
Pass	1 NT	Pass	3 ♠
Pass	4 ♠	All Pass	

West leads the queen of hearts. You win with the ace of hearts and cash two high spades; West follows with the three of spades and then discards the two of clubs.

Answers to Quiz for Chapter Six

1.

```
                North
                ♠ K Q 9 8
                ♡ 8 7 2
                ◇ A 10 6 4 3
                ♣ 2
West                         East
♠ 6 3                        ♠ 7 5 4
♡ K Q 6 4                    ♡ A 10 3
◇ K Q 9 8 5                  ◇ J 2
♣ J 5                        ♣ K 10 9 8 7
                South
                ♠ A J 10 2
                ♡ J 9 5
                ◇ 7
                ♣ A Q 6 4 3
```

West	North	East	South
			1 ♣
Pass	1 ◇	Pass	1 ♠
Pass	3 ♠	Pass	4 ♠
All Pass			

West leads the king of hearts. The defenders cash three heart tricks and then lead a spade.

Without the spade lead at trick four, you could crossruff for ten tricks. Since you will now be limited to seven spade winners, you must win *three* side tricks. The only good chance is the club finesse, so win the spade lead at trick four in the dummy and finesse the queen of clubs. After cashing your minor-suit aces, you can crossruff for ten tricks.

2.

```
                North
                ♠ K Q J 10
                ♡ A K 9 8 7 2
                ◇ 6 4
                ♣ 3
West                         East
♠ 9 7 3 2                    ♠ 8
♡ 10 4                       ♡ Q J 6 5
◇ Q 5 2                      ◇ K J 10 3
♣ K Q 8 6                    ♣ J 9 7 2
                South
                ♠ A 6 5 4
                ♡ 3
                ◇ A 9 8 7
                ♣ A 10 5 4
```

West	North	East	South
			1 ◇
Pass	1 ♡	Pass	1 ♠
Pass	4 NT	Pass	5 ♠
Pass	6 ♠	All Pass	

West leads the king of clubs.

The low trumps in your hand make it impossible to crossruff for twelve tricks, so the only chance is to make dummy the master hand and establish the heart suit.

After winning with the ace of clubs, lead a heart to dummy and ruff a low heart with a *low* spade. Now lead a spade to dummy and ruff another low heart with the *ace* of spades. The remaining hearts in dummy are now good, so draw the missing trumps and cash your remaining winners. As long as hearts divide no worse than 4-2 and spades no worse than 4-1, the contract is safe.

Note that you would fail if you led a trump, or cashed both top hearts, before you ruffed a heart in your hand. The exact sequence of plays is necessary.

3.

	North		
	♠ 6 4		
	♡ A 10 3 2		
	◇ Q 8 7 5		
	♣ A K 4		

West		East	
♠ Q J 10 9 8		♠ —	
♡ K 6		♡ Q J 9 8	
◇ A J 6 3		◇ K 10 9 4	
♣ 10 5		♣ Q J 7 3 2	

	South		
	♠ A K 7 5 3 2		
	♡ 7 5 4		
	◇ 2		
	♣ 9 8 6		

West	North	East	South
	1 ◇	Pass	1 ♠
Pass	1 NT	Pass	2 ♠
All Pass			

West leads the queen of spades and East discards the two of clubs.

The shocking spade division reveals that you have seven losers: three spades, two hearts, one diamond, and one club. The only chance to make your bid is to ruff three diamonds with small trumps in your hand. With three entries to dummy and the fortunate division of the side suits in the diagram, you can make your bid against any defense.

Win the first spade trick and lead a diamond. Suppose East wins this trick and leads the queen of hearts. Win with the ace of hearts, ruff a diamond, lead a club to dummy, ruff a diamond, lead another club to dummy, and ruff the last diamond. You now have eight tricks: five spades, one heart, and two clubs.

4.

	North		
	♠ 10 5 2		
	♡ 8 6 2		
	◇ A Q 4		
	♣ K 6 5 3		

West		East	
♠ 9		♠ Q J 8 7	
♡ J 9 5 3		♡ K Q 10	
◇ 10 8 7 6		◇ 9 5 3	
♣ Q 9 4 2		♣ J 10 8	

	South		
	♠ A K 6 4 3		
	♡ A 7 4		
	◇ K J 2		
	♣ A 7		

West	North	East	South
			1 ♠
Pass	2 ♠	Pass	4 ♠
All Pass			

West leads the three of hearts. You win with the ace of hearts and cash two high spades; West discards the five of hearts on the second spade lead.

After winning the first trick with the ace of hearts and cashing the ace and king of spades, you get the bad news that you must lose two spade tricks. You appear to have two inescapable heart losers, so the contract seems doomed. But look at it another way: You have six side winners (one heart, three diamonds, and two clubs), so you can make your bid if you can win four spade tricks. The plan is to ruff two clubs in your hand.

At trick four, cash the ace of clubs. Continue with a club to the king and a club ruff in your hand. Now cash *all three high diamonds* (if East has fewer than three diamonds, the contract cannot be made), with the lead winding up in dummy. Finally, lead dummy's last club for an "elopement play": If East ruffs the club, you will discard a heart and eventually win a spade trick; if East discards, you can ruff with a low spade.

Note that if you did not cash all of your diamond winners, East would be able to discard a diamond on the fourth round of clubs and set you.

5.   North
                         ♠ A 8 7
                         ♡ A K Q 6
                         ◊ A
                         ♣ A 10 8 6 3

West   East
♠ 6 5 4 3 2   ♠ —
♡ J 7 2   ♡ 10 8 4
◊ K Q 10 8   ◊ J 9 5 3
♣ J   ♣ K Q 9 7 5 4

                         South
                         ♠ K Q J 10 9
                         ♡ 9 5 3
                         ◊ 7 6 4 2
                         ♣ 2

West	North	East	South
	1 ♣	Pass	1 ♠
Pass	2 ♡	Pass	2 ♠
Pass	6 ♠	All Pass	

West leads the six of spades and East discards the four of clubs.

With the annoying trump lead and 5-0 split, the only chance to make the contract is to cross-ruff. But first you must cash *five* side winners since you can win only seven trump tricks.

After winning the first trick, your next five plays must be to cash the *three* top hearts and both minor suit aces. If West is able to ruff any of these tricks, you cannot make the contract. Here, though, West cannot ruff so you can crossruff the rest of the way for twelve tricks.

Note that if you played more than one round of clubs before cashing the ace, king, and queen of hearts, West could beat you by discarding a heart.

Also note that if West did not lead a trump, you could crossruff for *eight* trump tricks; then you could make your bid by cashing just *two* high hearts. Cashing the third heart would be a needless risk: If either defender had a doubleton heart, he could ruff and lead a trump.

6.   North
                         ♠ 10 9
                         ♡ A J
                         ◊ K Q J 7 3 2
                         ♣ 6 5 4

West   East
♠ 3   ♠ K 7 5 2
♡ 8 6 2   ♡ 7 4 3
◊ 10 9 5 4   ◊ 8 6
♣ A K 8 3 2   ♣ Q J 10 9

                         South
                         ♠ A Q J 8 6 4
                         ♡ K Q 10 9 5
                         ◊ A
                         ♣ 7

West	North	East	South
			1 ♠
Pass	2 ◊	Pass	2 ♡
Pass	2 ♠	Pass	4 NT
Pass	5 ◊	Pass	6 ♠
All Pass			

West leads the king and ace of clubs. You ruff, play a heart to dummy, and take two spade finesses. West discards a club on the second.

After you ruff the second club trick, lead a heart to dummy and take two spade finesses, East is left with the king-seven of spades and you with ace-queen-jack. Since there are no more spades in dummy, you must play for a trump coup. Lead dummy's last club and ruff in your hand to reduce your spade length to two — the same as East. Next cash the ace of diamonds, lead over to dummy's high heart, and play high diamonds. East is over a barrel: If he ruffs, you can overruff, draw his last trump, and win the rest of the tricks with high hearts; if he discards, you do the same and continue to lead high diamonds. If East continues to discard, you will win the last two tricks with the ace-queen over his king-seven.

Note that West could beat the contract if he did not help you reduce your trump holding by playing the second high club. Would you have been that smart?

7.   North
                        ♠ K J 9 8
                        ♡ Q J 5 4 3 2
                        ◇ A K
                        ♣ 7

West   East
♠ 5 4 3   ♠ 7
♡ 8 7 6   ♡ A K 10 9
◇ J 9 5   ◇ Q 10 6 2
♣ K J 9 2   ♣ 8 5 4 3

                        South
                        ♠ A Q 10 6 2
                        ♡ —
                        ◇ 8 7 4 3
                        ♣ A Q 10 6

West	North	East	South
	1 ♡	Pass	1 ♠
Pass	4 ♠	Pass	5 ♣
Pass	5 ◇	Pass	6 ♠
All Pass			

West leads the five of spades and East follows suit.

8.   North
                        ♠ A K
                        ♡ K 6 5 2
                        ◇ A 7 4
                        ♣ 9 8 7 3

West   East
♠ 3   ♠ Q 10 9 4
♡ Q J 9 8 3   ♡ 10 7
◇ K 5   ◇ Q J 8 6 2
♣ Q 10 6 4 2   ♣ J 5

                        South
                        ♠ J 8 7 6 5 2
                        ♡ A 4
                        ◇ 10 9 3
                        ♣ A K

West	North	East	South
	1 ♣	Pass	1 ♠
Pass	1 NT	Pass	3 ♠
Pass	4 ♠	All Pass	

West leads the queen of hearts. You win with the ace of hearts and cash two high spades; West follows with the three of spades and then discards the two of clubs.

Without the spade lead, you could cash your three minor-suit winners and then crossruff for twelve tricks. But the trump lead limits you to eight spade tricks. You may have considered taking a club finesse and then crossruffing, but this is an inferior line of play. A much better chance is to establish dummy's heart suit by ruffing in your hand, and then drawing trumps from dummy—a dummy reversal.

After winning the first spade trick in dummy, ruff a heart, lead a diamond to dummy, ruff a heart, lead a diamond to dummy, and ruff a heart (with the *ace* of spades if you have not already done so). There is only one high heart outstanding, so lead your last spade to dummy and cash a third round of spades to draw West's last trump. Now concede a heart trick to East, and claim the rest: The dummy is left with a trump and two good hearts.

Note that if hearts divide 5-2 (or worse), it may be impossible to establish the suit. But you will find this out when you ruff the third round in your hand. At this point you can alter your course: Ruff a diamond to get to dummy and try the club finesse; if it works, you can cash the ace of clubs and crossruff.

When West shows out on the second spade lead, it seems you must lose two spades and two diamonds, but again there is hope by ruffing in the long hand. If you can reduce your trump length so you have the same number as East (the jack-eight behind the queen-ten), you can hold your spade losers to one.

At tricks four and five, *cash the ace and king of clubs*. Now lead a heart to the king and play a low heart (or club) from dummy. If East ruffs, your troubles are over; so suppose he discards a diamond and you ruff with a low spade. Next play a diamond to dummy's ace and lead another heart (or club). Again, East discards and you ruff with a low spade. So far you have won nine tricks and still have the jack-eight of spades. Simply exit with a diamond and wait— you will score a tenth trick with the jack of spades.

If you did not cash the ace and king of clubs before ruffing hearts from dummy, East would discard a club on the third round of hearts; then your trump reduction and endplay would fail.

7

Going with the Odds

♣   ◇   ♡   ♠   ♣   ◇   ♡   ♠

In this chapter, you will find yourself in situations where two or three different lines of play are possible. It may be necessary to choose one line and ignore the other; or it may be possible to combine your chances: Try one line of play and, if it does not work, try another.

Choosing the Percentage Play

When it is necessary to decide between two or more possible lines of play, the obvious choice is the one that offers the best odds.

Which line of play would you adopt in the next twelve deals?

#1

Contract: four spades

Opening Lead: king of hearts

North
♠ 7 4
♡ A 6 5
◇ 9 6 5 3
♣ 10 7 4 2

South
♠ A Q J 10 9 8
♡ 9 4
◇ A Q J
♣ A Q

You have four possible losers, one in each suit. Since the ace of hearts is your only entry to dummy, you will be able to take only one finesse. Although it is true that one finesse is as likely to succeed as another, you should take the *club* finesse. If your right-hand opponent has the king of clubs, you eliminate one of your losers no matter how the suit divides.

Note that if you try the spade or diamond finesse and it works, you will still lose to the king if East has more than two cards in the suit.

#2   North
                                                    ♠ J 5 2
                                                    ♡ 4 3 2
                                                    ◊ A 8 7
Contract: four hearts   ♣ 9 7 6 5

Opening Lead: queen of diamonds   South
                                                    ♠ A Q
                                                    ♡ A Q J 10 9 7
                                                    ◊ K 9 4
                                                    ♣ A 3

Once again you have one possible loser in each suit and only one entry to dummy. But this time you should not plan to take any finesse. A far better line of play is to win the first trick with the king of diamonds, cash the ace of hearts (and draw the trumps if the king is singleton), cash the ace of spades, and lead the queen of spades to drive out the king. You will eventually get to dummy with the ace of diamonds and discard one of your losers on the jack of spades. Only if spades divide 6-2 or worse, or diamonds divide 6-1, is the contract in jeopardy (the opponents may get a ruff); but this is very unlikely.

#3   North
                                                    ♠ A 10
                                                    ♡ 7 6 5
                                                    ◊ 7 4 3
Contract: three notrump   ♣ 9 8 6 5 2

Opening Lead: three of spades   South
                                                    ♠ Q 5
                                                    ♡ A K Q 2
                                                    ◊ A Q 8 6
                                                    ♣ A K Q

You have eight winners: one spade, three hearts, one diamond, and three clubs. You play the ten of spades from dummy on the first trick, hoping West has led from the king; but East wins with the king and returns a spade to drive out your only stopper. There are two chances for a ninth trick: You can try the diamond finesse, or you can play for a 3-3 heart break—but you cannot do both. If you try the diamond finesse and it loses, the opponents will win enough spade tricks to set you. If you run the hearts first and they do not divide, you cannot get back to dummy for a diamond finesse. The percentage play is to finesse the queen of diamonds at trick three. The 50-percent chance that East has the king of diamonds is better than the 36-percent chance that hearts will divide 3-3.

#4   North
                             ♠ A Q 5 3 2
                             ♡ 6 4 2
                             ◊ 9 5 4

Contract: three notrump   ♣ 10 8

Opening Lead: three of hearts   South
                             ♠ 7 4
                             ♡ A 8 5
                             ◊ A J 10
                             ♣ A K Q J 9

You find out hearts divide 4-3 by ducking the first two rounds and winning the third with your ace. You have eight winners and can get a ninth if West has the king of spades or if East has the king or queen of diamonds. Since the odds are 3-to-1 in your favor that at least one of two missing cards will be onside, taking the double finesse in diamonds is a much better play than the spade finesse.

At trick four, enter the dummy with the ten of clubs and lead a diamond toward the ace-jack-ten. If East plays a low diamond, finesse the ten. Suppose West wins with the king or queen of diamonds, cashes the thirteenth heart (on which you discard a spade), and leads the ten of spades.

It may appear to be a tossup whether you should now take the spade finesse or the diamond finesse. But if you remember reading about Restricted Choice in Chapter 1 (see page 12), you know that the odds are heavily in favor of going up with the ace of spades and taking a second diamond finesse.

#5   North
                             ♠ A K 7 4 3
                             ♡ 6 5 2
                             ◊ 5 4

Contract: three notrump   ♣ 9 8 2

Opening Lead: king of hearts   South
                             ♠ 6 2
                             ♡ A 7 4 3
                             ◊ A K 10 9
                             ♣ A K Q

East follows suit to the first two rounds of hearts and discards a low club on the third lead as you win with the ace of hearts. You have eight winners and two chances for a ninth: Lead a low spade and duck in dummy, hoping for a 3-3 break; or take two finesses in diamonds. The 3-to-1 odds that East has at least one diamond honor make the choice clear.

Before leading a spade to get the lead in dummy, you have nothing to lose by playing your fourth heart. When West wins the trick, he may solve your problem by leading a diamond for you. Let's assume West is not obliging and that he switches to a club. You win and play a spade over to dummy's king. Now lead a diamond and finesse the nine (unless East puts up an honor). If West captures the nine of diamonds with the queen or jack, eventually you will get to dummy with the ace of spades and take a second diamond finesse. Only if West started with both the queen and jack of diamonds will you be set.

#6   North
                                              ♠ 8 7 6
                                              ♡ 9 3
                                              ◊ A 9 2
Contract: three notrump   ♣ A 8 6 5 4

Opening Lead: queen of hearts   South
                                              ♠ A J
                                              ♡ A K
                                              ◊ K 8 7 6 4
                                              ♣ 9 7 3 2

You have six winners: one spade, two hearts, two diamonds, and one club. Since you need *three* more tricks, you should cash the ace of clubs and, unless someone shows out, play another club. If clubs divide 2-2, you will win the three extra tricks you need when you regain the lead.

Note that the diamond suit offers only a chance for two extra tricks; so it is wrong to tackle diamonds, even though a 3-2 diamond split is far more likely than a 2-2 club split. If diamonds divide 3-2, you will still be set.

#7   North
                                              ♠ 7 4
                                              ♡ A Q 4
                                              ◊ K 9 6 5 2
Contract: three notrump   ♣ 8 7 3

Opening Lead: eight of spades   South
                                              ♠ A Q 3
                                              ♡ K 7 6
                                              ◊ Q 8 4
                                              ♣ K Q J 10

West	North	East	South
		1 ♠	1 NT
Pass	3 NT	All Pass	

You have five winners: two spades and three hearts. The bidding indicates that East has at least five spades and the two minor-suit aces, so you can afford to give up the lead only once more.

The club suit will provide only three tricks. So, if you try to establish clubs, you are playing safe to make sure you go down exactly one trick. East will win your club lead with the ace and knock out your last spade stopper. That leaves you with eight tricks. Whenever you lead a diamond, East will win with the ace and run the spade suit.

The correct line of play is to lead a diamond *through* East, forcing him to duck or waste his ace. As long as East has the ace of diamonds and the suit divides 3-2, you cannot be set.

Suppose this is the full deal:

```
                        North
                        ♠ 7 4
                        ♡ A Q 4
                        ◊ K 9 6 5 2
                        ♣ 8 7 3
     West                                      East
     ♠ 8 6 5                                   ♠ K J 10 9 2
     ♡ J 10 9 3                                ♡ 8 5 2
     ◊ 7 3                                     ◊ A J 10
     ♣ 9 5 4 2                                 ♣ A 6
                        South
                        ♠ A Q 3
                        ♡ K 7 6
                        ◊ Q 8 4
                        ♣ K Q J 10
```

After winning the first trick, lead a heart to dummy's queen and play a low diamond. If East goes up with the ace, you will have nine tricks when you regain the lead (two spades, three hearts, and four diamonds). If East ducks the diamond lead, win with the queen and then play clubs until the ace is driven out. Again, you have nine tricks (two spades, three hearts, one diamond, and three clubs).

#8	North
	♠ 7 6 4 2
	♡ 9 8 3
	◊ A Q J 10
Contract: six spades	♣ 5 2
Opening Lead: queen of hearts	South
	♠ A K Q 10 8
	♡ A
	◊ 7 3
	♣ A Q J 10 9

After winning the opening lead and drawing trumps in three rounds, you are left with two possible losers. It may appear that you need a successful finesse in one of the minor suits to make your bid (the odds are 3-to-1 in your favor that at least one finesse will work); but this time there is a line of play that will succeed even if both kings are offside. You have a 100-percent play.

At trick five, lead the ace of clubs (optional) and another club. Let's assume that West wins with the king of clubs and leads a diamond. You should win with the ace, ruff a heart to get back to your hand, and cash the three good clubs to discard three diamonds from dummy. Since the dummy has no more diamonds, your last diamond can be ruffed.

#9   North
                                                  ♠ A Q
                                                  ♡ J 7 6
                                                  ◊ Q 6 4 3
Contract: six diamonds   ♣ A 10 7 2

Opening Lead: king of clubs   South
                                                  ♠ J 9 5 2
                                                  ♡ A K Q
                                                  ◊ A 10 8 7 5 2
                                                  ♣ —

The question here is how to play the diamond suit. If you can afford to lose a diamond trick, there is a safety play to make sure you do not lose more than one trick. If you cannot afford a diamond loser, the percentage play (although the odds are against you) is to cash the ace and hope for a singleton king.

The only possible side loser is a spade, so you should find out whether or not you will lose a spade trick first. Ruff the opening lead and take the spade finesse. If the finesse fails, you will eventually cash the ace of diamonds. If the spade finesse works, take the safety play: Lead a diamond from dummy and finesse the ten if East plays the nine (in case he has king-jack-nine), or win with the ace if East plays the king or jack, or shows out. No matter how the suit divides, you will lose at most one trick.

#10   North
                                                  ♠ A K 7
                                                  ♡ 7 6 5 2
                                                  ◊ K J 3
Contract: five diamonds   ♣ K 10 9

Opening Lead: queen of spades   South
                                                  ♠ —
                                                  ♡ K Q
                                                  ◊ A Q 10 9 7 6 4
                                                  ♣ 8 5 3 2

The best contract is three notrump, but here you are in five diamonds. The key decision is what to discard on the ace and king of spades? If you discard two clubs, you are left with three possible losers: one heart and two clubs. The only hope to make your bid is to find West with the ace of clubs.

A much better play is to discard the king and queen of hearts on the high spades. Since you no longer have a heart loser, you can afford to lose two club tricks. After throwing the king and queen of hearts on the high spades and drawing trumps in two rounds, lead a club toward dummy. If West plays an honor, your troubles are over; so assume he plays a low club, you finesse the ten, and East wins with the queen or jack. When you regain the lead, play another low club toward dummy, intending to finesse the nine if West plays low.

The double finesse will limit your club losers to two tricks when West has either the queen or jack (or both) — 3-to-1 odds in your favor. You will also make your bid with the queen and jack offside if West has the ace of clubs and plays it when you lead toward dummy (something he must do if he has a singleton or a doubleton). These chances are diminished slightly by the possibility of a 3-0 trump break, but the recommended play is still a standout.

#11

Contract: four spades

Opening Lead: king of hearts

North
♠ 10 9 2
♡ A 5 3
◇ 7
♣ A Q 10 9 8 3

South
♠ A K J 8 7
♡ 10 6 4
◇ 10 8 2
♣ K J

In Chapter 1, you learned that the best way to play this spade suit is to cash the ace or king, then finesse for the queen. But in this deal you will immediately be set if the finesse fails: the opponents will cash two hearts and a diamond. A better play is to cash the ace and king of spades. If the queen falls under the ace or king, draw trumps and run the club suit for twelve tricks. If the queen does not fall (but both opponents follow suit), lead clubs until the player with the queen of spades ruffs. The contract is safe as long as he cannot ruff before you can discard one heart.

This line of play will fail if either defender has four spades to the queen, or three spades to the queen and a singleton or void in clubs; but it offers a better chance than the finesse.

#12

Contract: four spades

Opening Lead: queen of hearts

North
♠ A Q 3
♡ 7 4 2
◇ 8 6 5 4 3
♣ A 9

South
♠ K J 10 8 6 4
♡ A 6 5
◇ A Q
♣ 7 2

You have four losers and there are two chances to make this contract: Take a winning diamond finesse, or establish a long diamond in dummy to discard a loser. There are not enough entries to dummy to try both chances, so you must choose one. The diamond suit can be established if it divides no worse than 4-2 — an 84-percent chance (see the table on page 172). This is much better than relying on a finesse, which is only a 50-percent chance.

Suppose these are the four hands:

North
♠ A Q 3
♡ 7 4 2
◊ 8 6 5 4 3
♣ A 9

West
♠ 9 7 5
♡ Q J 10 9
◊ K 2
♣ J 10 8 3

East
♠ 2
♡ K 8 3
◊ J 10 9 7
♣ K Q 6 5 4

South
♠ K J 10 8 6 4
♡ A 6 5
◊ A Q
♣ 7 2

Win the opening heart lead and cash *one* high spade in your hand (this is a precaution to see if spades divide 4-0, in which case you must change your plan and take the diamond finesse). When both defenders follow to the spade lead, play the ace and queen of diamonds. Let's assume the opponents win with the king of diamonds, cash two heart tricks, and lead a club. Win with the ace of clubs, lead a diamond from dummy, and ruff with a *high* trump. East still has a high diamond, so lead a spade to dummy and ruff a fourth round of diamonds with a *high* trump. Now lead a spade to dummy to draw West's last trump and discard your losing club on the fifth diamond.

Note that if you use one of your spade entries to get to dummy and take a losing diamond finesse, you will be set even if diamonds divide 3-3. The opponents will cash two heart tricks, then lead a club to drive out dummy's ace. With the blank ace of diamonds in your hand and only one entry to dummy, the contract is hopeless.

Combining Your Chances

When two or more lines of play are available, it is not always necessary to choose between them. It may be possible to try one and, if it does not work, try another. With the knowledge that you have two or more chances to make your bid, how would you play the next twelve deals?

#13

Contract: six spades

Opening Lead: jack of diamonds

North
♠ K Q 7 5
♡ A Q 8 4
◊ 6 4 3
♣ Q 2

South
♠ A J 10 9 8 2
♡ 3
◊ A K 2
♣ A 8 7

There are two losers: one diamond and one club. If West has the king of clubs or the king of hearts, you will be able to discard the diamond loser and make the slam if you time the play correctly. After winning the opening lead and drawing trumps, lead a low club from your hand toward the queen. If West has the king of clubs and plays it, you will be able to discard one of dummy's diamonds on your ace of clubs (if he does not play his king of clubs, you will not lose a club trick). If East captures the queen of clubs with the king, you will eventually try the heart finesse so you can discard a diamond on the ace of hearts.

Note that if you took the heart finesse first, you would have no second chance if it failed.

#14	North
	♠ 10 8
	♡ 9 6 3 2
	◊ A Q 8 5
Contract: three notrump	♣ K J 7
Opening Lead: queen of spades	South
	♠ A K
	♡ K 8
	◊ 7 6 4 2
	♣ A Q 10 9 2

With eight winners in sight (two spades, one diamond, and five clubs) and only one more spade stopper, you can make your bid if West has the king of diamonds or if East has the ace of hearts. To give yourself both chances, you must try the heart finesse first. After winning the first trick with a high spade, play a club over to dummy and lead a heart toward your king. If the heart finesse fails, you can still rely on the diamond finesse — except in the very unlikely event that the opponents can (and do) run five heart tricks.

If you mistakenly try the diamond finesse first and East has the king, you will be set routinely even when the ace of hearts is onside.

#15	North
	♠ A J 10 4
	♡ 7 5
	◊ 6 3
Contract: three notrump	♣ A K J 10 3
Opening Lead: four of hearts	South
	♠ Q 9 2
	♡ K 10
	◊ A K J 10 5
	♣ 8 7 4

On the first trick, East plays the queen of hearts and you win with the king. You have six winners: one spade, one heart, two diamonds, and two clubs. Since you have no more heart stoppers, you must develop three additional tricks without giving up the lead. There are three suits that offer the possibility of three extra tricks. Which one would you try?

The answer is *all three*. First, cash the ace and king of clubs. If the queen falls, you have nine tricks. Second, cash the ace and king of diamonds. If that queen falls, you have nine tricks. If neither queen falls, your third and last chance will be a successful spade finesse. Lead the *nine* of spades first; if the finesse works, lead the queen of spades next. If West has four or more spades including the king, it will be necessary to retain the lead in your hand for a third finesse.

Note that it is important to cash the ace and king of clubs before the ace and king of diamonds. In case neither queen drops, the lead will be in your hand to try the spade finesse.

#16

Contract: three notrump

Opening Lead: seven of spades

North
♠ 6
♡ A 8 7 2
◇ A K 6 4 3
♣ 5 3 2

South
♠ A Q
♡ K 4 3
◇ 9 5 2
♣ A K 8 6 4

You have eight winners (two in each suit) and, with only one more spade stopper, can afford to give up the lead only once. A ninth trick is possible in clubs or diamonds if either suit divides 3-2, or in hearts if that suit divides 3-3. Here again you are able to try all three chances.

Suppose these are the four hands:

North
♠ 6
♡ A 8 7 2
◇ A K 6 4 3
♣ 5 3 2

West
♠ K 10 8 7 2
♡ J 9 5
◇ 10
♣ Q 10 9 7

East
♠ J 9 5 4 3
♡ Q 10 6
◇ Q J 8 7
♣ J

South
♠ A Q
♡ K 4 3
◇ 9 5 2
♣ A K 8 6 4

After winning the opening lead with the queen of spades, cash the ace and king of diamonds and the ace and king of clubs. If either suit divides 3-2, lead that suit again to drive out the high card and establish two extra tricks. As you can see here, both suits divide 4-1; so the only remaining hope is a 3-3 heart split. Lead a low heart and concede the trick; do *not* play the ace or king as you will need them for later entry cards. Whichever opponent wins the heart trick can cash two minor suit winners if he chooses, but that would give you an overtrick. So assume he leads another spade. Win with the ace and cash the king, ace, and thirteenth heart to make your bid — sometimes the least likely prospect is the only one that works.

#17   North
                                     ♠ A K
                                     ♡ 6 2
                                     ◊ K 10 9

Contract: three notrump   ♣ A Q J 8 4 3

Opening Lead: king of hearts   South
                                     ♠ J 10 3 2
                                     ♡ A 8
                                     ◊ A Q 4
                                     ♣ 10 7 5 2

Five clubs (or six clubs) is a better contract, but you reach three notrump. You have seven winners: two spades, one heart, three diamonds, and one club. Since your only heart stopper is being knocked out, you must develop two extra tricks without giving up the lead. There are two chances. Do you see them?

Suppose this is the full deal:

                          North
                          ♠ A K
                          ♡ 6 2
                          ◊ K 10 9
                          ♣ A Q J 8 4 3

West   East
♠ Q 5   ♠ 9 8 7 6 4
♡ K Q J 9 7   ♡ 10 5 4 3
◊ 8 7 6 3 2   ◊ J 5
♣ 6   ♣ K 9
                          South
                          ♠ J 10 3 2
                          ♡ A 8
                          ◊ A Q 4
                          ♣ 10 7 5 2

You will be set if you take the losing club finesse, but can make your bid if you cash the ace and king of spades. Since the queen drops, the jack and ten will be your eighth and ninth tricks. It is very unlikely (about a 10-percent chance) that the queen of spades will drop under the ace-king, but it is a free shot. If the queen doesn't drop, you can still make your bid if the club finesse works. Two chances are better than one.

Sometimes one of the chances to make your contract is so remote that it is overlooked. For example:

#18   North
                                       ♠ 7 5 4
                                       ♡ K 3
                                       ◇ A K Q 2
Contract: six hearts   ♣ K 10 6 5

Opening Lead: ten of diamonds   South
                                       ♠ K 10
                                       ♡ A Q J 10 7 4
                                       ◇ 8 6 5
                                       ♣ A 2

To make this bid you must limit your spade losers to one, and it is possible to combine three chances to achieve this. Before looking at the full deal, do you see the three possibilities?

                          North
                          ♠ 7 5 4
                          ♡ K 3
                          ◇ A K Q 2
                          ♣ K 10 6 5
West   East
♠ A Q 9 8 3   ♠ J 6 2
♡ 6 2   ♡ 9 8 5
◇ 10 9   ◇ J 7 4 3
♣ 9 7 4 3   ♣ Q J 8
                          South
                          ♠ K 10
                          ♡ A Q J 10 7 4
                          ◇ 8 6 5
                          ♣ A 2

The three chances are: The ace of spades is onside, the diamonds divide 3-3, or the ten of clubs can be established for a discard. The last is remote, but it is the only one that works as the cards lie.

After winning the opening diamond lead, the best sequence of plays to give yourself all three chances is to draw trumps, cash the ace and king of clubs, and trump a third round of clubs in your hand. Since the queen and jack of clubs fall, you can discard a losing spade on the ten of clubs.

If the ten of clubs does not set up for a discard, the next play is to test the diamond suit to see if it divides 3-3 so you can discard a spade on the thirteenth diamond. If that fails, as a last resort you will lead a spade from dummy in the hope that East has the ace.

#19

North
♠ A 3 2
♡ 8 6 5 4
◇ 10 9 7
♣ A K 7

Contract: six spades

Opening Lead: queen of hearts

South
♠ K Q J 10 9 7 4
♡ A K 2
◇ K 8
♣ 6

You have three losers (one heart and two diamonds) and can discard the heart loser on dummy's second high club. There are two possible ways to avoid losing two diamonds: either the hearts divide 3-3, or East has the ace of diamonds. The correct line of play to give yourself both chances is to win the first heart trick, cash two high trumps in your hand (the ace in dummy will be needed for an entry), cash the other high heart, lead a club to dummy, and discard your losing heart on the second high club. Now lead a third round of hearts and ruff in your hand. If hearts divide 3-3, you will discard a diamond on the last heart. Otherwise, you will have to find the ace of diamonds onside.

#20

North
♠ 3 2
♡ 8 5 4
◇ A 7 6 3 2
♣ A K Q

Contract: seven spades

Opening Lead: king of diamonds

South
♠ A K Q J 10 9 5
♡ A Q
◇ —
♣ 8 7 3 2

You have two possible losers (the queen of hearts and a club) and one of them can be discarded on the ace of diamonds — but which one? If you discard the queen of hearts, you give up on the heart finesse. If you discard a club, you will be parting with a winner if clubs divide 3-3. Before reading further, which would you discard?

The answer is neither — at least, not yet. To complicate matters further, you can establish dummy's fifth diamond if that suit divides 4-4.

Here is the best play to cater to all chances: Play a low diamond from dummy, ruffing the first trick in your hand; then lead four rounds of trumps, discarding two *hearts* from dummy. Next lead a club to dummy, ruff a diamond, lead another club to dummy, and ruff another diamond with your last trump.

The remaining cards are:

North
♠ —
♡ 8
◇ A 7
♣ A

South
♠ —
♡ A Q
◇ —
♣ 8 7

Lead a club to the ace. If the eight of clubs is good, discard the queen of hearts on the ace of diamonds and claim. Otherwise, discard your club on the ace of diamonds. Now there are only two cards left: If the seven of diamonds is good, claim; otherwise, take the heart finesse *unless* East's last card is known to be a club or a diamond — then play the *ace* of hearts.

#21

Contract: six notrump

Opening Lead: ten of hearts

North
♠ J 9 8 5 2
♡ K Q
◇ A Q 10
♣ Q J 3

South
♠ A 10
♡ A J 2
◇ K J 4 3
♣ A 10 9 6

You have nine winners (one spade, three hearts, four diamonds, and one club) and have two chances to get the three extra tricks you need: in clubs, if East has the king; or in spades, if East has both missing honors, or a singleton or doubleton honor. If you try the club finesse first, you will automatically be set if the finesse fails. So you should begin by testing the spade suit.

Win the opening heart lead in dummy and lead a low spade. If East plays the king or queen, you have twelve tricks simply by winning with ace and driving out the other spade honor. But suppose East follows with a low spade, you finesse the ten, and West wins with the king or queen. As soon as you regain the lead, play the ace of spades. If the missing spade honor drops, you have twelve tricks. Otherwise, you will fall back on the club finesse.

Also note that if the opponents allow you to win the first spade trick with the ten, you will switch to clubs and make your bid whether the finesse works or not.

#22

Contract: three notrump

Opening Lead: jack of hearts

North
♠ 10 9 6 3
♡ A 7
◇ A Q J 10 8 7
♣ 4

South
♠ A 4
♡ K 2
◇ 9 3 2
♣ K Q 8 7 5 3

You have only four winners: one spade, two hearts, and one diamond. It is tempting to win with the king of hearts and take a diamond finesse, but you will be held to eight tricks if the finesse fails. A much better play is to win the first trick in dummy and lead a club. Three things might happen:

1. If you are allowed to win the first club trick with the king or queen, switch to diamonds. Now that you have stolen a club trick, you can win nine tricks even if the diamond finesse fails.
2. If East goes up with the ace of clubs and the suit divides 3-3, you have nine tricks without needing the diamond finesse. You will win one spade, two hearts, one diamond, and *five* clubs.
3. If East goes up with the ace of clubs and clubs do not divide 3-3, or if West captures your club honor with the ace, you can still make your bid if the diamond finesse works.

#23

Contract: three notrump

Opening Lead: queen of spades

North
♠ 5 4
♡ 8 3
◇ 6 5 2
♣ A Q J 10 9 7

South
♠ A K
♡ A 10 9 7
◇ A K 8 4 3
♣ 6 5

You have six winners (two spades, one heart, two diamonds, and one club) and the only suit that can produce three extra tricks is clubs. So your play at trick two is automatic: Lead a club and finesse the queen. It wins. What would you do now?

Suppose this is the full deal:

North
♠ 5 4
♡ 8 3
◊ 6 5 2
♣ A Q J 10 9 7

West
♠ Q J 10 8 7
♡ K J 6
◊ Q 10 9
♣ 4 2

East
♠ 9 6 3 2
♡ Q 5 4 2
◊ J 7
♣ K 8 3

South
♠ A K
♡ A 10 9 7
◊ A K 8 4 3
♣ 6 5

As you can see, East has the king of clubs. You would have had ten easy tricks if he had won the first club lead, so his decision to duck was good defense. If you mistakenly return to your hand and try a second club finesse, East will win with the king and return a spade. Since you have no more entries to dummy, the contract would then be hopeless.

You should be aware that East may be holding up with the king of clubs; this is a common maneuver. Fortunately, you can now win nine tricks without running the club suit if diamonds divide 3-2. After winning with the queen of clubs, play the ace, king, and another diamond. When you regain the lead, take your nine tricks (two spades, one heart, four diamonds, and two clubs); *do not* take a second club finesse.

When you cash the ace and king of diamonds, if you find the suit does not divide 3-2, you should try a second club finesse. Then you will succeed if clubs break 3-2 and the king is onside.

#24

Contract: three notrump

Opening Lead: six of spades

North
♠ A 2
♡ 10 9 3
◊ K 8 7 6 4 3
♣ 9 5

South
♠ K 10
♡ A J 8 5
◊ A Q
♣ A K 6 3 2

You have eight winners (two spades, one heart, three diamonds, and two clubs) and two excellent chances to make your bid: if diamonds divide 3-2, or if East has at least one heart honor. To give yourself both chances, you must make a fancy play. After winning the first trick in your hand with the king of spades, cash the ace of diamonds, lead the queen of diamonds, and *overtake* it with the king in dummy. If both defenders follow to the second diamond, you can win ten tricks simply by leading another diamond to establish the suit.

If diamonds divide 4-1, you cannot establish the suit (this is also true if you did not overtake the queen). The purpose of overtaking in dummy (even though it will cost you a trick if the suit divides 3-2) is to give you the second entry you will need to take two heart finesses.

Suppose these are the four hands:

```
                      North
                      ♠ A 2
                      ♡ 10 9 3
                      ◊ K 8 7 6 4 3
                      ♣ 9 5
        West                          East
        ♠ J 9 7 6 4                   ♠ Q 8 5 3
        ♡ Q 7 2                       ♡ K 6 4
        ◊ J 10 9 5                    ◊ 2
        ♣ 8                           ♣ Q J 10 7 4
                      South
                      ♠ K 10
                      ♡ A J 8 5
                      ◊ A Q
                      ♣ A K 6 3 2
```

With the lead in dummy at trick four, lead the ten of hearts and let it ride. Presumably West will win with the queen and return a spade to dummy's ace. All that remains is to finesse East out of his king of hearts and you have nine tricks.

As you can see, if you do not overtake the queen of diamonds with the king, the contract is hopeless. With the lead in your hand, you might try for a ninth trick by playing clubs, hoping for a 3-3 break; but that is a poor percentage play and deservedly fails.

The Percentage Table for Suit Distribution of Outstanding Cards

2 cards will divide		3 cards will divide	
1-1	52 percent	2-1	78 percent
2-0	48 percent	3-0	22 percent
4 cards will divide		**5 cards will divide**	
3-1	50 percent	3-2	68 percent
2-2	40 percent	4-1	28 percent
4-0	10 percent	5-0	4 percent
6 cards will divide		**7 cards will divide**	
4-2	48 percent	4-3	62 percent
3-3	36 percent	5-2	31 percent
5-1	15 percent	6-1	6 percent
6-0	1 percent	7-0	1 percent

(Percentages are rounded to whole numbers for convenience.)

It is not necessary or recommended that you try to memorize this table. But it will be helpful to note and remember this general principle: When the opponents have an *odd* number of cards, they most likely will divide as evenly as possible; but when the opponents have an *even* number of cards, they most likely will not divide evenly—except that two cards are a slight favorite to divide 1-1.

Quiz for Chapter Seven

1.

	North
	♠ 3 2
	♡ 10 5 4
	◇ A K 8 7 5 3
	♣ 8 6

	South
	♠ A K
	♡ A 8 6 3
	◇ 4 2
	♣ A K 7 4 2

West	North	East	South
			1 ♣
Pass	1 ◇	Pass	1 ♡
Pass	2 ◇	Pass	3 NT
All Pass			

West leads the six of spades.

2.

	North
	♠ 3 2
	♡ A 5 4
	◇ A K 8 7 5 3
	♣ 8 6

	South
	♠ A K
	♡ 10 8 6 3
	◇ 4 2
	♣ A K 7 4 2

West	North	East	South
			1 ♣
Pass	1 ◇	Pass	1 ♡
Pass	3 ◇	Pass	3 NT
All Pass			

West leads the six of spades.

3.

	North
	♠ 10 8 3
	♡ J 5
	◇ A K Q 7
	♣ 6 5 4 2

	South
	♠ K Q J
	♡ A K
	◇ 6 4 3
	♣ A 10 9 8 7

West	North	East	South
			1 NT
2 ♡	3 NT	All Pass	

West leads the seven of hearts.

4.

	North
	♠ 9 7 4
	♡ A K 6 2
	◇ Q J 3
	♣ K Q 5

	South
	♠ A Q 3
	♡ J 5
	◇ A K 10 9
	♣ A J 7 6

West	North	East	South
			1 ◇
Pass	1 ♡	Pass	2 NT
Pass	6 NT	All Pass	

West leads the ten of clubs.

5.   North
          ♠ 9 6 5 2
          ♡ A 7 6 3
          ◇ 4 3
          ♣ A K Q

          South
          ♠ K Q
          ♡ K Q J 10 9 8
          ◇ A Q
          ♣ 8 5 2

West	North	East	South
	1 ♣	Pass	1 ♡
Pass	2 ♡	Pass	4 NT
Pass	5 ♡	Pass	6 ♡
All Pass			

West leads the ten of clubs.

6.   North
          ♠ Q J 8 6
          ♡ 9 5
          ◇ A 4 3
          ♣ A Q 7 2

          South
          ♠ 10 9 7 5 4 2
          ♡ A J 10
          ◇ K 8 2
          ♣ 6

West	North	East	South
Pass	1 ♣	Pass	1 ♠
Pass	2 ♠	Pass	4 ♠
All Pass			

West leads the queen of diamonds.

7.   North
          ♠ K 7 2
          ♡ J 10 9 8
          ◇ K 5 4
          ♣ A Q 6

          South
          ♠ A 8 6 5
          ♡ A K Q 4 3
          ◇ A 3 2
          ♣ 7

West	North	East	South
			1 ♡
Pass	3 ♡	Pass	6 ♡
All Pass			

West leads the queen of diamonds.
Hearts divide 3-1.

8.   North
          ♠ A 10 4 3
          ♡ J 7 2
          ◇ A Q 5
          ♣ A J 6

          South
          ♠ K Q J 9 8 5
          ♡ A K 10
          ◇ 7
          ♣ K Q 2

West	North	East	South
	1 NT	Pass	3 ♠
Pass	4 ♠	Pass	4 NT
Pass	5 ♠	Pass	7 ♠
All Pass			

West leads the ten of clubs.

Answers to Quiz for Chapter Seven

1.
```
                North
                ♠ 3 2
                ♡ 10 5 4
                ◊ A K 8 7 5 3
                ♣ 8 6
West                          East
♠ Q J 8 6 5                   ♠ 10 9 7 4
♡ Q J 9 7                     ♡ K 2
◊ 10                          ◊ Q J 9 6
♣ Q 10 3                      ♣ J 9 5
                South
                ♠ A K
                ♡ A 8 6 3
                ◊ 4 2
                ♣ A K 7 4 2
```

West	North	East	South
			1 ♣
Pass	1 ◊	Pass	1 ♡
Pass	2 ◊	Pass	3 NT
All Pass			

West leads the six of spades.

You have seven winners and can get the extra tricks you need in diamonds if the suit divides 3-2 (a 68-percent chance), or in clubs if that suit divides 3-3 (a 36-percent chance). Clearly, the odds substantially favor tackling the diamond suit.

The best play at trick two is to duck a diamond trick to the enemy. (If you play the ace or king, you never can win more than two diamond tricks because the dummy lacks an outside entry.) When the opponents lead another spade to clear the suit, you will play your last diamond to dummy. If the diamonds divide 3-2, the rest of the diamonds will be good tricks. But, as you can see in the diagram, diamonds divide 4-1 and you will be set. Clubs happen to divide 3-3, and you would have made your bid if you went after the club suit. Tough luck, but the percentage play does not always succeed. If you made this contract, you need bridge lessons badly.

2.
```
                North
                ♠ 3 2
                ♡ A 5 4
                ◊ A K 8 7 5 3
                ♣ 8 6
West                          East
♠ Q J 8 6 5                   ♠ 10 9 7 4
♡ Q J 9 7                     ♡ K 2
◊ 10                          ◊ Q J 9 6
♣ Q 10 3                      ♣ J 9 5
                South
                ♠ A K
                ♡ 10 8 6 3
                ◊ 4 2
                ♣ A K 7 4 2
```

West	North	East	South
			1 ♣
Pass	1 ◊	Pass	1 ♡
Pass	3 ◊	Pass	3 NT
All Pass			

West leads the six of spades.

The only difference between this hand and the last is that the ace of hearts in now in the dummy. This provides a side entry to dummy, so you can find out how the diamond suit divides *before* giving up the lead. Now you have two chances to make your bid: diamonds divide 3-2, or clubs divide 3-3.

After winning the spade lead, cash the ace and king of diamonds. If both opponents follow suit (diamonds divide 3-2), lead a third diamond to establish the suit and make your bid with an overtrick. But when West shows out on the second diamond lead, you must abandon that suit and try clubs. Since clubs are divided 3-3, you can establish two extra club tricks by giving up one trick along the way. If both suits divide badly, you will be set; but at least you will have given yourself both chances.

3.

	North		
	♠ 10 8 3		
	♡ J 5		
	◇ A K Q 7		
	♣ 6 5 4 2		

West		East
♠ A 5 4		♠ 9 7 6 2
♡ Q 10 8 7 6 2		♡ 9 4 3
◇ 9 2		◇ J 10 8 5
♣ K Q		♣ J 3

	South		
	♠ K Q J		
	♡ A K		
	◇ 6 4 3		
	♣ A 10 9 8 7		

West	*North*	*East*	*South*
			1 NT
2 ♡	3 NT	All Pass	

West leads the seven of hearts.

You have six winners (two hearts, three diamonds, and one club) and must establish three more tricks without giving up the lead more than once. If diamonds divide 3-3, you can win a trick with dummy's fourth diamond and two more by driving out the ace of spades. If clubs divide 2-2, you can develop three tricks by conceding a club trick.

Which one should you try? The answer is *both*—by cashing the ace, king, and queen of diamonds first. If diamonds divide 3-3, you have a sure road to nine tricks by cashing the thirteenth diamond and then driving out the ace of spades. If diamonds do not divide 3-3, you need *three* more tricks; so the only chance to make your bid is to tackle the club suit and hope for a 2-2 split.

4.

	North		
	♠ 9 7 4		
	♡ A K 6 2		
	◇ Q J 3		
	♣ K Q 5		

West		East
♠ K J 8		♠ 10 6 5 2
♡ 10 8 3		♡ Q 9 7 4
◇ 7 5 4		◇ 8 6 2
♣ 10 9 8 2		♣ 4 3

	South		
	♠ A Q 3		
	♡ J 5		
	◇ A K 10 9		
	♣ A J 7 6		

West	*North*	*East*	*South*
			1 ◇
Pass	1 ♡	Pass	2 NT
Pass	6 NT	All Pass	

West leads the ten of clubs.

There are eleven top tricks (one spade, two hearts, four diamonds, and four clubs) and two chances for a twelfth: a successful spade finesse, or a successful heart finesse. To give yourself both chances, you must try the heart finesse first.

Win the opening club lead in dummy and play a *low* heart toward the jack. (Note that you cannot gain by leading the jack from your hand; West would cover if he had the queen.) Since East has the queen, you will win a third heart trick with your jack—so you don't need the spade finesse.

Note that if West holds the queen of hearts, you will still be able to try the spade finesse. The contract will succeed unless West has both the king of spades and the queen of hearts; the odds are 3-to-1 in your favor.

5.
        North
        ♠ 9 6 5 2
        ♡ A 7 6 3
        ◇ 4 3
        ♣ A K Q

West	East
♠ A 8 4 3	♠ J 10 7
♡ 5 4	♡ 2
◇ K J 10 6 2	◇ 9 8 7 5
♣ 10 9	♣ J 7 6 4 3

        South
        ♠ K Q
        ♡ K Q J 10 9 8
        ◇ A Q
        ♣ 8 5 2

West	North	East	South
	1 ♣	Pass	1 ♡
Pass	2 ♡	Pass	4 NT
Pass	5 ♡	Pass	6 ♡
All Pass			

West leads the ten of clubs.

There is no way to escape losing a trick to the ace of spades, so the key to making the contract is to avoid a diamond loser. The contract is easily made if the diamond finesse works, but there is a less obvious chance which should be tried first: Establish the nine of spades.

After winning the opening club lead, draw the missing trumps without playing the ace of hearts. Now lead a spade. Suppose West wins with the ace and leads another club (there is no better defense), which you win in dummy. Next win the remaining high spade, lead a club to dummy, and ruff the third round of spades in your hand. Since the jack and ten of spades fall, the nine is now good and you can discard your queen of diamonds. This extra chance is a long shot, but you have nothing to lose by trying.

It is interesting to note what might happen if East has the ace of spades. At the point you lead a spade, East will win with the ace and return a *diamond* (the logical play). Now you cannot try both chances. The diamond finesse should be taken because it offers a much better chance than the jack and ten of spades falling.

6.
        North
        ♠ Q J 8 6
        ♡ 9 5
        ◇ A 4 3
        ♣ A Q 7 2

West	East
♠ A K	♠ 3
♡ Q 7 6 2	♡ K 8 4 3
◇ Q J 10 5	◇ 9 7 6
♣ 9 8 3	♣ K J 10 5 4

        South
        ♠ 10 9 7 5 4 2
        ♡ A J 10
        ◇ K 8 2
        ♣ 6

West	North	East	South
Pass	1 ♣	Pass	1 ♠
Pass	2 ♠	Pass	4 ♠
All Pass			

West leads the queen of diamonds.

You have four losers (two spades, one heart, and one diamond), and the only chance to make the contract is to avoid the diamond loser. You have two choices: Finesse the queen of clubs and hope that West has the king, or take two heart finesses and hope that East has at least one honor (king or queen). The club finesse is an even chance, while the heart finesses offer 3-to-1 odds in your favor; so there is no doubt as to the better play.

Win the opening diamond lead with the ace and finesse the ten of hearts. West wins with the queen of hearts and leads the ten of diamonds, which you win with the king. Now lead a club to dummy's *ace* and finesse the jack of hearts. Since this finesse works, you can discard dummy's losing diamond on the ace of hearts and make your bid.

Note that you must play hearts before touching trumps, else the opponents will be able to cash their diamond trick before you can get the discard.

7.   North
          ♠ K 7 2
          ♡ J 10 9 8
          ◇ K 5 4
          ♣ A Q 6

West   East
♠ Q 10 9   ♠ J 4 3
♡ 7   ♡ 6 5 2
◇ Q J 10 6   ◇ 9 8 7
♣ 9 8 5 4 2   ♣ K J 10 3

          South
          ♠ A 8 6 5
          ♡ A K Q 4 3
          ◇ A 3 2
          ♣ 7

West	North	East	South
			1 ♡
Pass	3 ♡	Pass	6 ♡
All Pass			

West leads the queen of diamonds. Hearts divide 3-1.

The only chance to make your bid is to avoid a diamond loser, and this can be done in two ways: If the club finesse works, you can discard a diamond from your hand on the ace of clubs; if the spades divide 3-3, you can discard a diamond from dummy on your fourth spade. This time you can try *both* chances if you test the spade suit first.

Win the opening diamond lead in *dummy* (if spades do not divide, you will need the ace of diamonds as an entry to take the club finesse), draw trumps in three rounds, cash the ace and king of spades, and lead a third spade. Since the spades divide 3-3, the fourth spade in your hand is a good trick and the rest is easy. If the spades did not divide, you would try the club finesse.

Note that it is important to cash the ace and king of spades *before* conceding a spade trick to find out how the suit divides. If you give up a spade trick before cashing the ace and king, West may win the spade and lead a *club*; then you cannot try both chances. You must decide right then and there whether to finesse the queen of clubs or to play for the spade break.

8.   North
          ♠ A 10 4 3
          ♡ J 7 2
          ◇ A Q 5
          ♣ A J 6

West   East
♠ 7 2   ♠ 6
♡ Q 6   ♡ 9 8 5 4 3
◇ 9 8 6 4 3   ◇ K J 10 2
♣ 10 9 8 5   ♣ 7 4 3

          South
          ♠ K Q J 9 8 5
          ♡ A K 10
          ◇ 7
          ♣ K Q 2

West	North	East	South
	1 NT	Pass	3 ♠
Pass	4 ♠	Pass	4 NT
Pass	5 ♠	Pass	7 ♠
All Pass			

West leads the ten of clubs.

You have one loser (in hearts) and two obvious chances to avoid losing it: the heart finesse, or the diamond finesse so you can discard your losing heart. The problem is you cannot try both finesses — if one fails you are finished — but there is a better line of play than just taking a stab at one finesse or the other.

After drawing trumps, lead the *jack of hearts* in the hope that East has the queen and plays it — most players would cover the honor. If East does not cover, cash the ace and king of hearts and hope for a singleton or doubleton queen. If that fails, cash all of your trumps and clubs (perhaps an opponent will throw away the queen of hearts) before you take the diamond finesse.

8

Clues from the Opening Lead and the Bidding

♣   ◇   ♡   ♠   ♣   ◇   ♡   ♠

The opening lead and the bidding (or lack of it) sometimes give the declarer valuable information about the defenders' hands. The declarer may learn the location of certain high cards or how a suit will divide. On occasion, a defender may mislead the declarer by making an unorthodox lead or bid, but in real life this rarely happens — a defender who violates his partnership agreements is more apt to fool his partner than the declarer. These sources of information have been tried and proven to be reliable, and they are indispensable to a good declarer.

Clues from the Opening Lead

Before studying full deals, here are four elementary suit combinations to show how information is derived from the opening lead:

A.	North J 3 2	B.	North K J 8
West K led		West 10 led	
	South A 5 4		South A 3 2

A. The lead of the king indicates that West has the queen. If so, you can get two tricks in the suit by winning with the ace and leading toward the jack.

B. If West has the nine, as the lead of the ten suggests, you can win three tricks in the suit by covering the ten with the jack. If East plays the queen, win with the ace; later you can finesse the eight.

C.	North		D.	North
	J 3 2			7 4
West			West	
9 led			3 led	
	South			South
	A K 8			A 10 2

C. The nine-spot is usually the leader's highest card from a short suit, so you should assume that East has the queen and ten. If so, you can win three tricks in the suit. First, you must cover the nine with the jack and, if East plays the queen, win with the ace. This leaves you with the king-eight behind East's ten, so you can win a trick with the eight by leading from dummy and finessing.

D. The three-spot lead suggests that West has at most four cards in the suit. If West held a longer suit, he would not lead his lowest card. (This assumes that West has led his fourth-highest card, the usual procedure from a four-card or longer suit.) This lead does not give you an extra trick in the suit, as the lead in the first three illustrations did, but learning that the missing eight cards are probably divided 4-4 could guide you into the winning line of play—as you shall see in later illustrations.

The following eight hands show how clues derived from the opening lead can be used to help you make your contract. Since honor-card leads are fairly obvious, all of these illustrations are spot-card leads, beginning with the *nine*.

#1

North
♠ A K Q 10
♡ Q 3
◇ 7 2

Contract: four spades

♣ A 10 9 8 4

Opening Lead: nine of hearts

South
♠ 9 8 7 6 4
♡ A J 8
◇ K 5
♣ 5 3 2

West	North	East	South
	1 ♣	1 ♡	1 ♠
2 ◇	3 ♠	4 ◇	4 ♠
All Pass			

Assuming spades divide no worse than 3-1, you have four losers: two diamonds and two clubs. You can avoid one of the diamond losers even with the ace of diamonds offside. Can you figure out how to do it?

West would not lead the nine of hearts if he held the king or ten, so you should conclude that they are in the East hand. If you play the heart suit correctly, you can establish a third heart trick in your hand to discard one of your losing diamonds in the dummy.

Here is the full deal:

North
♠ A K Q 10
♡ Q 3
◇ 7 2
♣ A 10 9 8 4

West
♠ J 5 3
♡ 9 2
◇ A Q 9 8 6 4
♣ 7 6

East
♠ 2
♡ K 10 7 6 5 4
◇ J 10 3
♣ K Q J

South
♠ 9 8 7 6 4
♡ A J 8
◇ K 5
♣ 5 3 2

First, you must cover the nine of hearts with the *queen* (a key play); East contributes the king and you, the ace. After drawing the trumps in three rounds, lead a heart from dummy and finesse the *eight*. You can now discard a diamond from dummy on the jack of hearts.

#2

Contract: six spades

Opening Lead: nine of hearts

North
♠ K Q 9 8 7
♡ 10 8 2
◇ 6 5
♣ A Q 3

South
♠ A J 10 6 3
♡ A Q 6 4
◇ A Q 2
♣ 5

With the heart lead, you have two losers: one heart and one diamond. Your plan should be to make the slam without risking the diamond finesse. This can be done by establishing the fourth heart in your hand to discard a diamond from dummy. If hearts divide 3-3, there is no problem. But the nine-of-hearts lead appears to be from a doubleton or a singleton; so you should play the hand on that basis.

Suppose these are the four hands:

```
                              North
                              ♠ K Q 9 8 7
                              ♡ 10 8 2
                              ◇ 6 5
                              ♣ A Q 3
          West                                      East
          ♠ 5 2                                     ♠ 4
          ♡ 9                                       ♡ K J 7 5 3
          ◇ K J 4 3                                 ◇ 10 9 8 7
          ♣ 10 8 7 6 4 2                            ♣ K J 9
                              South
                              ♠ A J 10 6 3
                              ♡ A Q 6 4
                              ◇ A Q 2
                              ♣ 5
```

The first important play is to cover the nine-of-hearts lead with dummy's ten, East plays the king (no defense is better), and you win with the ace. After drawing two rounds of trumps, lead the eight of hearts from dummy, East covers with the jack (otherwise he will not get a heart trick) and you win with the queen. Since West shows out, you know the remaining hearts are:

```
                              North
                              ♡ 2
          West                                      East
          ♡ —                                       ♡ 7 5 3
                              South
                              ♡ 6 4
```

The next heart lead must come from the dummy, so cross to the ace of clubs and play the two of hearts. East wins with the seven of hearts, establishing your six as a good trick. When you regain the lead, discard dummy's losing diamond on the six of hearts and claim the rest of the tricks.

It would have been interesting if West had the nine-seven doubleton. At the point at which you led the eight from dummy and East covered with the jack, the seven would drop and the remaining hearts would be:

```
                              North
                              ♡ 2
          West                                      East
          ♡ —                                       ♡ 5 3
                              South
                              ♡ 6 4
```

By going to dummy and leading the two, you can take the deepest finesse in history — the two-three-four! Not only do you avoid a heart loser, but also you still can discard a diamond on the six of hearts and make a grand slam. Wow!

The lead of a nine is almost always from a short suit, but lower spot cards are not as easy to read — they could be low from a three-card suit, or fourth best from a four-card or longer suit. However, the lead of an eight is usually readable by noting the missing higher cards.

For example:

#3   North
                                       ♠ 6 4
                                       ♡ J 10
                                       ◊ A K 9 7 3

Contract: six spades   ♣ 9 7 5 2

Opening Lead: eight of clubs   South
                                       ♠ A K Q J 10 9
                                       ♡ A K
                                       ◊ 8 5 4
                                       ♣ A J

Without a club lead, your plan would be to concede a diamond trick to establish the suit so you can discard your losing club. With the club lead, you must do just the opposite: Establish the club suit so you can discard your losing diamond.

Your goal is to figure out the club distribution. The lead of the eight appears to be the highest card from a short suit; but it also would be correct for West to lead the eight from Q 10 8 or K 10 8. You will find out which when clubs are played a second time.

Suppose the four hands are:

                              North
                              ♠ 6 4
                              ♡ J 10
                              ◊ A K 9 7 3
                              ♣ 9 7 5 2

West   East
♠ 8 7 5 3   ♠ 2
♡ Q 6 4 2   ♡ 9 8 7 5 3
◊ Q 10 2   ◊ J 6
♣ 8 3   ♣ K Q 10 6 4
                              South
                              ♠ A K Q J 10 9
                              ♡ A K
                              ◊ 8 5 4
                              ♣ A J

East plays the queen of clubs on the first trick, and you win with the ace. Now lead four (or five) rounds of trumps, but *do not discard any clubs from dummy*. Then lead the jack of clubs. West plays the three and East wins with the king. The only club honor still missing is the ten and East should have it (West is unlikely to lead the eight from 10 8 x or 10 8 x x — the normal lead is low). When you regain the lead, play a diamond over to dummy and lead the nine of clubs. If East plays a low club, discard your diamond loser; if

East covers with the ten, ruff it, return to dummy with a high diamond, and discard a diamond on the seven of clubs.

The Rule Of Eleven: This is a helpful rule that may be applied at both notrump and trump contracts, but only when you can assume that a defender has made a fourth-best lead (fourth highest card in the suit led).[1] It can be used by both the leader's partner and the declarer. Here is how it works: Subtract the card led from eleven. The result is the number of cards held by the other three players (other than the leader) that are *higher* than the card led.

This rule is based on simple arithmetic: If the ace, king, queen, and jack had numbers, the cards of a suit would be numbered from two to fourteen. If you subtract any card from fourteen, you find out how many higher cards there are in the suit. If a fourth-best lead has been made, the leader has exactly three higher cards in his own hand. So, rather than subtracting from fourteen and then subtracting three, you simply subtract from eleven.

The next three deals illustrate how this information can be useful:

#4

North
- ♠ A Q 10 2
- ♡ A K J
- ◇ A 10 5 4
- ♣ J 3

Contract: three notrump

Opening Lead: seven of spades

South
- ♠ 8 5 3
- ♡ Q 10 9
- ◇ 7 2
- ♣ A 6 5 4 2

West	North	East	South
	1 ◇	Pass	1 NT
Pass	3 NT	All Pass	

The success of this contract hinges on which spade you play from dummy on the first trick. Before looking at the four hands, which spade would you select?

---

1. Many experts and a few followers do not lead fourth best, in which case the Rule of Eleven cannot be used. However, those who employ a different method must in some way make this information available to their opponents.

North
♠ A Q 10 2
♡ A K J
◇ A 10 5 4
♣ J 3

West
♠ K J 9 7 4
♡ 7 3 2
◇ Q J 6
♣ 8 7

East
♠ 6
♡ 8 6 5 4
◇ K 9 8 3
♣ K Q 10 9

South
♠ 8 5 3
♡ Q 10 9
◇ 7 2
♣ A 6 5 4 2

Presumably, West's lead of the seven is his fourth highest, so this is a case for the Rule of Eleven. By subtracting seven from eleven, you learn that the other three hands (North, East, and South) have four spades higher than the seven. Since the dummy has the ace-queen-ten and you have the eight, East has none; in which case he cannot prevent you from winning the first trick with the eight.

The right play from dummy at trick one is the two of spades. After winning with the eight, you can finesse the ten, and later the queen. This gives you four spade tricks to add to your five top tricks in the other suits. If your first spade play from dummy is not the two, you cannot win four spade tricks and you will be set.

#5

North
♠ A Q 9 2
♡ A Q J
◇ A K 8 5
♣ 7 6

Contract: three notrump

Opening Lead: four of spades

South
♠ 7 6 5
♡ K 10 9
◇ 7 6 3
♣ A 8 5 2

West	North	East	South
	1 ◇	Pass	1 NT
Pass	3 NT	All Pass	

Here again you have received a favorable lead and can make your bid if you handle the spade suit wisely. More specifically, you have six winners outside the spade suit and need *three* spade tricks. If you subtract the card led (the four) from eleven, you get seven. You see six cards higher than the four between your hand and dummy, so East has *one* higher. It figures to be the jack or ten (rather than the king or eight), because the normal lead from J 10 8 4 or K J 10 4 is the jack, not the four. Therefore, to win three spade tricks, you should play the two from dummy and allow East to win the first trick with his jack or ten.

Here is the full deal:

                              North
                              ♠ A Q 9 2
                              ♡ A Q J
                              ◇ A K 8 5
                              ♣ 7 6
        West   East
        ♠ K 10 8 4   ♠ J 3
        ♡ 7 3 2   ♡ 8 6 5 4
        ◇ 4 2   ◇ Q J 10 9
        ♣ K 9 4 3   ♣ Q J 10
                              South
                              ♠ 7 6 5
                              ♡ K 10 9
                              ◇ 7 6 3
                              ♣ A 8 5 2

As you can see, after East wins the jack of spades, the dummy is left with the A Q 9 behind the K 10 8. You can use the two entries to your hand to finesse first the nine and then the queen. If your first play from dummy is any spade but the two, you cannot win three spade tricks and the contract is lost.

The Rule of Eleven should not be used when the lead is the lowest outstanding card in a suit, as there is an easier way to derive whatever information is available.
    For example:

#6   North
                                      ♠ 5 4 2
                                      ♡ K 8
                                      ◇ K Q 10 7 6
Contract: three notrump   ♣ J 10 3

Opening Lead: three of spades   South
                                      ♠ A 7
                                      ♡ A Q 5
                                      ◇ J 9 2
                                      ♣ A Q 9 8 4

Suppose East wins the first trick with the ten of spades and then leads the queen of spades to your ace. You have five winners (one spade, three hearts, and one club) and must decide whether to develop the four needed tricks in clubs or diamonds. If spades divide 5-3, your only chance is a successful club finesse; if you lead a diamond, the opponents can win the ace of diamonds and four spade tricks. If spades divide 4-4, it is safe to give up the lead to the ace of diamonds because the opponents can win only three spade tricks; you can make your bid without risking the club finesse.
    What you need to know is how the spade suit is going to divide, and the opening lead is the clue. Since the two is in the dummy, West has led his lowest spade; presumably he would not lead his lowest if he held more than four cards in the suit, and he is unlikely to

be leading from a shorter suit. So spades figure to divide 4-4, and you should tackle the diamond suit.[2]

Suppose this is the full deal:

North
♠ 5 4 2
♡ K 8
◇ K Q 10 7 6
♣ J 10 3

West
♠ K 9 6 3
♡ J 9 2
◇ 8 4 3
♣ K 6 5

East
♠ Q J 10 8
♡ 10 7 6 4 3
◇ A 5
♣ 7 2

South
♠ A 7
♡ A Q 5
◇ J 9 2
♣ A Q 9 8 4

As you can see, the contract is cold if you drive out the ace of diamonds. Since the club finesse fails, you will be set if you take it; the opponents can win three spades, one diamond, and one club. However, the club finesse would be the right play if you judged spades were dividing 5-3.

In the next hand, the lead of the two is a subtle clue to the winning line. Before reading the explanation, how would you play the club suit?

#7

North
♠ 7 6 3
♡ Q J 10
◇ K 8
♣ K J 9 5 2

Contract: three notrump

Opening Lead: two of diamonds

South
♠ Q 9
♡ A K 8
◇ A 7 3
♣ A 10 6 4 3

West	North	East	South
			1 NT
Pass	3 NT	All Pass	

---

2. The Rule of Eleven reveals the same information: Three – the card led – subtracted from eleven leaves eight higher spades; you see four of them, so East has the other four. But you must admit that recognizing that West has led his lowest card is an easier way to predict the 4-4 split.

You have ten tricks if you can run the club suit, but you can be set if you lose a trick to the queen of clubs. The only thing to worry about is a 3-0 split, something that happens 22 percent of the time. If West is void in clubs, your first play must be the king; if East is void, your first play must be the ace. The challenge is to figure out which player is more likely to have a club void, and the opening lead is a clue. West apparently has led from a four-card suit. Since it is normal to lead one's longest suit, you should assume that West has no five-card or longer suit, in which case it would be impossible for West to have a void suit. Consequently, your first club play should be the *ace*.

Here are the four hands:

```
                          North
                          ♠ 7 6 3
                          ♡ Q J 10
                          ◇ K 8
                          ♣ K J 9 5 2
        West                              East
        ♠ A 5 2                           ♠ K J 10 8 4
        ♡ 9 6 5                           ♡ 7 4 3 2
        ◇ Q 10 4 2                        ◇ J 9 6 5
        ♣ Q 8 7                           ♣ —
                          South
                          ♠ Q 9
                          ♡ A K 8
                          ◇ A 7 3
                          ♣ A 10 6 4 3
```

Yes, an original spade lead would be fatal, but West's lead of the two of diamonds is normal. If your first club play is the ace, you can finesse West out of his queen and win ten tricks. If your first club play is the king, you must lose a club trick to the queen and the opponents can set you if they run the spade suit.

If you don't know when you're in trouble, you can't save yourself. Do you see the danger in the following deal?

```
#8                        North
                          ♠ 2
                          ♡ K 10 8 6 5 3
                          ◇ A J 7 4
Contract: six spades      ♣ 9 4

Opening Lead: four of hearts   South
                          ♠ K Q J 10 9 4 3
                          ♡ A 7
                          ◇ —
                          ♣ A K Q J
```

On the surface, it appears that the only loser is the ace of spades. But how about the four-of-hearts opening lead? You should be aware that West may have led a singleton and you are subject to a heart ruff.

Suppose this is the layout:

                North
                ♠ 2
                ♡ K 10 8 6 5 3
                ◇ A J 7 4
                ♣ 9 4

West   **East**
♠ 7 6 5   ♠ A 8
♡ 4   ♡ Q J 9 2
◇ K 9 8 5 2   ◇ Q 10 6 3
♣ 10 6 3 2   ♣ 8 7 5

                South
                ♠ K Q J 10 9 4 3
                ♡ A 7
                ◇ —
                ♣ A K Q J

As you can see, you can be set if you lead a spade at trick two; East can win with the ace and give West a heart ruff. You can prevent this by winning the first trick in dummy with the king of hearts and cashing the ace of diamonds to discard the ace of hearts. Now when East wins with the ace of spades and leads a heart, you can ruff with a high trump in your hand.

Clues from the Bidding

In the next twelve deals, it is the bidding that discloses information about the defenders' hands. Deals 9 through 14 reveal how to locate missing high cards, while deals 15 through 20 reveal how suits will divide.

#9   **North**
                         ♠ K 2
                         ♡ 6 3
                         ◇ A K 7 5 4

Contract: three notrump   ♣ K 8 5 2

Opening Lead: two of hearts   **South**
                         ♠ Q J 7 5
                         ♡ A Q
                         ◇ 6 3 2
                         ♣ A 9 4 3

West	North	East	South
	1 ◇	1 ♡	1 ♠
Pass	2 ♣	Pass	3 NT
All Pass			

You have six winners: two hearts, two diamonds, and two clubs. You must develop three more tricks and can afford to give up the lead only once. There are two chances: Establish three spade tricks, or steal *one* spade trick and then develop two extra diamond tricks. To accomplish this, you must lead a *low* spade through the player who has the ace to prevent him from capturing one of your honors. Which defender should you play for the ace of spades? The answer is obvious. East made a bid and is therefore a big favorite to have the ace. Here are the four hands so you can see how the contract can be made if East has the ace of spades and diamonds divide 3-2.

North
♠ K 2
♡ 6 3
◇ A K 7 5 4
♣ K 8 5 2

West
♠ 10 9 8 6
♡ 7 5 4 2
◇ 10 8
♣ Q J 10

East
♠ A 4 3
♡ K J 10 9 8
◇ Q J 9
♣ 7 6

South
♠ Q J 7 5
♡ A Q
◇ 6 3 2
♣ A 9 4 3

After winning the first trick, play a diamond to dummy's king and lead the *two* of spades. If East goes up with the ace, you have nine tricks: three spades, two hearts, two diamonds, and two clubs. If East plays a low spade, you will win with the queen (or jack) and abandon spades. Now lead a diamond to dummy's ace to find out the suit divides 3-2, then concede a diamond trick to the opponents. Again you have nine tricks: one spade, two hearts, four diamonds, and two clubs.

#10

Contract: four hearts

Opening Lead: king of spades

North
♠ 8 6 5
♡ A 9
◇ 5 4 3
♣ A Q 6 4 2

South
♠ A J
♡ K Q J 6 5 4
◇ K 8 7
♣ 7 3

West	North	East	South
		1 ♠	2 ♡
Pass	3 ♡	Pass	4 ♡
All Pass			

After West leads the king of spades, East is marked with the ace of diamonds and king of clubs; he needs both of those cards to have an opening bid. Therefore, you can see four possible losers: one spade, one club, and two diamonds — one too many. Since you do not have sufficient entries in dummy to establish the club suit, the only hope is to discard a diamond on the *queen* of clubs. You can succeed if East has no more than two clubs.

Suppose these are the four hands:

```
                        North
                        ♠ 8 6 5
                        ♡ A 9
                        ◇ 5 4 3
                        ♣ A Q 6 4 2
        West                            East
        ♠ K 7                           ♠ Q 10 9 4 3 2
        ♡ 10 3 2                        ♡ 8 7
        ◇ 10 9 6 2                      ◇ A Q J
        ♣ J 9 8 5                       ♣ K 10
                        South
                        ♠ A J
                        ♡ K Q J 6 5 4
                        ◇ K 8 7
                        ♣ 7 3
```

After winning with the ace of spades and drawing three (or four) rounds of trumps, lead a club and *duck* in dummy; this is the key play. Suppose East defends as well as possible by winning with the ten of clubs, cashing the queen of spades, and leading another spade, which you ruff. Now play a club to dummy's ace (dropping the king), discard a diamond on the queen of clubs, and lead a diamond toward your king.

You may think it was very lucky to find East with a doubleton club. Actually, the odds were in favor of it. Since West was dealt only two spades while East was dealt six, West figured to have greater length in any of the other three suits.

#11

Contract: four spades

Opening Lead: jack of hearts

```
                        North
                        ♠ 10 8 7
                        ♡ 9 5 2
                        ◇ A J 10
                        ♣ J 6 5 3

                        South
                        ♠ A Q J 9 6 5
                        ♡ K 4
                        ◇ K Q 8
                        ♣ Q 2
```

West	North	East	South
		Pass	1 ♠
Pass	2 ♠	Pass	4 ♠
All Pass			

North's two-spade bid was minimal, but, with the heart lead, you can make your bid if you avoid a spade loser. Suppose East wins the first trick with the ace of hearts, cashes the ace of clubs, and leads another club, which West wins with the king. At this point you should realize West has the king of spades. Before reading on, can you figure out why?

Here is the full deal:

```
                        North
                        ♠ 10 8 7
                        ♡ 9 5 2
                        ◇ A J 10
                        ♣ J 6 5 3
West                                        East
♠ K                                         ♠ 4 3 2
♡ J 10 8 7                                  ♡ A Q 6 3
◇ 6 4 3                                     ◇ 9 7 5 2
♣ K 9 8 7 4                                 ♣ A 10
                        South
                        ♠ A Q J 9 6 5
                        ♡ K 4
                        ◇ K Q 8
                        ♣ Q 2
```

East has shown up with two aces and he is known to have the queen of hearts because West led the jack. If East had the king of spades as well, he would have 13 quality high-card points and would not have passed originally. Therefore, West has the king of spades and you should not try the spade finesse. Your only hope is to lay down the ace and find West with a singleton king.

#12

```
                        North
                        ♠ K Q 9 2
                        ♡ 8 7 6 4
Contract: three spades   ◇ K J
                        ♣ 10 5 3

Opening Lead: king of clubs   South
                        ♠ A J 10 8 7 3
                        ♡ K Q
                        ◇ 9 5 2
                        ♣ 6 4
```

West	North	East	South
1 ◇	Pass	1 ♡	1 ♠
2 ♣	2 ♠	3 ♣	3 ♠
All Pass			

West begins by playing the king, ace, and queen of clubs, and you ruff the third lead. You have lost two clubs and must lose one heart, so you cannot afford to lose more than one diamond. If the diamond honors are divided, you will eventually have to guess whether West has the ace or queen. An analysis of the bidding may help you guess correctly. Your opponents have 21 high-card points (since your side has 19), and the opponents' bidding suggests that West has 12 to 15 and East 6 to 9. Now let's count points to see how this will help you locate the ace and queen of diamonds.

West has shown up with the ace, king, and queen of clubs (9 high-card points), so he should have 3 to 6 more if the above analysis is correct. If West has the ace of hearts, then East has the ace of diamonds. If East has the ace of hearts, West probably has the ace of diamonds. Therefore, you should find out who has the ace of hearts before playing diamonds. After ruffing the third round of clubs, draw two rounds of trumps, and lead a heart to your king. Suppose this is the layout:

```
                     North
                     ♠ K Q 9 2
                     ♡ 8 7 6 4
                     ◇ K J
                     ♣ 10 5 3
     West                              East
     ♠ 5 4                             ♠ 6
     ♡ A 3                             ♡ J 10 9 5 2
     ◇ Q 10 8 7 6                      ◇ A 4 3
     ♣ A K Q 2                         ♣ J 9 8 7
                     South
                     ♠ A J 10 8 7 3
                     ♡ K Q
                     ◇ 9 5 2
                     ♣ 6 4
```

When West shows up with the ace of hearts, it is evident that East has the ace of diamonds. The bidding would not be logical if West had both red aces; West would have bid more and East may not have bid even once, let alone twice, with only one queen and two jacks. The indicated play is to finesse the *jack* of diamonds and hope that West has the queen.

Note that the defense could have been better. If West had led a low diamond at trick two or three, you would have to guess whether to play the king or jack before you could find out who had the ace of hearts.

#13

Contract: two spades

Opening Lead: four of clubs

```
                     North
                     ♠ K Q 5
                     ♡ 8 7 6 4
                     ◇ 7 5 2
                     ♣ 9 3 2

                     South
                     ♠ A J 10 9 8 2
                     ♡ J 3
                     ◇ K 6 4
                     ♣ A J
```

West	North	East	South
1 ♡	Pass	1 NT	2 ♠
All Pass			

On the first trick, East plays the king of clubs and you win with the ace. With six losers (two hearts, three diamonds, and one club) the only chance to make your bid is to limit your diamond losers to two. If West has three or more diamonds including the ace, your task is essentially hopeless. But if East has the ace, or if West has a singleton or doubleton ace, you can win a trick with the king if you can determine who has the ace. A review of the bidding should help you figure it out.

The opponents have 21 high-card points between them and West should have 12 to 15 while East has 6 to 9. East has shown up with the king of clubs and probably has the king of hearts (West would have chosen a heart lead from ace-king or king-queen as a more attractive choice than a club away from the queen). If East has the king of clubs and the king of hearts, then West should have the ace of diamonds — otherwise he would not have enough to open the bidding.

Suppose the four hands are:

                              North
                              ♠ K Q 5
                              ♡ 8 7 6 4
                              ◇ 7 5 2
                              ♣ 9 3 2
West   East
♠ 7 3   ♠ 6 4
♡ A Q 10 9 5   ♡ K 2
◇ A J   ◇ Q 10 9 8 3
♣ Q 10 6 4   ♣ K 8 7 5
                              South
                              ♠ A J 10 9 8 2
                              ♡ J 3
                              ◇ K 6 4
                              ♣ A J

There is no hurry to play diamonds. First draw two rounds of trumps, then lead a heart to verify the location of the king. East does have the king of hearts, so it is clearly right to play West for the ace of diamonds. When diamonds are led, do not play the king until the third round. Since West must play his ace on the second diamond lead, you will score a trick with your king.

#14

Contract: two spades

Opening Lead: king of clubs

North
♠ J 7 5 3
♡ 10 8 2
◇ K J 9
♣ 8 7 6

South
♠ K Q 10 9 8
♡ K Q
◇ A 4 2
♣ 5 4 3

West	North	East	South
1 NT	Pass	2 ♡	2 ♠
All Pass			

You have five top losers (one spade, one heart, and three clubs), so you must avoid losing a diamond trick to make your bid. Since West opened the bidding with one no-trump, you should be optimistic about the diamond finesse working. However, you should not play diamonds until you learn as much as possible about the defenders' hands. West's opening one-notrump bid showed 16 to 18 high-card points, so East has 3 to 5, which may include the queen of diamonds.

West cashes the ace, king, and queen of clubs and the ace of hearts, and then he leads a low heart. You win the fifth trick with the king of hearts and lead the king of spades, which West wins with the ace. Note that West has shown up with 17 high-card points (ace, king, queen of clubs, ace of hearts, and ace of spades). If he holds the queen of diamonds as well, he has 19 points. Therefore, East should have the queen of diamonds, and the normal diamond finesse will fail. You still have a chance to make your bid by a technique called a *backward finesse*.

Suppose these are the four hands:

North
♠ J 7 5 3
♡ 10 8 2
◇ K J 9
♣ 8 7 6

West
♠ A 4 2
♡ A 6 3
◇ 10 7 6
♣ A K Q 9

East
♠ 6
♡ J 9 7 5 4
◇ Q 8 5 3
♣ J 10 2

South
♠ K Q 10 9 8
♡ K Q
◇ A 4 2
♣ 5 4 3

At the point that West wins with the ace of spades, he leads a heart, which you ruff. The first diamond play must be from dummy, so draw trumps ending in dummy and play the *jack* of diamonds. If East plays low, you will win a trick with the jack. If East covers with the queen, win with the ace and finesse through West for the ten. You will fail if East has both the queen and ten, but the backward finesse is the only logical play once you have concluded that East has the queen.[3]

#15

		North	
		♠ 10 6	
		♡ A 7 4 2	
		◇ A Q 8 5	
Contract: four spades		♣ Q 9 3	

Opening Lead: queen of hearts

South
♠ Q J 9 8 4 2
♡ K 3
◇ K
♣ K J 10 5

West	*North*	*East*	*South*
			1 ♠
2 ♡	2 NT	Pass	3 ♠
Pass	4 ♠	All Pass	

You are off three top tricks (two spades and one club), and the contract is secure unless the opponents can get a ruff. The most probable danger is that East has a singleton heart; West is likely to have a six-card suit for his two-level overcall. There is an easy way to avoid the heart ruff: After winning the first trick with the king of hearts, overtake the king of diamonds with dummy's ace and lead the queen of diamonds to discard your last heart.

Suppose these are the four hands:

North
♠ 10 6
♡ A 7 4 2
◇ A Q 8 5
♣ Q 9 3

West
♠ A K
♡ Q J 10 9 8 5
◇ 7 3 2
♣ A 6

East
♠ 7 5 3
♡ 6
◇ J 10 9 6 4
♣ 8 7 4 2

South
♠ Q J 9 8 4 2
♡ K 3
◇ K
♣ K J 10 5

---

3. A backward finesse requires *two* cards to be in the right places, so it is a poor percentage play unless you are convinced that the normal finesse will fail.

Note that West could give East a heart ruff if you led a trump before discarding a heart on the queen of diamonds. But once you shed your heart, they can win only three tricks.

#16

Contract: four hearts

Opening Lead: queen of spades

North
♠ K 6 4
♡ J 9 2
◇ K 7 2
♣ A 10 8 4

South
♠ A 7 5
♡ K Q 10 8 6 4
◇ A 3
♣ 6 5

West	North	East	South
1 ♠	Pass	Pass	2 ♡
Pass	3 ♡	Pass	4 ♡
All Pass			

It appears that you have just three losers (one spade, one heart, and one club), but if West has a six-card spade suit and the ace of hearts, he can give his partner a spade ruff. If East has a singleton spade, you cannot prevent this ruff; but you can arrange it so that he cannot ruff one of your winning spade tricks by playing the *king* from dummy on the first trick.

Suppose these are the four hands:

North
♠ K 6 4
♡ J 9 2
◇ K 7 2
♣ A 10 8 4

West
♠ Q J 10 9 8 3
♡ A 5
◇ 6 4
♣ K Q 7

East
♠ 2
♡ 7 3
◇ Q J 10 9 8 5
♣ J 9 3 2

South
♠ A 7 5
♡ K Q 10 8 6 4
◇ A 3
♣ 6 5

After winning the first trick with the king of spades, lead a heart, which West wins with the ace. If West leads another spade and East ruffs, you will play a low spade from your hand; East will have trumped your loser. Note that if you win the first trick with the ace of spades, you will be set; when West leads the second spade, your king will be trapped and ruffed by East.

It is true that there is no way of knowing whether West has five or six spades, but your contract is safe in either case by playing the king at trick one.

#17

Contract: four spades

Opening Lead: king of hearts

North
♠ J 5 4
♡ A 9 6 3
◇ A K 7
♣ 10 8 2

South
♠ A K 10 9 8 2
♡ 7 4
◇ 9 5
♣ A 6 3

West	North	East	South
3 ♡	Pass	Pass	3 ♠
Pass	4 ♠	All Pass	

You can see three obvious losers (one heart and two clubs), so you will be set if you lose a trump trick. The three-heart opening bid suggests that West has a seven-card suit, in which case East is void. The first key play is a *low* heart from dummy on the first trick; you must not allow East to ruff the ace of hearts. If West continues to lead hearts, you must continue to play low from dummy and ruff the third heart in your hand. You will have lost two hearts instead of one, but you will get the trick back later by discarding a club loser on the ace of hearts.

Now for a second problem: How should you play the spade suit? The percentage play with nine cards missing the queen is to cash one top honor, then, if both defenders follow suit, cash the other top honor and hope for a 2-2 split. This is the correct play *if you know nothing about the opponents' distribution*. But here you know a great deal and the odds should be figured as follows: West was dealt seven hearts and has six other cards, while East was dealt no hearts and has thirteen other cards. The odds are 13-to-6 in favor of East having any one card outside the heart suit—and this includes the queen of spades. (These odds fluctuate *slightly* as cards are played in turn, but the great disparity makes East a strong favorite to hold the queen of spades.) The first spade play is to cash the ace or king in case West has a singleton queen. When both defenders follow with low cards, lead a diamond to dummy and finesse through East for the queen of spades. If West was dealt a doubleton queen of spades, you will be set; but finessing is your best shot.

This line of play will succeed in the following layout:

North
♠ J 5 4
♡ A 9 6 3
♢ A K 7
♣ 10 8 2

West
♠ 6
♡ K Q J 10 8 5 2
♢ 4 3
♣ Q 9 7

East
♠ Q 7 3
♡ —
♢ Q J 10 8 6 2
♣ K J 5 4

South
♠ A K 10 9 8 2
♡ 7 4
♢ 9 5
♣ A 6 3

On the next deal the clue comes from a takeout double.

#18

Contract: four spades

Opening Lead: ten of hearts

North
♠ A 10 6 4
♡ 8 7 3
♢ A K J 9
♣ A K

South
♠ K Q 8 2
♡ 6 4 2
♢ Q 7 3 2
♣ 6 5

West	North	East	South
	1 ♢	Double	1 ♠
Pass	4 ♠	All Pass	

East wins the first three heart tricks (West following suit), and then he leads the jack of clubs, which you win in dummy. You must avoid a spade loser to make your bid and the bidding is enlightening: A takeout double describes a hand with length in the three unbid suits (especially unbid major suits) and shortness in the opening bidder's suit. Good card reading suggests that East was dealt a four-card spade suit, or at least J x x, and you should play accordingly.

Your first spade play should be the ace. Let's say the opponents follow suit with the three and the five. Now lead the ten of spades, intending to finesse if East plays low. If East covers with the jack, win with the king; if West shows out, return to dummy with a club and finesse again (your queen and eight of spades are behind the nine and seven).

Here are the four hands:

North
♠ A 10 6 4
♡ 8 7 3
◇ A K J 9
♣ A K

West
♠ 3
♡ 10 9 5
◇ 10 8 6 5
♣ Q 7 4 3 2

East
♠ J 9 7 5
♡ A K Q J
◇ 4
♣ J 10 9 8

South
♠ K Q 8 2
♡ 6 4 2
◇ Q 7 3 2
♣ 6 5

Note that the East hand is ideally suited for a takeout double and the recommended line of play succeeds. You would be set only if East doubled with three (or fewer) small spades — very unlikely, although anything is possible.

#19

Contract: six spades

Opening Lead: king of diamonds

North
♠ Q 6 5
♡ A K J 5 3 2
◇ A 7 4
♣ 2

South
♠ A K J 10 9 7
♡ 6
◇ J 3 2
♣ K J 5

West	North	East	South
			1 ♠
Double	Redouble	2 ♣	Pass
Pass	2 ♡	Pass	3 ♠
Pass	6 ♠	All Pass	

The best chance to make this slam is to establish the heart suit so you can discard four of your five minor-suit losers. If the missing hearts divide 3-3 or there is a doubleton queen, the suit is easily established by ruffing one heart in your hand; but the takeout double of one spade suggests that West has four hearts to the queen. Since you do not have enough entries to ruff more than one heart, and will need *four* discards, the best plan is to take a first-round heart finesse.

Suppose the four hands are:

North
♠ Q 6 5
♡ A K J 5 3 2
♢ A 7 4
♣ 2

West
♠ 8
♡ Q 10 9 4
♢ K Q 10 6
♣ A Q 8 7

East
♠ 4 3 2
♡ 8 7
♢ 9 8 5
♣ 10 9 6 4 3

South
♠ A K J 10 9 7
♡ 6
♢ J 3 2
♣ K J 5

Win the first trick with the ace of diamonds, and lead a spade to your king. Cash the jack of spades (optional), then finesse the jack of hearts. Now ruff a low heart in your hand to establish the remaining four hearts in dummy. Finally, lead a spade to the queen to draw East's last trump and discard four losers on the heart suit.

If East had the queen of hearts, you would be set two tricks. But with so few high cards missing, West is an overwhelming favorite to hold that card.

#20

Contract: four spades

Opening Lead: two of hearts

North
♠ Q 10
♡ 6 4
♢ 10 7 5 4
♣ A 9 8 4 3

South
♠ A K J 9 8 4
♡ A K 7 5
♢ 3 2
♣ 6

West	North	East	South
			1 ♠
Pass	1 NT	2 ♡	3 ♠
Pass	4 ♠	All Pass	

You have two inevitable diamond losers and must hold your heart losers to one if you are going to make your bid. West's two-of-hearts lead is obviously a singleton — he cannot have three cards and, with a doubleton, he would have led the higher card.

Most players overlook the winning play in cases like this. They try to win as many tricks as they can, rather than the number of tricks they need to make their bid. Before looking at the full deal, can you figure out the right play?

North
♠ Q 10
♡ 6 4
◇ 10 7 5 4
♣ A 9 8 4 3

West
♠ 7 3 2
♡ 2
◇ J 9 8 6
♣ K Q 10 7 5

East
♠ 6 5
♡ Q J 10 9 8 3
◇ A K Q
♣ J 2

South
♠ A K J 9 8 4
♡ A K 7 5
◇ 3 2
♣ 6

If you draw trumps, you will eventually lose two hearts. If you play the ace and king of hearts before drawing trumps, West will ruff the second one; then he can beat you by leading a trump. The sure-fire road to ten tricks is to win the first heart and *lead a low heart at trick two*. Although the contract cannot be beaten with any defense, suppose East wins the heart trick, and leads a trump. The contract is now safe if you win with the king of spades, ruff your remaining low heart in the dummy, and then return to your hand with a club ruff to draw trumps.

Quiz for Chapter Eight

1.
	North		
	♠ 3 2		
	♡ 7 4		
	◇ A K Q		
	♣ K J 7 5 3 2		

	South		
	♠ A K Q J 10 8		
	♡ K 6 5 2		
	◇ 10 8 3		
	♣ —		

West	North	East	South
	1 ♣	1 ♡	1 ♠
Pass	2 ♣	Pass	4 ♠
All Pass			

West leads the nine of hearts, East wins with the ace and then leads the queen of hearts.

2.
	North		
	♠ J 10 8		
	♡ J 9 6 2		
	◇ J 5 3		
	♣ Q 7 6		

	South		
	♠ A K Q		
	♡ A Q 10 3		
	◇ Q 9 7		
	♣ K 10 5		

West	North	East	South
			2 NT
Pass	3 NT	All Pass	

West leads the four of clubs, you play low from dummy and East puts in the nine.

3.
	North		
	♠ Q 6 4		
	♡ Q 10		
	◇ A Q J 5		
	♣ K 9 7 3		

	South		
	♠ A J 7 5 3		
	♡ 9 8		
	◇ K 7 4 2		
	♣ A 4		

West	North	East	South
	1 ◇	Dbl	Rdbl
1 ♡	Pass	Pass	1 ♠
Pass	2 ♠	Pass	4 ♠
All Pass			

West leads the four of hearts. East wins the first two tricks with the king and ace of hearts, and then leads the queen of clubs.

4.
	North		
	♠ K Q 9 5		
	♡ A 6		
	◇ Q J 7 2		
	♣ A K J		

	South		
	♠ A J 10 7 6 3		
	♡ Q J 2		
	◇ K 9 5		
	♣ 8		

West	North	East	South
	2 NT	Pass	3 ♠
Pass	4 ♠	Pass	4 NT
Pass	5 ♡	Pass	6 ♠
All Pass			

West leads the ten of hearts.

5.   North   6.   North
            ♠ A Q 9 2   ♠ A K 8 5
            ♡ A J 6   ♡ 7 4 3
            ◇ 8 4   ◇ 9 6 5 2
            ♣ K 7 5 3   ♣ K 6

            South   South
            ♠ 5   ♠ 6 3
            ♡ K Q 10 9 7 2   ♡ K Q J 9 8 5
            ◇ 5 3   ◇ A 7 3
            ♣ A 6 4 2   ♣ A 4

West	North	East	South
	1 ♣	1 ♠	2 ♡
2 ♠	3 ♡	Pass	4 ♡
All Pass			

West	North	East	South
			1 ♡
1 ♠	1 NT	Pass	3 ♡
Pass	4 ♡	All Pass	

West leads the jack of spades.

West leads the queen of spades, which you win in dummy. You play a heart, West wins with the ace of hearts and returns the jack of spades.

7.   North   8.   North
            ♠ A J 9   ♠ 4
            ♡ K J 4   ♡ 8 3
            ◇ J 5 3 2   ◇ Q 10 8 7 2
            ♣ Q J 7   ♣ K J 9 5 3

            South   South
            ♠ K Q 3   ♠ A K Q J 10 9 2
            ♡ A Q 9 8 5 2   ♡ A 9 6
            ◇ A K 7 4   ◇ A K
            ♣ —   ♣ A

West	North	East	South
			1 ♡
Pass	2 NT	Pass	3 ♡
Pass	4 ♡	Pass	6 ♡
All Pass			

West	North	East	South
		3 ♡	6 ♠
All Pass			

West leads the eight of diamonds.

West leads the two of hearts.

Answers to Quiz for Chapter Eight

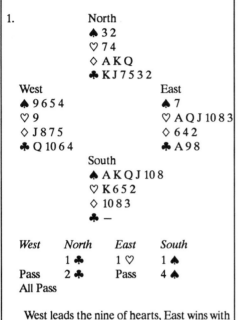

1.
       North
       ♠ 3 2
       ♡ 7 4
       ◇ A K Q
       ♣ K J 7 5 3 2
West   East
♠ 9 6 5 4   ♠ 7
♡ 9   ♡ A Q J 10 8 3
◇ J 8 7 5   ◇ 6 4 2
♣ Q 10 6 4   ♣ A 9 8
       South
       ♠ A K Q J 10 8
       ♡ K 6 5 2
       ◇ 10 8 3
       ♣ —

West	North	East	South
	1 ♣	1 ♡	1 ♠
Pass	2 ♣	Pass	4 ♠
All Pass			

West leads the nine of hearts, East wins with the ace and then leads the queen of hearts.

If you cover the queen of hearts with the king at trick two, West will ruff and you will be set; you cannot escape the loss of four heart tricks since dummy's trumps are too low to be of consequence. It may seem more likely that East has *five* hearts instead of six, but there is a safe way to make the contract in either case.

The winning play is to duck the second heart trick; let East win with his queen. If East leads another heart, play low again and West will ruff (else you will ruff in dummy); but that is the last trick for the defense. Whatever West leads next, you will win the trick, draw trumps, and claim the rest.

2.
       North
       ♠ J 10 8
       ♡ J 9 6 2
       ◇ J 5 3
       ♣ Q 7 6
West   East
♠ 9 7 4   ♠ 6 5 3 2
♡ 8 5   ♡ K 7 4
◇ A 4 2   ◇ K 10 8 6
♣ A J 8 4 3   ♣ 9 2
       South
       ♠ A K Q
       ♡ A Q 10 3
       ◇ Q 9 7
       ♣ K 10 5

West	North	East	South
			2 NT
Pass	3 NT	All Pass	

West leads the four of clubs, you play low from dummy and East puts in the nine.

There is little hope to make this contract if you lose a heart trick, so you desperately need an entry to dummy to try the heart finesse. The key play is to win the first trick with the *king* of clubs so the queen will be an entry if West has the ace. Next, lead a club right back. Whether West takes his ace or not, you will reach dummy with the queen and take the winning heart finesse. This gives you nine tricks: three spades, four hearts, and two clubs.

If you mistakenly win the first trick with the ten of clubs, you can be set with good defense. West can prevent you from getting to dummy by ducking if you lead the king of clubs, or by going up with his ace if you lead your low club.

There is very little risk in winning the first trick with the king of clubs. It is a reasonable conclusion that West led his fourth best club, so (by the Rule of Eleven) there are seven higher clubs in the other three hands. You have six between your hand and dummy, so East's nine is his only card above the six. Further evidence of West's fourth-best lead is that if West has led top of nothing, East's normal play from A J 9 x would be the *jack* (not the nine) at trick one.

3.

	North		
	♠ Q 6 4		
	♡ Q 10		
	◇ A Q J 5		
	♣ K 9 7 3		

West		East	
♠ 8		♠ K 10 9 2	
♡ J 6 5 4 2		♡ A K 7 3	
◇ 10 9 3		◇ 8 6	
♣ 8 6 5 2		♣ Q J 10	

	South		
	♠ A J 7 5 3		
	♡ 9 8		
	◇ K 7 4 2		
	♣ A 4		

West	North	East	South
	1 ◇	Dbl	Rdbl
1 ♡	Pass	Pass	1 ♠
Pass	2 ♠	Pass	4 ♠
All Pass			

West leads the four of hearts. East wins the first two tricks with the king and ace of hearts, and then leads the queen of clubs.

You can afford to lose one spade trick, but not two. You cannot go wrong if spades divide 3-2; but East made a takeout double, so he is likely to have four spades. If West has a singleton two and East has ♠ K 10 9 8, there is no hope; but you can succeed if West holds a singleton ten, nine, or eight.

Win the third trick in dummy with the king of clubs and lead the *queen* of spades. East must cover with the king (else your task is easy) and West drops the eight. Next lead a *low* spade from your hand and East wins with the nine. You now have jack-seven-five and East has ten-two. Regardless of what East leads, he cannot stop you from getting to dummy with a high diamond to take the winning spade finesse.

4.

	North		
	♠ K Q 9 5		
	♡ A 6		
	◇ Q J 7 2		
	♣ A K J		

West		East	
♠ 4		♠ 8 2	
♡ 10 9 8 3		♡ K 7 5 4	
◇ A 10 3		◇ 8 6 4	
♣ Q 7 5 4 2		♣ 10 9 6 3	

	South		
	♠ A J 10 7 6 3		
	♡ Q J 2		
	◇ K 9 5		
	♣ 8		

West	North	East	South
	2 NT	Pass	3 ♠
Pass	4 ♠	Pass	4 NT
Pass	5 ♡	Pass	6 ♠
All Pass			

West leads the ten of hearts.

The ace of diamonds is a sure loser, so to make this contract you must not lose a heart trick. There are two possibilities: You can take the heart finesse; or you can go up with the ace of hearts and try the club finesse—if West has the queen, you can discard two hearts on the ace and king of clubs.

Which finesse is more likely to work? You would be a poor psychologist if you thought the heart finesse, because few defenders would choose to lead from a holding of K 10 9, while the ten from 10 9 8 is an attractive choice.

The logical play is to win the first trick with the ace of hearts, draw trumps in two rounds, lead a club from your hand, and finesse the jack. If East has the queen of clubs and West has the king of hearts, you will have been swindled by West's daring lead; but bridge isn't a game for sissies.

5.

	North		
	♠ A Q 9 2		
	♡ A J 6		
	◇ 8 4		
	♣ K 7 5 3		

West		East
♠ J 10 3		♠ K 8 7 6 4
♡ 5		♡ 8 4 3
◇ K 10 9 7 6		◇ A Q J 2
♣ Q J 9 8		♣ 10

	South		
	♠ 5		
	♡ K Q 10 9 7 2		
	◇ 5 3		
	♣ A 6 4 2		

West	North	East	South
	1 ♣	1 ♠	2 ♡
2 ♠	3 ♡	Pass	4 ♡
All Pass			

West leads the jack of spades.

You have four possible losers (two diamonds and two clubs), and it looks as though you will need a 3-2 club break to make your bid. If you do your card reading, you should notice another chance: establishing a spade trick in dummy to discard one of your losers. The bidding suggests that East was dealt five spades and West three. If West is making a normal lead, he should have J 10 x, in which case dummy's nine of spades can be made into a winner.

Win the first trick with the ace of spades and ruff a low spade in your hand. Now draw three rounds of trumps ending in dummy, and lead the *queen* of spades. Assume East covers with the king (else you will discard a diamond), you ruff, and West drops the ten. The nine of spades is now a good trick, so lead a club to dummy's king and discard a diamond.

Note that you have nothing to lose by playing this way. If West does not have the ♠ J 10 x, the contract can still be made if clubs divide 3-2.

6.

	North		
	♠ A K 8 5		
	♡ 7 4 3		
	◇ 9 6 5 2		
	♣ K 6		

West		East
♠ Q J 10 9 4 2		♠ 7
♡ A		♡ 10 6 2
◇ K 8 4		◇ Q J 10
♣ Q 7 5		♣ J 10 9 8 3 2

	South		
	♠ 6 3		
	♡ K Q J 9 8 5		
	◇ A 7 3		
	♣ A 4		

West	North	East	South
			1 ♡
1 ♠	1 NT	Pass	3 ♡
Pass	4 ♡	All Pass	

West leads the queen of spades, which you win in dummy. You play a heart, West wins with the ace of hearts and returns the jack of spades.

As you can see, East has a singleton spade and he will ruff if you play dummy's high spade at trick three. Since you must lose two diamonds, you will be set one trick.

West's overcall should alert you to the possibility of East's singleton. Once aware, you should see a foolproof way to make your bid *no matter how the spades divide*. Simply duck the spade at trick three and allow West to win with his jack. If West continues with another spade, duck again and ruff in your hand. After drawing the remaining trumps, you will eventually discard one of your losing diamonds on the high spade.

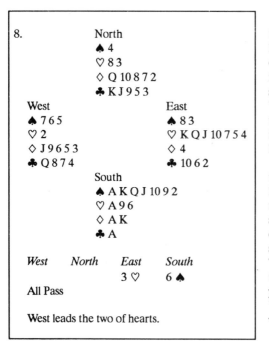

7.
North
♠ A J 9
♡ K J 4
◇ J 5 3 2
♣ Q J 7

West
♠ 10 7 6 2
♡ 10 6 3
◇ 8
♣ K 10 9 5 4

East
♠ 8 5 4
♡ 7
◇ Q 10 9 6
♣ A 8 6 3 2

South
♠ K Q 3
♡ A Q 9 8 5 2
◇ A K 7 4
♣ —

West	North	East	South
			1 ♡
Pass	2 NT	Pass	3 ♡
Pass	4 ♡	Pass	6 ♡
All Pass			

West leads the eight of diamonds.

To make this slam, you must hold your diamond losers to one. The eight-of-diamonds lead is probably a singleton, in which case the only way to avoid two diamond losers is to promote the seven of diamonds into a trick. The first play from dummy should be the *jack*; East plays the queen and you win with the ace. Now draw three rounds of trumps ending in dummy and lead a diamond; East plays the nine (if he plays the six, you will finesse the seven) and you win with the king. You are left with seven-four behind East's ten-six, so you can win a trick with the seven by leading another diamond from dummy. (Note you also could duck when East plays the nine, retaining the king-seven behind the ten-six, and planning to finesse the seven later.)

There is only one holding where playing the jack of diamonds at trick one would cost you the contract: if West made the abnormal lead of the eight from the 10 9 8 6, in which case East would have the singleton queen. But that possibility is too extraordinary to worry about.

Without a diamond lead, a good declarer would be set with the unlucky suit division shown in the diagram. The normal play of cashing the ace and king of diamonds would leave him with two losers.

8.
North
♠ 4
♡ 8 3
◇ Q 10 8 7 2
♣ K J 9 5 3

West
♠ 7 6 5
♡ 2
◇ J 9 6 5 3
♣ Q 8 7 4

East
♠ 8 3
♡ K Q J 10 7 5 4
◇ 4
♣ 10 6 2

South
♠ A K Q J 10 9 2
♡ A 9 6
◇ A K
♣ A

West	North	East	South
		3 ♡	6 ♠
All Pass			

West leads the two of hearts.

The only chance to make this contract is to get to dummy so you can discard your two losing hearts on the king of clubs and queen of diamonds. The three-heart opening bid indicates that East has a seven-card heart suit, and the opening lead confirms this; West would not lead the two from a doubleton, so he must have a singleton. With this information, you can make your bid if West has at least three spades.

East plays the ten of hearts on the first trick and you win with the ace. Now cash two high trumps, then the ace and king of diamonds and the ace of clubs. The stage is now set: Lead your two of spades to throw West on lead. Since West has no more hearts or spades, he must lead a club or a diamond. This puts the lead in dummy, permitting you to discard your two losing hearts and make your slam. Only if East has more spades than West will you be set, and this is unlikely in view of the heart split.

9

How to Count the Suits and the Squeeze Play

♣   ◇   ♡   ♠   ♣   ◇   ♡   ♠

How to Count the Suits

Figuring out how many cards each defender was dealt in one or more suits is often the key to the winning line of play. But it is not necessary to keep a mental record of every suit in every deal; this would tire you out needlessly. It is when you wish to know how one particular suit is divided that keeping track of one or more other suits is apt to be useful information.

When a defender fails to follow suit, you learn the exact distribution of the suit led. Other sources of information to help you count suits are the opponents' bidding, leads, discards, and signals. Here are seven hands in which it is important to count the suits and show how to use this information to your advantage.

Counting One Suit

#1

Contract: six notrump

Opening Lead: jack of spades

North
♠ 8 4 3
♡ J 5
◇ K J 10
♣ A Q 8 7 2

South
♠ A K
♡ A 7 2
◇ A Q 9 5
♣ K 10 6 3

You have twelve tricks if you can run the club suit, so only a 4-0 club break poses a problem. If West has four clubs, you can win five club tricks if your first play is the king. If East has four clubs, your first play must be the ace or queen.

Although the 4-0 split will happen only 10 percent of the time, you have nothing to lose by trying to figure out which defender is more likely to have four clubs before leading the suit. The only side suit you can count for sure is diamonds, so, after winning the first trick, run the diamond suit to see how it divides. On the third diamond lead, West shows out—West started with two diamonds and East with four. Since West has eleven cards in the other three suits, while East has nine, there is a greater chance that West has four clubs. Your first club play should be the *king.*

Suppose this is the full deal:

North
♠ 8 4 3
♡ J 5
♢ K J 10
♣ A Q 8 7 2

West
♠ J 10 9 7
♡ K 6 3
♢ 8 2
♣ J 9 5 4

East
♠ Q 6 5 2
♡ Q 10 9 8 4
♢ 7 6 4 3
♣ —

South
♠ A K
♡ A 7 2
♢ A Q 9 5
♣ K 10 6 3

When East shows out on the first club lead, it is an easy task to run the club suit by finessing West out of the jack-nine. If your first club play were the ace or queen, you would be set.

If it developed that East and West each were dealt three diamonds, you would be left with a pure guess as to which club honor to play first.

#2

Contract: three notrump

Opening Lead: two of hearts

North
♠ 8 2
♡ 6 5 3
♢ K 10 9 7
♣ A K 4 3

South
♠ A 10 7 5
♡ A Q
♢ A Q 4
♣ 9 8 6 2

With the heart lead, you have eight winners (one spade, two hearts, three diamonds, and two clubs), and each minor suit offers a possible ninth—clubs if the suit divides 3-2, and diamonds if you can locate the jack. Since there are optional ways to play diamonds, you should try the club suit first. When you cash the ace and king of clubs, West discards a spade on the second lead. That chance fizzled. When you lead diamonds, both defenders follow to the ace and queen, and West follows when you lead a low diamond toward dummy, but the jack of diamonds has not appeared. Should you finesse the ten or play the king? You will be set if you make the wrong decision.

With no information about the enemy distribution, the percentage play would be the king. But here you discovered that West had only one club to East's four, which leaves West with three extra unknown cards, or chances to hold the jack of diamonds. Even considering that East has not yet played to the trick, West still has two extra unknown cards; so the odds favor finessing the ten.

Here are the four hands:

```
                         North
                         ♠ 8 2
                         ♡ 6 5 3
                         ◇ K 10 9 7
                         ♣ A K 4 3
       West                              East
       ♠ K 9 6 3                         ♠ Q J 4
       ♡ J 10 4 2                        ♡ K 9 8 7
       ◇ J 8 5 2                         ◇ 6 3
       ♣ 7                               ♣ Q J 10 5
                         South
                         ♠ A 10 7 5
                         ♡ A Q
                         ◇ A Q 4
                         ♣ 9 8 6 2
```

There is another clue that West began with four diamonds: The two-of-hearts opening lead indicated a four-card heart suit, so West's original distribution figures to be 4-4-4-1. If he began with five spades and three diamonds, his normal lead would have been a spade.

Counting Two Suits

#3

Contract: three notrump

Opening Lead: three of spades

```
                         North
                         ♠ 10 7 6
                         ♡ A 9 2
                         ◇ A 10 9 4
                         ♣ 10 8 3

                         South
                         ♠ K J
                         ♡ 10 5 4
                         ◇ K J 8 3 2
                         ♣ A K Q
```

After winning the first trick with ace of spades, East returns the nine of spades and West follows with the two, suggesting he has led from a five-card suit. You must run the diamond suit to make your bid; if you lose a trick to the queen of diamonds, the opponents can win enough spade tricks to set you.

Your quest is to figure out how the diamonds divide. Should you cash the top diamonds and hope the queen falls? Or should you finesse East or West for the queen? At the moment, the odds lean toward finessing East for the queen—he was dealt only three spades while West was dealt five—but you should cash your club winners before you decide. This turns out to be revealing, as West discards a heart on the second club lead. You now have a count on two suits: West was dealt five spades and one club, while East was dealt three spades and six clubs. Therefore, West started with seven red cards to East's four, so the odds are 7-to-4 that West has the queen of diamonds.[1] The percentage play is to cash the king of diamonds and, if the queen does not fall, finesse through West for the queen.

Here is a likely layout of the four hands:

```
                        North
                        ♠ 10 7 6
                        ♡ A 9 2
                        ◊ A 10 9 4
                        ♣ 10 8 3
        West                                East
        ♠ Q 8 4 3 2                         ♠ A 9 5
        ♡ K J 6 3                           ♡ Q 8 7
        ◊ Q 7 5                             ◊ 6
        ♣ 7                                 ♣ J 9 6 5 4 2
                        South
                        ♠ K J
                        ♡ 10 5 4
                        ◊ K J 8 3 2
                        ♣ A K Q
```

Counting All Four Suits

#4   North
                                 ♠ 10 8
                                 ♡ 7 6 3
                                 ◊ A K Q 4
Contract: three notrump   ♣ A 8 5 2

Opening Lead: four of spades   ♠ J 6 5
                                 ♡ A K
                                 ◊ 7 6 5 2
                                 ♣ K Q 9 3

---

1. These are the odds prior to playing diamonds. At the actual moment of decision (when West follows low to the second diamond lead), the odds are only 6-to-4 because West has played one more card than East.

It looks like you will be set before you get the lead. But East wins the first two tricks with the king and queen of spades and switches to the queen of hearts (obviously, he has no more spades). If either diamonds or clubs divide 3-2, you have nine tricks. Since there are optional lines of play if clubs divide 4-1, you should tackle the diamond suit first.

You find out that diamonds divide 4-1 when East discards a heart on the second lead. But at least you learned that West began with six spades and four diamonds. If you now cash your second high heart, West will follow suit to reveal that he started with two hearts. Therefore, West has at most one club, and the contract is safe if your next play is the *ace* of clubs.

Before explaining further, here are the four hands:

                    North
                    ♠ 10 8
                    ♡ 7 6 3
                    ◇ A K Q 4
                    ♣ A 8 5 2
West   East
♠ A 9 7 4 3 2   ♠ K Q
♡ 9 5   ♡ Q J 10 8 4 2
◇ J 10 9 8   ◇ 3
♣ 6   ♣ J 10 7 4
                    South
                    ♠ J 6 5
                    ♡ A K
                    ◇ 7 6 5 2
                    ♣ K Q 9 3

When West plays his only club on dummy's ace, you know that East is left with jack-ten-seven. Lead a club from dummy and finesse the *nine*. Note that it does East no good to split his jack-ten — you can win and return to dummy with a diamond to finesse again.

#5   North
                            ♠ 7 5
                            ♡ 9 8 4
                            ◇ A Q 10 8 6 2
Contract: six notrump   ♣ A 10

Opening Lead: three of spades   South
                            ♠ K 10 2
                            ♡ A K 6 5
                            ◇ K 7
                            ♣ K Q J 4

West	North	East	South
		3 ♠	3 NT
Pass	4 NT	Pass	6 NT
All Pass			

East wins the first trick with the ace of spades, and returns the queen of spades to your king, as West discards a low club. As you expected from the bidding, spades are 7-1. The only chance to make your bid is to run the diamond suit. Should you cash three top diamonds in the hope the jack falls? Or should you take a second-round finesse for the jack? The normal percentage play for this suit combination is to lead out the three top honors, but the extraordinary spade division makes it a closer choice.

Before playing diamonds, you should cash your side winners to see what you can learn about the distribution. East follows suit to three rounds of clubs, two high hearts, and the king of diamonds. You now have a complete count on East's hand. He was dealt seven spades, three clubs, two hearts, and one diamond. West must have the three remaining diamonds, so finessing the ten is a sure thing.

Here are the four hands:

<pre>
                          North
                          ♠ 7 5
                          ♡ 9 8 4
                          ◇ A Q 10 8 6 2
                          ♣ A 10
        West   East
        ♠ 3   ♠ A Q J 9 8 6 4
        ♡ Q J 7 2   ♡ 10 3
        ◇ J 9 4 3   ◇ 5
        ♣ 9 8 6 5   ♣ 7 3 2
                          South
                          ♠ K 10 2
                          ♡ A K 6 5
                          ◇ K 7
                          ♣ K Q J 4
</pre>

The next deal features a two-way finesse.

#6   North
                                  ♠ 7 6 2
                                  ♡ 9 8 5
                                  ◇ A 10 8 7
Contract: seven notrump   ♣ K 7 6

Opening Lead: jack of spades   South
                                 ♠ A K Q
                                 ♡ A K Q
                                 ◇ K J 9 3
                                 ♣ A Q 8

You need four diamond tricks to make your grand slam and must "guess" which way to finesse for the queen. Here again you should try to count as many suits as possible to learn as much as you can about the enemy distribution.

You do this by cashing the ace, king, and queen in all three side suits. East shows out on the third spade lead and the third heart lead, so both of those suits divide five for West and two for East. West shows out on the third club lead, so he was dealt two clubs to East's five. Since you can count three suits, you automatically have a count of the fourth: West began with five spades, five hearts, two clubs — and consequently *one* diamond. East began with two spades, two hearts, five clubs — and consequently *four* diamonds. In bridge terminology, when you know the exact distribution of all four suits, you can "count the hand."

Here is the full layout:

```
                         North
                         ♠ 7 6 2
                         ♡ 9 8 5
                         ◇ A 10 8 7
                         ♣ K 7 6
         West                              East
         ♠ J 10 9 5 3                      ♠ 8 4
         ♡ J 7 6 4 3                       ♡ 10 2
         ◇ 4                               ◇ Q 6 5 2
         ♣ 10 2                            ♣ J 9 5 4 3
                         South
                         ♠ A K Q
                         ♡ A K Q
                         ◇ K J 9 3
                         ♣ A Q 8
```

Since you know that West began with one diamond and East with four, there is no longer a guess to make your bid. Your first diamond play should be the *ace*, then, if West does not drop the queen, lead the ten of diamonds and take the marked finesse through East.

It was good luck on this deal that all three side suits divided 5-2 so you could count the hand. But even if just one suit had lopsided distribution, the odds would favor finessing the defender who was short in that suit for the queen of diamonds. If both defenders had followed suit throughout, you would have been left with a guess as to which way to finesse.

Conceding a Trick to Obtain a Count

Sometimes it is necessary to concede a trick to the opponents in order to find out how a suit divides.

For example:

#7

Contract: six notrump

Opening Lead: jack of Spades

```
                         North
                         ♠ 7 6 2
                         ♡ 9 8 5
                         ◇ A 10 8 7
                         ♣ K 7 6

                         South
                         ♠ A K Q
                         ♡ A K 4
                         ◇ K J 9 3
                         ♣ A Q 8
```

Again you must guess the location of the queen of diamonds, but this time the bid is six notrump. Suppose the suits divide as they did in the last hand:

North
♠ 7 6 2
♡ 9 8 5
◊ A 10 8 7
♣ K 7 6

West
♠ J 10 9 5 3
♡ Q J 7 6 3
◊ 4
♣ 10 2

East
♠ 8 4
♡ 10 2
◊ Q 6 5 2
♣ J 9 5 4 3

South
♠ A K Q
♡ A K 4
◊ K J 9 3
♣ A Q 8

If you cash your eight winners in the side suits (three spades, three clubs, and two hearts), you will find out that West began with five spades and two clubs, and East began with five clubs and two spades, but you will learn nothing about the heart division. You cannot find out that hearts divide 5-2 unless the suit is led *three times*. The solution is to lose one heart trick before you cash the ace and king. As good a play as any is to concede a heart trick to the opponents at trick two. Eventually you will cash the ace and king to reveal that hearts divide 5-2. Then you can make your bid by playing the same way as you did in illustration 6.

The Squeeze Play

Many squeeze plays occur by accident. The declarer cashes winners in one or more long suits to force the defenders to discard. It is his hope that someone will make a bad discard to give him an extra trick. During one of the later tricks, a defender may have a discarding problem and perhaps start squirming in his chair; it is then that the declarer first realizes that he may have a squeeze.

Cashing winners in long suits is good technique and often does present discarding problems for the defenders. But declarer must be properly prepared, or he may find that it is too late to execute a legitimate squeeze. A skillful declarer must recognize and preserve his *threat cards*, and cash his winners in the proper order so he can *maintain communication* between his hand and dummy. Most squeeze plays also require that declarer is able to win *all but one* of the remaining tricks.

Here are twelve deals that show how to plan and execute squeeze plays:

#8   North
                                      ♠ 9 3
                                      ♡ J 6 4 3
                                      ◇ K Q 6 5

Contract: seven notrump   ♣ 10 9 8

Opening Lead: king of hearts   South
                                        ♠ A K Q J
                                      ♡ A 7 2
                                      ◇ A 4
                                      ♣ A K Q J

You have twelve winners and no apparent chance for a thirteenth. (Someone bid too much.) But you should not give up, as there may be a squeeze. Only one defender can hold as many as four diamonds; if he bears down to three, you can win a trick with dummy's fourth diamond. West's opening lead makes it obvious that he has the queen of hearts; if he throws it away, you can win a trick with the jack. Of course, no good defender will discard so foolishly *unless he has to*; and that is the essence of a squeeze play. If you run *all* of your winners in the black suits, West will be in trouble if this is the full deal:

                                  North
                                  ♠ 9 3
                                  ♡ J 6 4 3
                                  ◇ K Q 6 5
                                  ♣ 10 9 8

West   East
♠ 7 6 5   ♠ 10 8 4 2
♡ K Q 10   ♡ 9 8 5
◇ J 9 8 7   ◇ 10 3 2
♣ 4 3 2   ♣ 7 6 5
                                South
                                  ♠ A K Q J
                                  ♡ A 7 2
                                  ◇ A 4
                                  ♣ A K Q J

After winning the first trick with the ace of hearts, cash four spades and four clubs. This is the ending you will reach before you lead your last club:

                                        North
                                        ♠ —
                                        ♡ J
                                        ◊ K Q 6 5
                                        ♣ —

West   East

♠ —
♡ Q   (falling asleep)
◊ J 9 8 7
♣ —

                                        South
                                        ♠ —
                                        ♡ 7 2
                                        ◊ A 4
                                        ♣ J

Now cash your last club. If West discards a diamond, you will throw away the jack of hearts from dummy; if West discards the queen of hearts, you will throw a diamond. Either way, all the tricks are yours.

Dummy's jack of hearts and fourth diamond are threat cards. Since both threat cards are in the same hand, only one defender (West) can be squeezed; if East held the queen of hearts and four diamonds, he would discard *after* the dummy and the squeeze would fail. In the next deal, the threat cards are in *separate hands*, so it is possible to squeeze either defender.

#9   North
                                        ♠ K Q 6 3 2
                                        ♡ A 7
                                        ◊ Q 10 9
Contract: six notrump   ♣ K Q 8

Opening Lead: eight of diamonds   South
                                        ♠ A 7
                                        ♡ K Q 5 4 3
                                        ◊ K J 2
                                        ♣ A J 10

East wins the first trick with the ace of diamonds and returns a diamond at trick two. You have eleven winners and a twelfth is available in spades or hearts if either suit divides 3-3. But you should not rush into leading spades and hearts to find out how they divide. If you cash the *minor-suit winners* first, you can also make your bid if either defender has four (or more) cards in each major suits. That defender will be squeezed.

Suppose these are the four hands:

```
                          North
                          ♠ K Q 6 3 2
                          ♡ A 7
                          ◇ Q 10 9
                          ♣ K Q 8
      West                                    East
      ♠ 10 5                                  ♠ J 9 8 4
      ♡ 9 6                                   ♡ J 10 8 2
      ◇ 8 7 6 4                               ◇ A 5 3
      ♣ 9 5 4 3 2                             ♣ 7 6
                          South
                          ♠ A 7
                          ♡ K Q 5 4 3
                          ◇ K J 2
                          ♣ A J 10
```

When you cash your last minor-suit winner, East must part with a spade or a heart. Note that your two threat cards — the fourth heart and the fourth spade — are in different hands, which means that either defender can be squeezed. You can verify this by switching the East-West hands.

If you mistakenly cash two or three spades *and* two or three hearts before cashing all of your clubs and diamonds, you sever your communication — you can no longer reach both threat cards and there is no squeeze. East will simply hold on to the appropriate stopper, according to which hand wins the last minor-suit trick.

Rectifying the Count

In most cases a squeeze cannot be executed until you can win all but one of the remaining tricks. Therefore, you may have to lose one or more tricks deliberately early in the play to "rectify" the situation (i.e., to squeeze for a twelfth trick, first lose one trick; to squeeze for a tenth trick, first lose three tricks; etc.).

Here are two illustrations:

```
#10                            North
                               ♠ A 7 6
                               ♡ 5 3 2
                               ◇ 8 4 3
Contract: six notrump          ♣ A Q 4 2

Opening Lead: king of diamonds South
                               ♠ K Q J 5
                               ♡ A K Q 7
                               ◇ A 9 6
                               ♣ K 7
```

You have eleven winners, and the heart suit will provide the twelfth if that suit divides 3-3. There is also a chance for a squeeze. Suppose you win with the ace of diamonds and cash four spade tricks.

Here is the full deal:

```
                        North
                        ♠ A 7 6
                        ♡ 5 3 2
                        ◇ 8 4 3
                        ♣ A Q 4 2
        West                            East
        ♠ 10 9 8 2                      ♠ 4 3
        ♡ 9 4                           ♡ J 10 8 6
        ◇ K Q J 7                       ◇ 10 5 2
        ♣ 6 5 3                         ♣ J 10 9 8
                        South
                        ♠ K Q J 5
                        ♡ A K Q 7
                        ◇ A 9 6
                        ♣ K 7
```

When you cash your four spade winners, East will simply discard two diamonds. You cannot force him to part with a heart or a club, so your squeeze will not work.

The problem is that you cannot win all but one of the remaining tricks. In order to squeeze East, four spades and *two* diamonds must be played to reduce him to seven cards. The only way to do this is to duck the first diamond trick — rectify the count. If you then cash the ace of diamonds and four spades, East will have to come down to seven cards and part with a heart or a club.

#11   North
                                        ♠ A K Q 2
                                        ♡ 6 5 4 3
                                        ◇ A 9
Contract: three notrump   ♣ 9 8 7

Opening Lead: king of clubs   South
                                        ♠ 9 8
                                        ♡ A 7 2
                                        ◇ K Q 6 5
                                        ♣ A 4 3 2

You have eight winners, and a 3-3 club break appears to be the only chance for a ninth. But there are squeeze possibilities, the most promising being to use the fourth spade in dummy and the fourth diamond in your hand as threat cards and find one defender with four or more cards in each of those suits. But you first must rectify the count — in this case, lose exactly four tricks.

Suppose you duck the first two club leads. West leads a third club and East discards a heart, so you learn that clubs are 4-2. You must lose two more tricks, so duck again. West then switches to the king of hearts (no other defense is better), and you play low once more. You now have rectified the count by losing the first four tricks.

Let's look at a layout that would reward this skillful play.

                          North
                          ♠ A K Q 2
                          ♡ 6 5 4 3
                          ◊ A 9
                          ♣ 9 8 7

West   East
♠ 10 5 3   ♠ J 7 6 4
♡ K Q J   ♡ 10 9 8
◊ 7 4 2   ◊ J 10 8 3
♣ K Q J 10   ♣ 6 5

                          South
                          ♠ 9 8
                          ♡ A 7 2
                          ◊ K Q 6 5
                          ♣ A 4 3 2

Assume West leads a heart to your ace at trick five (nothing matters). At this point everyone has eight cards and East still protects both diamonds and spades. Now cash the ace of clubs! East must discard a spade or a diamond – it took a lot of work, but you finally squeezed him. The rest of the tricks are yours.

In some cases it is impossible (or inconvenient) to rectify the count. A squeeze might work by running your long suit and forcing an opponent to discard.

Here is one example:

#12   North
                                     ♠ 8 3
                                     ♡ A J 4
                                     ◊ K Q 7 2
Contract: three notrump   ♣ 10 9 6 5

Opening Lead: six of spades   South
                                     ♠ K 9 7 2
                                     ♡ K Q 9 6
                                     ◊ A 5
                                     ♣ K Q 4

West	*North*	*East*	*South*
		1 ♠	1 NT
Pass	3 NT	All Pass	

East wins the first trick with the ace of spades and returns the queen of spades, which you duck. Then he continues with the jack of spades to your king, as West discards a club. You have eight winners and will be set if you try to get the ninth trick by leading a club; East is marked with the ace of clubs from the bidding and he will be able to cash two more spade tricks.

There is no way to rectify the count, and the contract may appear hopeless; but you have nothing to lose by cashing your four heart winners. If you do so, you will squeeze East if he has four or more diamonds.

Suppose these are the four hands:

                                    North
                                    ♠ 8 3
                                    ♡ A J 4
                                    ◇ K Q 7 2
                                    ♣ 10 9 6 5
            West   East
            ♠ 6 4   ♠ A Q J 10 5
            ♡ 10 8 7 5   ♡ 3 2
            ◇ 9 4 3   ◇ J 10 8 6
            ♣ 8 7 3 2   ♣ A J
                                    South
                                    ♠ K 9 7 2
                                    ♡ K Q 9 6
                                    ◇ A 5
                                    ♣ K Q 4

East must discard twice when you cash four heart tricks, but he has only one safe discard: the jack of clubs. If he discards a spade on the fourth heart, you can win a ninth trick by driving out the ace of clubs; East no longer has enough spades to set you. If he discards a diamond, dummy's fourth diamond becomes a winner.

The Pseudo Squeeze

Good technique in the early going may enable you to make an impossible contract. For example:

#13   North
                                        ♠ 10 9 8
                                        ♡ A Q 3
                                        ◇ A Q 5
Contract: six notrump   ♣ A 10 7 6

Opening Lead: king of spades   South
                                        ♠ A 5 4
                                        ♡ K 7 6 2
                                        ◇ K 8 3
                                        ♣ K Q J

West	*North*	*East*	*South*
			1 NT
Pass	6 NT	All Pass	

Once again you are one trick short; you have eleven winners and need twelve. If hearts divide 3-3, all is well; otherwise you will need a squeeze, or an error from a defender. The first step is to rectify the count by ducking the first trick. Suppose West continues with the queen of spades and you win with the ace. Dummy's ten of spades and your fourth heart are both threat cards; if one defender has the jack of spades and the long hearts, he will be squeezed.

Suppose, though, that this is the full deal:

                          North
                          ♠ 10 9 8
                          ♡ A Q 3
                          ◇ A Q 5
                          ♣ A 10 7 6
        West   East
        ♠ K Q J 2   ♠ 7 6 3
        ♡ 5 4   ♡ J 10 9 8
        ◇ 7 6 2   ◇ J 10 9 4
        ♣ 9 8 5 3   ♣ 4 2
                          South
                          ♠ A 5 4
                          ♡ K 7 6 2
                          ◇ K 8 3
                          ♣ K Q J

As you can see, West has the jack of spades and East has the long hearts, so the contract cannot be made. But note the problem East will have if you immediately cash four club tricks. He can discard his last spade on the third club lead, but what should he discard on the fourth club? East does not know whether you have four hearts or four diamonds in your hand, and he may decide to discard a heart — in which case you can win four heart tricks.

When a defender is confronted with a discarding problem but can beat the contract if he makes the right discard, it is called a "pseudo squeeze." Note that even the pseudo squeeze would fail if you did not rectify the count.

Creating a Threat Card

The declarer may have to do some manipulating to establish a threat card for a squeeze. The next two deals illustrate this.

#14   North
                                 ♠ K 9 8 7 3
                                 ♡ A 5 2
                                 ◇ K
Contract: seven hearts   ♣ 7 6 4 3

Opening Lead: ten of diamonds   South
                                 ♠ A 5 2
                                 ♡ K Q J 10 9 4
                                 ◇ A Q
                                 ♣ A K

You have only one loser — a spade — and no obvious way to get rid of it. Your only chance is a squeeze play. (Have you noticed that overbidders need to be more efficient at squeeze plays than accurate bidders?) The third spade is one of your threat cards and the other can be created in clubs. After winning the ace (or king) of diamonds, cash the king and queen of hearts (both follow), cash the ace and king of clubs, lead a heart to the ace, and *ruff* a club. The last is a key play; it creates the *fourth* club as a threat card — only one defender can protect it. Now cash your high diamond and the rest of your hearts except one to reach this four-card ending:

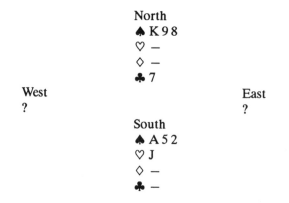

North
♠ K 9 8
♡ —
◊ —
♣ 7

West
?

East
?

South
♠ A 5 2
♡ J
◊ —
♣ —

When you play your last heart and throw a spade from dummy, neither defender can hold three spades and the high club. If dummy's club is not good, just play the king, ace, and another spade — either the third spade is good, or you go down. The odds are against one defender having four or more clubs and the long spades, and you are likely to be set in spite of your superior play — but that's what happens when you bid too much.

#15

North
♠ A Q 9
♡ A K
◊ J 6 5 3
♣ A K Q 2

Contract: seven diamonds

Opening Lead: jack of spades

South
♠ 7
♡ 10 6
◊ A K Q 10 9 7
♣ 8 5 4 3

If clubs divide 3-2 (a 68-percent chance), you have thirteen tricks, so it would be foolish to take the spade finesse. After winning the first trick with the ace of spades and drawing trumps, you cash the ace and king of clubs. Trouble — East shows out on the second lead. Since clubs divide 4-1, the only remaining hope is to squeeze West. But where is the second threat card?

West's opening jack-of-spades lead indicates that he probably has the ten but not the king. If this card reading is accurate, you can make your bid by creating the nine of spades as a threat card.

Here are the four hands with the expected spade division:

North
♠ A Q 9
♡ A K
◇ J 6 5 3
♣ A K Q 2

West
♠ J 10 8 5 4
♡ Q 3 2
◇ 4
♣ J 9 7 6

East
♠ K 6 3 2
♡ J 9 8 7 5 4
◇ 8 2
♣ 10

South
♠ 7
♡ 10 6
◇ A K Q 10 9 7
♣ 8 5 4 3

The last trick was won in dummy with a high club, so lead the *queen* of spades. Let's assume that East covers with his king of spades and you ruff. (If East does not cover, you can discard your losing club.)

Now West can be squeezed if you cash the high hearts and then run your diamonds. After ten tricks have been played (before you cash your last diamond), this will be the ending:

North
♠ 9
♡ —
◇ —
♣ Q 2

West
♠ 10
♡ —
◇ —
♣ J 9

East

(immaterial)

South
♠ —
♡ —
◇ 9
♣ 8 5

When you cash your last diamond, West must discard the ten of spades or a club ahead of the dummy. In either case, you have the rest of the tricks.

The Suicide Squeeze

#16   North
                                                ♠ 7 6 3
                                                ♡ K 2
                                                ◇ K Q 7 4
Contract: three notrump   ♣ K 8 5 4

Opening Lead: four of hearts   South
                                                ♠ A K 5 4
                                                ♡ J 8 5
                                                ◇ A 3
                                                ♣ A 7 6 2

On the first trick, you play a low heart from dummy, East contributes the ten, and you win with the jack. This gives you eight winners, and it appears that the best chance for a ninth is to develop an extra club trick. The trouble with that plan is you must lose a club trick. Then you will be set if the opponents can win four heart tricks.

A better plan is to let the opponents run their heart suit immediately. This will not set you (West's lead, presumably fourth-best, indicates a four- or five-card suit, but not six). If the opponents run four heart tricks, they will rectify the count for you and a squeeze may develop. If hearts divide 4-4, the opponents can win only three heart tricks; then you will still be able to develop a ninth trick in clubs if that suit divides 3-2.

Suppose these are the four hands:

```
                        North
                        ♠ 7 6 3
                        ♡ K 2
                        ◇ K Q 7 4
                        ♣ K 8 5 4
        West                            East
        ♠ 9 8 2                         ♠ Q J 10
        ♡ Q 9 7 4 3                     ♡ A 10 6
        ◇ 10 8 6                        ◇ J 9 5 2
        ♣ J 9                           ♣ Q 10 3
                        South
                        ♠ A K 5 4
                        ♡ J 8 5
                        ◇ A 3
                        ♣ A 7 6 2
```

At trick two, lead a heart to East's ace, then assume East returns a heart and West runs the rest of the suit. East cannot afford to discard a diamond or a club; he will have to discard two spades. You discard a spade and two clubs from dummy and a spade and a club from your hand. This is a likely layout after five hearts have been played:

```
                          North
                          ♠ 7 6
                          ♡ —
                          ◊ K Q 7 4
                          ♣ K 8
        West                              East
        ♠ 9 8 2                           ♠ Q
        ♡ —                               ♡ —
        ◊ 10 8 6                          ◊ J 9 5 2
        ♣ J 9                             ♣ Q 10 3
                          South
                          ♠ A K 5
                          ♡ —
                          ◊ A 3
                          ♣ A 7 6
```

Suppose West leads a spade at trick six (nothing matters) and you win with the king. Now cash the ace of spades and East is squeezed — either dummy's fourth diamond or your third club will provide the ninth trick. Since West contributed to his own side being squeezed, this is called a *suicide squeeze.*

If West does not cash all of his hearts (very unlikely), the squeeze will fail. But then you can revert to your original plan — to establish the club suit. Play ace, king, and another club; West cannot get the lead, so your fourth club will be your ninth trick.

Take note that it is often a winning strategy to concede tricks to the enemy in the early going, provided they cannot win enough tricks to set the contract. Although the eventual benefit is not always obvious at the time you concede the tricks, the opponents may give you a trick by making a bad lead, a bad discard, or by allowing a squeeze to develop.

Communication Problems

You may miss the opportunity for a squeeze if you do not cash your winners in the right rotation. Here are two examples:

#17   North
                                  ♠ A K Q J
                                  ♡ 7 5
                                  ◊ 9 4 2
Contract: seven notrump   ♣ 10 8 4 2

Opening Lead: ten of hearts   South
                                  ♠ 7 2
                                  ♡ A K Q
                                  ◊ A K 6 5 3
                                  ♣ A K Q

You have twelve winners and can make the grand slam if the jack of clubs falls under the ace-king-queen, or by a squeeze if either defender has three or more diamonds and the guarded jack of clubs. All true—but you must maintain communication for your potential tricks.

The first step is to cash the ace, king, and queen of clubs. Assume the jack does not drop, so you must resort to the squeeze. Your two threat cards are the ten of clubs in dummy and the third diamond in your hand. In order to reach both threat cards after the squeeze, you must cash the major-suit winners *ending in dummy*. This means, you must run the hearts before the spades. This is the ending you will reach with *North* on lead:

North
♠ —
♡ —
◇ 9 4
♣ 10

South
♠ —
♡ —
◇ A K 6
♣ —

If the ten of clubs is not good, just play the ace, king, and another diamond. You will win a trick with the six of diamonds if one defender was dealt the long diamonds and the jack of clubs; otherwise someone will still have three diamonds and you will be set. Your fate depends on the lie of the opponents' cards; but if it is possible to make the contract, this line of play will succeed.

Note the importance of the lead being in *dummy* in the three-card ending. If you cash your spade winners before your hearts, you can never get back to dummy to win a trick with the ten of clubs. Also note that the ace and king of diamonds were not cashed until the very end; at least one high diamond must be preserved to get back to your hand in case the third diamond becomes a winner.

#18

Contract: six spades

Opening Lead: jack of clubs

North
♠ 9 8 5
♡ A 10 4 2
◇ A K Q 7
♣ 6 3

South
♠ A K Q J 10 7
♡ Q 9 3
◇ 8 5
♣ K Q

East wins the first trick with the ace of clubs and leads a second club to your king. The best chance to win twelve tricks is to find one defender with the king of hearts and four (or more) diamonds, in which case you can squeeze him and win a trick with your queen of hearts or dummy's fourth diamond.

Here is a layout where the squeeze can be executed:

North
♠ 9 8 5
♡ A 10 4 2
◇ A K Q 7
♣ 6 3

West
♠ 6 3 2
♡ J 5
◇ 6 4 3
♣ J 10 9 8 2

East
♠ 4
♡ K 8 7 6
◇ J 10 9 2
♣ A 7 5 4

South
♠ A K Q J 10 7
♡ Q 9 3
◇ 8 5
♣ K Q

Suppose you decide to run the spade suit. After five spades have been led, here is the situation:

North
♠ —
♡ A 10
◇ A K Q 7
♣ —

West

(immaterial)

East
♠ —
♡ K 8
◇ J 10 9 2
♣ —

South
♠ 7
♡ Q 9 3
◇ 8 5
♣ —

If you lead the seven of spades and discard the ten of hearts from dummy, East must blank his king of hearts to protect the diamond suit. But what good does that do you? The answer is *no good* at all; after you cash the ace of hearts, you cannot get back to your hand to win a trick with the queen of hearts. What went wrong?

The problem is that the ace of hearts blocks your communication. The solution is to cash the ace of hearts *before* you run the spade suit. If you do so, you will reach this ending before you cash your last spade:

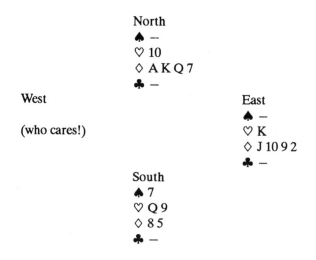

North
♠ —
♡ 10
♢ A K Q 7
♣ —

West

(who cares!)

East
♠ —
♡ K
♢ J 10 9 2
♣ —

South
♠ 7
♡ Q 9
♢ 8 5
♣ —

Now when you lead your last spade and throw a heart from dummy, East is really squeezed.

Any unblocking play to set up a squeeze, such as cashing the ace of hearts early in this deal, is called a "Vienna Coup."

The Double Squeeze

It is sometimes possible to squeeze both opponents.
For example:

#19

Contract: seven diamonds

Opening Lead: king of hearts

North
♠ K J 7 5 3
♡ J 8 2
♢ 6 4
♣ K 9 6

South
♠ A 4
♡ A
♢ A K Q J 10 9 8
♣ A 7 2

This is the last example and I could not quit without showing you one double squeeze. The ingredients needed are a threat card against each opponent and a common threat card against both opponents.

Your only possible losing trick is a club. Before thinking about a squeeze, you should test the spade suit; you may be able to establish a spade winner. Win the opening heart lead, draw trumps in three rounds, cash the ace and king of spades, and ruff a spade. No luck—West shows out on the third spade lead, so that plan did not work. At this stage, however, an expert would visualize that the contract can be made by a double squeeze.

Before explaining further, here are the four hands:

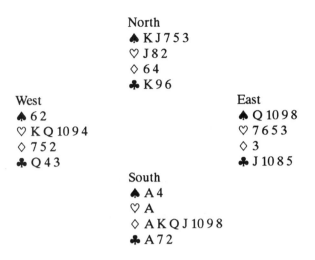

North
♠ K J 7 5 3
♡ J 8 2
◇ 6 4
♣ K 9 6

West
♠ 6 2
♡ K Q 10 9 4
◇ 7 5 2
♣ Q 4 3

East
♠ Q 10 9 8
♡ 7 6 5 3
◇ 3
♣ J 10 8 5

South
♠ A 4
♡ A
◇ A K Q J 10 9 8
♣ A 7 2

West's opening lead marked him with the queen of hearts, so the jack of hearts is a threat against West. East is known to have the queen of spades, so the jack of spades is a threat against East. The common threat is the third club in your hand. Cash two more diamonds to reach this four-card ending:

North
♠ J
♡ J
◇ —
♣ K 9

West
♠ —
♡ Q
◇ —
♣ Q 4 3

East
♠ Q
♡ —
◇ —
♣ J 10 8

South
♠ —
♡ —
◇ 10
♣ A 7 2

When you lead your last diamond, West is forced to throw a club (if he parts with the queen of hearts, dummy's jack is good); so dummy's jack of hearts is no longer of any use and you discard it. Now it is East's turn and he also must throw a club (if he parts with the queen of spades, dummy's jack is good). Both defenders are now down to two clubs, so you can win the last three club tricks. If you want to show off, lead the seven of clubs to the king, the nine of clubs to the ace, and claim the last trick with the *two* of clubs — the lowest card in the deck.

Quiz for Chapter Nine

1.
North
♠ A 9 6 4
♡ J 3 2
◇ 7
♣ A K J 10 8

South
♠ K Q J 10 8 7
♡ A
◇ A K Q
♣ 9 3 2

West	North	East	South
	1 ♣	Pass	1 ♠
Pass	2 ♠	Pass	4 NT
Pass	5 ♡	Pass	5 NT
Pass	6 ◇	Pass	7 ♠
All Pass			

West leads the king of hearts.

2.
North
♠ A Q 6 5
♡ A K 3
◇ 7 2
♣ 10 9 6 4

South
♠ K 2
♡ Q 7 6 4
◇ A 6 5 4 3
♣ A 3

West	North	East	South
			1 ◇
Pass	1 ♠	Pass	1 NT
Pass	3 NT	All Pass	

West wins the first trick with the king of diamonds, then leads the queen of diamonds and East discards the two of clubs.

3.
North
♠ 9 5
♡ 10 7 4
◇ A Q 2
♣ A Q J 6 3

South
♠ Q J 10
♡ K Q J 9 6 5 3
◇ J
♣ 10 7

West	North	East	South
		1 NT	2 ♡
Pass	4 ♡	All Pass	

West leads the two of spades and East wins the king. East then cashes the ace of spades and switches to the ace and another heart.

The one-notrump opening bid shows 16-18 points.

4.
North
♠ A 10 4
♡ A 5 3
◇ Q 7
♣ K 10 9 8 2

South
♠ K Q J 7 3
♡ K Q J 8
◇ 4
♣ A J 5

West	North	East	South
			1 ♠
Pass	2 ♣	Pass	2 ♡
Pass	3 ♠	Pass	4 NT
Pass	5 ♡	Pass	6 ♠
All Pass			

West leads the ace and another diamond.

5.

North
♠ A Q 7
♡ A K
◇ K Q 3 2
♣ K 9 6 3

South
♠ K J 10 9 8 4
♡ Q
◇ 6 4
♣ A 8 4 2

West	North	East	South
	2 NT	Pass	3 ♠
Pass	4 ♠	Pass	4 NT
Pass	5 ♡	Pass	6 ♠
All Pass			

West leads the jack of diamonds, dummy plays the queen, and East wins with the ace. East returns a diamond to dummy's king.

6.

North
♠ K Q 7 2
♡ Q 10 5
◇ 9 7 5
♣ 8 4 3

South
♠ A 6
♡ A K J 3 2
◇ J 8 4
♣ A Q 6

West	North	East	South
			1 ♡
Dbl	2 ♡	Pass	4 ♡
All Pass			

West leads the king, ace, and another diamond. East wins the third round with the queen and switches to the ten of clubs.

7.

North
♠ 10 7
♡ 9 6
◇ A 6 5 4 2
♣ A 5 4 3

South
♠ A K Q
♡ K J 10
◇ K J 8 3
♣ 10 6 2

West	North	East	South
1 ♡	Pass	Pass	Dbl
Pass	2 ◇	Pass	2 NT
Pass	3 NT	All Pass	

West leads the king, queen, and jack of clubs, and you win the third trick with the ace. East follows suit twice and then discards the two of spades.

8.

North
♠ K 9 6 5
♡ A 6 5
◇ A 5 3
♣ Q 4 3

South
♠ A Q J 10 4 3
♡ K Q 3
◇ J 7 6
♣ A

West	North	East	South
			1 ♠
Pass	3 ♠	Pass	4 ♣
Pass	4 ◇	Pass	6 ♠
All Pass			

West leads the king of diamonds.

Answers to Quiz for Chapter Nine

1.   North
                     ♠ A 9 6 4
                     ♡ J 3 2
                     ◇ 7
                     ♣ A K J 10 8
   West   East
   ♠ 3   ♠ 5 2
   ♡ K Q 10 5   ♡ 9 8 7 6 4
   ◇ J 9 8 6 2   ◇ 10 5 4 3
   ♣ 7 6 4   ♣ Q 5
                     South
                     ♠ K Q J 10 8 7
                     ♡ A
                     ◇ A K Q
                     ♣ 9 3 2

West	North	East	South
	1 ♣	Pass	1 ♠
Pass	2 ♠	Pass	4 NT
Pass	5 ♡	Pass	5 NT
Pass	6 ◇	Pass	7 ♠
All Pass			

   West leads the king of hearts.

Obviously you must avoid a club loser to make your grand slam. The normal percentage play with eight cards in a suit is to finesse for the queen, but in this case the finesse is unnecessary. The king-of-hearts lead marks West with the queen of hearts; if he also holds the queen of clubs, he can be squeezed. The squeeze is no better than the finesse if West actually has the queen of clubs, but it gives you the additional chance to make your bid if East has a doubleton queen.

After winning the first trick with the ace of hearts, draw trumps, and then ruff a heart (in case the queen falls). Now cash three diamonds and all but one of your trumps, leaving dummy with the jack of hearts and the ace-king-jack of clubs. When you cash your last spade, West must discard something besides the queen of hearts, in which case you will discard the jack of hearts from dummy. West no longer can have three clubs (one of his last three cards is the queen of hearts), so the club finesse can never gain. When you cash the ace and king of clubs, the queen will come tumbling down unless East has *three* clubs to the queen.

2.   North
                     ♠ A Q 6 5
                     ♡ A K 3
                     ◇ 7 2
                     ♣ 10 9 6 4
   West   East
   ♠ 9 8 3   ♠ J 10 7 4
   ♡ 5 2   ♡ J 10 9 8
   ◇ K Q J 10 9   ◇ 8
   ♣ Q J 8   ♣ K 7 5 2
                     South
                     ♠ K 2
                     ♡ Q 7 6 4
                     ◇ A 6 5 4 3
                     ♣ A 3

West	North	East	South
			1 ◇
Pass	1 ♠	Pass	1 NT
Pass	3 NT	All Pass	

   West wins the first trick with the king of diamonds. He leads the queen of diamonds at trick two and East discards the two of clubs.

You have eight winners and can win a ninth if hearts divide 3-3; but there is no hurry to test that suit. The best approach is to lose four tricks early to rectify the count, in case a squeeze develops.

Suppose you duck the second diamond trick and West continues to lead the suit (there is no way to beat the contract as the cards lie). You allow West to win the third and fourth diamond tricks as both dummy and East discard clubs.

West's play at trick five is immaterial, but suppose he leads a club to your ace. Everyone has eight cards left, and East still holds four hearts and four spades. A *sixth* minor-suit card must be led to execute the squeeze, so cash your ace of diamonds and discard dummy's last club. East must unguard one of the major suits and give you the contract-fulfilling ninth trick.

3.

North
- ♠ 9 5
- ♡ 10 7 4
- ◇ A Q 2
- ♣ A Q J 6 3

West
- ♠ 8 7 6 2
- ♡ 8
- ◇ 9 8 5 4 3
- ♣ 5 4 2

East
- ♠ A K 4 3
- ♡ A 2
- ◇ K 10 7 6
- ♣ K 9 8

South
- ♠ Q J 10
- ♡ K Q J 9 6 5 3
- ◇ J
- ♣ 10 7

West	North	East	South
		1 NT	2 ♡
Pass	4 ♡	All Pass	

West leads the two of spades and East wins the king. East then cashes the ace of spades and switches to the ace and another heart. The one-notrump opening bid shows 16-18 points.

Either minor-suit finesse is bound to fail—East must have both kings to justify his opening bid—so the only chance to make your bid is a squeeze. One threat card is the queen of diamonds. The other must be the *ten* of clubs, since you cannot have both threat cards in dummy if your are going to squeeze East.

You also have a communication problem. The ace of clubs is unnecessary as an entry, and it will block the suit—if the ten of clubs becomes a winner, you will not be able to get back to your hand. *Cash the ace of clubs* (the Vienna Coup) at trick five, then cash all of your major-suit winners. Your last two cards will be the jack of diamonds and ten of clubs; dummy will have the ace-queen of diamonds; and East cannot keep both the king-ten of diamonds and the king of clubs. He is squeezed and you will win the rest.

True, the contract can be made without cashing the ace of clubs early. Lead all of your major suit winners except for *one* heart, reducing dummy to the ace-queen-two of diamonds and ace of clubs. If East keeps the king-ten of diamonds and the king-nine of clubs, you can ruff out his king of diamonds. If he keeps the king-ten-seven of diamonds and the blank king of clubs, you can cash the ace of clubs. Unfortunately, you must *guess* what to do. If you cash the ace of clubs early, there is no need to guess.

4.

North
- ♠ A 10 4
- ♡ A 5 3
- ◇ Q 7
- ♣ K 10 9 8 2

West
- ♠ 9 2
- ♡ 7 6
- ◇ A 10 9 8 6
- ♣ Q 6 4 3

East
- ♠ 8 6 5
- ♡ 10 9 4 2
- ◇ K J 5 3 2
- ♣ 7

South
- ♠ K Q J 7 3
- ♡ K Q J 8
- ◇ 4
- ♣ A J 5

West	North	East	South
			1 ♠
Pass	2 ♣	Pass	2 ♡
Pass	3 ♠	Pass	4 NT
Pass	5 ♡	Pass	6 ♠
All Pass			

West leads the ace and another diamond.

You will make your bid if you guess which defender has the queen of clubs. You can make an *educated* guess if you find out how the spades and hearts divide before tackling the club suit.

After ruffing the second diamond lead, draw the trumps, then cash your heart winners. West shows out on the third lead of both suits. There is no way to count the diamond suit, so the best you can do is to calculate the odds with the information you have. West started with two spades and two hearts, so he has nine other cards. East started with three spades and four hearts, so he has six other cards. The odds are 9-to-6 (or 3-to-2) that West has the queen of clubs.

The percentage play is to cash the ace of clubs first—in case East has a singleton queen—and then to take the finesse through West.

5.   North
      ♠ A Q 7
      ♡ A K
      ◇ K Q 3 2
      ♣ K 9 6 3

West   East
♠ 6 3 2   ♠ 5
♡ J 9 7 6 5   ♡ 10 8 4 3 2
◇ J 10 9   ◇ A 8 7 5
♣ J 7   ♣ Q 10 5

      South
      ♠ K J 10 9 8 4
      ♡ Q
      ◇ 6 4
      ♣ A 8 4 2

West	North	East	South
	2 NT	Pass	3 ♠
Pass	4 ♠	Pass	4 NT
Pass	5 ♡	Pass	6 ♠
All Pass			

West leads the jack of diamonds, dummy plays the queen, and East wins with the ace. East returns a diamond to dummy's king.

6.   North
      ♠ K Q 7 2
      ♡ Q 10 5
      ◇ 9 7 5
      ♣ 8 4 3

West   East
♠ J 10 9 8   ♠ 5 4 3
♡ 4   ♡ 9 8 7 6
◇ A K 6 3   ◇ Q 10 2
♣ K J 5 2   ♣ 10 9 7

      South
      ♠ A 6
      ♡ A K J 3 2
      ◇ J 8 4
      ♣ A Q 6

West	North	East	South
			1 ♡
Dbl	2 ♡	Pass	4 ♡
All Pass			

West leads the king, ace, and another diamond. East wins the third round with the queen and switches to the ten of clubs.

You can discard a club on dummy's king of hearts, but that still leaves you with one club loser. The only chance is a squeeze, which will succeed if the defender with the long clubs has four or more diamonds.

Cash five rounds of trumps and discard two clubs from the dummy. Next lead a heart to dummy and *ruff* a diamond—the key play, as it creates dummy's fourth diamond as a threat card, which only East can protect as the cards lie. Now lead a club to dummy, and the three-card ending will be:

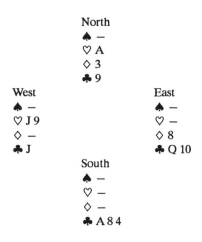

      North
      ♠ —
      ♡ A
      ◇ 3
      ♣ 9

West   East
♠ —   ♠ —
♡ J 9   ♡ —
◇ —   ◇ 8
♣ J   ♣ Q 10

      South
      ♠ —
      ♡ —
      ◇ —
      ♣ A 8 4

When you lead dummy's ace of hearts, East must part with the high diamond or a club and you will win the rest of the tricks.

Answer to Problem 6

Do *not* take the club finesse. West's takeout double indicates that he has the king of clubs and four spades; in which case you have a squeeze.

After winning with the ace of clubs, you must cash *all five trumps* to squeeze West. (Many of my students are reluctant to play their *last* trump; they treat it like an insurance policy, or their last dollar in the bank.) When you cash the fifth heart, West must come down to four cards. Since he cannot keep four spades and the king of clubs, you will win the crucial tenth trick with dummy's fourth spade or the queen of clubs.

7.

	North	
	♠ 10 7	
	♡ 9 6	
	◇ A 6 5 4 2	
	♣ A 5 4 3	
West		**East**
♠ J 9 4		♠ 8 6 5 3 2
♡ A Q 8 5 2		♡ 7 4 3
◇ 7		◇ Q 10 9
♣ K Q J 9		♣ 8 7
	South	
	♠ A K Q	
	♡ K J 10	
	◇ K J 8 3	
	♣ 10 6 2	

West	North	East	South
1 ♡	Pass	Pass	Dbl
Pass	2 ◇	Pass	2 NT
Pass	3 NT	All Pass	

West leads the king, queen, and jack of clubs, and you win the third trick with the ace. East follows suit twice and then discards the two of spades.

You need five diamond tricks to make your bid, so the challenge here is to count the other suits to figure out how the diamond suit will divide.

You already know nine of West's cards: You learned that he started with four clubs when East showed out on the third lead, and his opening one-heart bid marks him with at least five hearts. (Even if he were not playing "five-card majors," the normal opening bid with four hearts and four clubs is one club.) To learn more about West's hand, you should *cash your spade winners*. West follows suit three times, so he has at most one diamond.

In order to win five diamond tricks, you must be careful not to block the suit. Lead the *eight* of diamonds to dummy's ace, then take the marked finesse through East and collect your five diamond tricks.

8.

	North	
	♠ K 9 6 5	
	♡ A 6 5	
	◇ A 5 3	
	♣ Q 4 3	
West		**East**
♠ 8 7		♠ 2
♡ 10 9 2		♡ J 8 7 4
◇ K Q 10 8		◇ 9 4 2
♣ K 8 7 2		♣ J 10 9 6 5
	South	
	♠ A Q J 10 4 3	
	♡ K Q 3	
	◇ J 7 6	
	♣ A	

West	North	East	South
			1 ♠
Pass	3 ♠	Pass	4 ♣
Pass	4 ◇	Pass	6 ♠
All Pass			

West leads the king of diamonds.

Your only losers are two diamonds tricks. The opening lead marks West with the queen of diamonds. If he also has the king of clubs, you will have a squeeze — and that is your only good chance to make your bid. If you win the first trick, you will give up a critical entry to dummy, so *duck* the diamond lead. (This also rectifies the count, so you can win all but one of the remaining tricks.) Suppose West shifts to the ten of hearts (no other lead can beat you). You should draw trumps, cash the ace of clubs, cross to dummy, ruff a club (in case the king falls), and then lead the rest of your winners.

When you play your last spade, West will hold the queen-ten of diamonds and the king of clubs; dummy will have the ace-five of diamonds and the queen of clubs. Whatever West discards, dummy throws from the opposite suit. The rest of the tricks are yours.

10
The Throw-In Play

♣　◇　♡　♠　♣　◇　♡　♠

A throw-in play (also called an endplay) should be considered when you have a suit combination that is apt to produce more winning tricks if it is led by an opponent, or when you have ample trumps and will get a ruff and discard if an opponent leads a suit in which you and dummy are void.

The ingredients needed are a losing trick to concede the lead, and one or more losing tricks elsewhere — one of which you hope to avoid because of an opponent's lead.

In order for a throw-in play to succeed, you must first remove all safe exit cards from one or both opponents' hands. This process is called "stripping the hand." Then the opponent must lead a suit that will benefit you.

Throw In Either Opponent

#1

Contract: four spades

Opening Lead: king of diamonds

North
♠ 10 9 7 3 2
♡ Q 8 4
◇ A 3
♣ J 6 5

South
♠ A K Q 6 5
♡ A K J
◇ 9 2
♣ Q 4 3

You have one inevitable diamond loser and will be set if you lose three club tricks. The suit combination in clubs is one of many in which you will do better if the opponents lead it first.

Let's look at the four hands to get the picture:

North
♠ 109732
♡ Q84
♢ A3
♣ J65

West
♠ J4
♡ 1073
♢ KQ85
♣ A972

East
♠ 8
♡ 9652
♢ J10764
♣ K108

South
♠ AKQ65
♡ AKJ
♢ 92
♣ Q43

As long as the opponents adhere to the rules "second hand low" and "cover an honor with an honor," you will lose three club tricks if you lead the suit first. But if either defender leads a club, you will lose only two tricks.

You can throw the opponents on lead with a diamond, but *first* you must take away their safe exit cards. This is done by winning the first trick, drawing trumps, and cashing three rounds of hearts. Now lead the diamond. Whoever wins must lead a club for you, or give you a ruff and discard. Either way, you will lose only two club tricks and make your contract.

Here are some samples of suit combinations that you should avoid leading if you can induce an opponent to do so:

North	North	North	North
A J x	A J x	A 10 x	A 9 x

South	South	South	South
K 10 x	K 9 x	K 9 x	Q 8 x

North	North	North	North
A 10 x	Q x x	Q 9 x	J x x

South	South	South	South
J x x	K 10 9	K 8 x	K x x

Throw In One Opponent

Sometimes it is important that you lose the lead to one particular defender in order to gain a trick.

For example:

#2   North
                                            ♠ K J 7 6
                                            ♡ A 2
                                            ◊ K Q 3 2
Contract: six spades   ♣ 8 5 4

Opening Lead: queen of hearts   South
                                            ♠ A Q 10 8 4
                                            ♡ K 7
                                            ◊ A 7 4
                                            ♣ A Q 3

The only losers are two club tricks. The club finesse is an obvious chance, but reserve it as a last resort. Win the first trick with the king of hearts, draw trumps in three rounds, and cash three top diamonds to see how that suit divides. You were hoping for a 3-3 diamond split so you could discard a club, but East shows out on the third diamond. This is *good news*. You can make your contract without risking the club finesse – via a throw-in play.

Suppose this is the full deal:

                        North
                        ♠ K J 7 6
                        ♡ A 2
                        ◊ K Q 3 2
                        ♣ 8 5 4

West   East
♠ 3   ♠ 9 5 2
♡ Q J 10 4   ♡ 9 8 6 5 3
◊ J 10 9 8   ◊ 6 5
♣ K 7 6 2   ♣ J 10 9
                        South
                        ♠ A Q 10 8 4
                        ♡ K 7
                        ◊ A 7 4
                        ♣ A Q 3

You must complete the stripping process, so cash your ace of hearts. Now lead the last diamond from dummy and *discard the three of clubs*. When West wins the trick, he must lead a club into your ace-queen, or a heart which gives you a ruff and discard.

#3

North
♠ A K 4
♡ J 7 6 4
◇ A 2
♣ 6 5 3 2

Contract: six hearts

Opening Lead: jack of diamonds

South
♠ 8 2
♡ A K Q 10 8
◇ K 7 3
♣ A J 10

Unless West has the king and queen of clubs, you can make your bid by taking two club finesses. But if hearts divide favorably, you can guarantee your contract by executing a throw-in play.

Suppose the four hands are:

North
♠ A K 4
♡ J 7 6 4
◇ A 2
♣ 6 5 3 2

West
♠ J 10 9 3
♡ 5 2
◇ J 10 9 4
♣ K Q 7

East
♠ Q 7 6 5
♡ 9 3
◇ Q 8 6 5
♣ 9 8 4

South
♠ 8 2
♡ A K Q 10 8
◇ K 7 3
♣ A J 10

Win the first trick with the ace of diamonds, draw two rounds of trumps, strip out the spades (ruffing the third in your hand), and strip out the diamonds (ruffing the third in dummy). With the lead in dummy (important), the stage is set: Lead a club and finesse the ten, endplaying West. He must lead a club into your ace-jack, or give you a ruff and discard.

Note that the success of your throw-in play requires that you draw only *two* rounds of trumps, otherwise you will not have at least one trump left in each hand after stripping out the spades and diamonds—hence you cannot profit from a ruff and discard. The friendly 2-2 trump break makes it easy. Suppose instead that West shows out on the second heart lead. The recommended line of play will still succeed provided you do not draw the third trump and East cannot ruff one of your winners along the way. If West has more than two trumps, you must rely on the double finesse in clubs.

#4   North
                                            ♠ 10 6 3
                                            ♡ A J
                                            ◇ 8 7 5 4 2
Contract: four spades   ♣ A K 7

Opening Lead: king of hearts   South
                                            ♠ A K 8 7 5 4
                                            ♡ 9 2
                                            ◇ K 3
                                            ♣ Q 6 2

You win the first trick with the ace of hearts and cash the ace and king of spades, but West discards a low heart on the second spade. Before looking at the four hands, how would you play?

                                            North
                                            ♠ 10 6 3
                                            ♡ A J
                                            ◇ 8 7 5 4 2
                                            ♣ A K 7
        West   East
        ♠ 2   ♠ Q J 9
        ♡ K Q 7 3   ♡ 10 8 6 5 4
        ◇ A 10 9 6   ◇ Q J
        ♣ 9 8 5 4   ♣ J 10 3
                                            South
                                            ♠ A K 8 7 5 4
                                            ♡ 9 2
                                            ◇ K 3
                                            ♣ Q 6 2

You must lose a heart and a spade, so the object is not to lose two diamond tricks. You can manage this even if West has the ace of diamonds; he can be endplayed since he is marked with the queen of hearts by his opening lead. First cash the ace, king, and queen of clubs; then play a heart to put West on lead. If he leads a diamond, you will win a trick with the king; if he leads a heart or a club, you will ruff in dummy and discard a diamond from your hand.

#5

Contract: four hearts

Opening Lead: king of diamonds

North
♠ 7 6 4
♡ Q J 10 3
◇ A 10 8
♣ A K 9

South
♠ K 9
♡ A K 8 7 4
◇ 9 6 5
♣ Q 3 2

West	North	East	South
	1 ♣	Pass	1 ♡
1 ♠	2 ♡	Pass	4 ♡
All Pass			

You have four losers (two spades and two diamonds), and prospects are gloomy because the bidding makes it probable that West has the ace of spades. Nevertheless, you can make the contract by endplaying West if the diamonds are divided favorably.

Here is a layout in which the contract is makable:

North
♠ 7 6 4
♡ Q J 10 3
◇ A 10 8
♣ A K 9

West
♠ A Q J 10 3
♡ 9 5
◇ K Q
♣ J 8 7 6

East
♠ 8 5 2
♡ 6 2
◇ J 7 4 3 2
♣ 10 5 4

South
♠ K 9
♡ A K 8 7 4
◇ 9 6 5
♣ Q 3 2

Win the first trick with the ace of diamonds, draw trumps in two rounds, and cash three club tricks so West cannot lead those suits safely. Then exit with a diamond to throw West on lead. West must play a spade to establish your king, or his last club to give you a ruff and discard.

It was fortunate to find the diamonds divided so that East could not gain the lead to play a spade through your king; but you had nothing to lose by trying the throw-in play. Note also that you would succeed if West held any number of diamonds including the king-queen-jack.

In the next deal, you must time your plays carefully to preserve your chances for a throw-in play.

#6   North
                                                ♠ J 10
                                                ♡ Q 8 6 5 3
                                                ◇ 7 5 2
Contract: four hearts   ♣ A K 9

Opening Lead: king of spades   South
                                                ♠ A 3
                                                ♡ A K 9 7 4
                                                ◇ A Q 6
                                                ♣ 8 5 2

With an obvious loser in spades and clubs, the fate of this hand depends on holding your diamond losers to one. The challenge is to make your bid when West has the king of diamonds, and this can be done. How? You guessed it – by a throw-in play. The stripping process, however, is a bit tricky.

Suppose these are the four hands:

```
                        North
                        ♠ J 10
                        ♡ Q 8 6 5 3
                        ◇ 7 5 2
                        ♣ A K 9
    West                                      East
    ♠ K Q 9 4                                 ♠ 8 7 6 5 2
    ♡ J 2                                     ♡ 10
    ◇ K 8 3                                   ◇ J 10 9 4
    ♣ J 7 6 3                                 ♣ Q 10 4
                        South
                        ♠ A 3
                        ♡ A K 9 7 4
                        ◇ A Q 6
                        ♣ 8 5 2
```

Win the first trick with the ace of spades, draw trumps, then play the ace, king, and another club. Assume East wins with the queen and leads the jack of diamonds (if he leads a spade, West is endplayed immediately). You must *win with the ace*; otherwise, another diamond lead will set you. Now lead your spade. West must win the trick and he has no safe exit card – a diamond lead will establish your queen, and anything else gives you a ruff and discard.

Forcing a Ruff and Discard

Sometimes you do not have a suit combination that will benefit from a lead by an opponent. In that event, the only way to gain a trick by a throw-in play is to force an opponent to give you a "ruff and a sluff." [1] Note the following two deals:

#7

Contract: six hearts

Opening Lead: king of diamonds

	North
	♠ A Q 5
	♡ K 9 7 3
	◊ A 10
	♣ A K Q 2
	South
	♠ K 10 3
	♡ A 8 6 5 2
	◊ 4
	♣ 8 7 4 3

The slam is easily made if trumps divide 2-2, or if clubs divide 3-2. Suppose you start by winning with the ace of diamonds and cashing the ace and king of hearts. West discards a diamond on the second heart lead, so East has a sure heart trick. *Before testing the club suit*, you should ruff the ten of diamonds in your hand and cash three spade tricks. Now cash your high clubs and you can make your bid even if West has four or five clubs.

With the cards as follows, this line of play is necessary.

	North	
	♠ A Q 5	
	♡ K 9 7 3	
	◊ A 10	
	♣ A K Q 2	
West		East
♠ 8 6 2		♠ J 9 7 4
♡ J		♡ Q 10 4
◊ K Q 9 7 3		◊ J 8 6 5 2
♣ J 10 9 5		♣ 6
	South	
	♠ K 10 3	
	♡ A 8 6 5 2	
	◊ 4	
	♣ 8 7 4 3	

If East ruffs the second or third club, he must give you a ruff and discard. If East does not ruff one of your clubs, just throw him on the lead with a *trump* to achieve the same ending.

---

1. A "ruff and a sluff" is a slangy (but popular) term for a "ruff and discard." Both mean exactly the same thing.

Note that if you did not ruff the ten of diamonds and cash three spade tricks before cashing more than one high club, East could ruff the second club and exit safely. West eventually would get a club trick to set you.

#8   North
                                         ♠ Q 9 6 5
                                         ♡ A 10 8 7
                                         ◇ A K 8
Contract: six spades   ♣ 7 3

Opening Lead: queen of hearts   South
                                         ♠ A K J 10 8 7
                                         ♡ 6 4 3 2
                                         ◇ 7
                                         ♣ A K

You can discard one of your heart losers on the king of diamonds, but that still leaves you with two losers. Win the first trick with the ace of hearts, as East follows with the five. The opening lead suggests that West has the jack of hearts and East the king. If so, the heart suit is blocked and the opponents cannot cash two heart tricks due to a lack of communication. You can make your bid by forcing the opponents to yield a ruff and discard.

Here is a probable layout:

                          North
                          ♠ Q 9 6 5
                          ♡ A 10 8 7
                          ◇ A K 8
                          ♣ 7 3
        West   East
        ♠ 3   ♠ 4 2
        ♡ Q J 9   ♡ K 5
        ◇ 10 9 5 4   ◇ Q J 6 3 2
        ♣ Q J 8 6 2   ♣ 10 9 5 4
                          South
                          ♠ A K J 10 8 7
                          ♡ 6 4 3 2
                          ◇ 7
                          ♣ A K

Draw two rounds of trumps and strip the North-South hands of clubs and diamonds. Then lead a heart to put East on lead. East must play a club or a diamond, and you will discard the last heart from your hand and ruff in dummy.

It gets more interesting if West chooses a different opening lead. Suppose he selects a club originally (instead of the queen of hearts). Your best play is to lead a heart to the ace at trick *two*. In order to defeat you, West must play the *nine* and East must unblock the *king*—otherwise you will make your bid by playing as above. The reason for leading a heart early is to make it difficult for a defender to unblock. If you draw trumps and strip the hand first, the opponents are more likely to visualize the heart situation and defend correctly.

Guarding Against a Bad Break

Sometimes a throw-in play can be used as a precaution to guard against a bad break in a side suit.

Here are two examples:

#9   North
                            ♠ Q 9 8 3
                            ♡ 9 6
                            ♢ A K 10 7

Contract: four spades   ♣ A 4 2

Opening Lead: two of diamonds   South
                            ♠ A K J 10 2
                            ♡ Q 7
                            ♢ 6 5 4 3
                            ♣ K 8

You should suspect that the two-of-diamonds lead is a singleton. If so, East must hold ♢ Q J 9 8 and you have two diamond losers. Your plan should be to avoid one of these losers by a throw-in play.

Suppose these are the four hands:

	North	
	♠ Q 9 8 3	
	♡ 9 6	
	♢ A K 10 7	
	♣ A 4 2	
West		East
♠ 7 6 5		♠ 4
♡ K J 8 5 2		♡ A 10 4 3
♢ 2		♢ Q J 9 8
♣ J 10 9 3		♣ Q 7 6 5
	South	
	♠ A K J 10 2	
	♡ Q 7	
	♢ 6 5 4 3	
	♣ K 8	

Win the first trick with the ace of diamonds, draw three rounds of trumps, and strip the clubs by cashing the king and ace, and ruffing the third round. Now lead a heart and allow the opponents to win their two heart tricks. If West wins the second heart, he must give you a ruff and discard. So suppose East wins the second heart and leads the queen of diamonds. If you win this trick, you must lose two diamond tricks. So the winning play is to *duck*. East is endplayed, forced either to lead a diamond from his jack-nine into dummy's king-ten, or to give you a ruff and discard.

Note that the contract cannot be made if the defense begins by cashing two heart tricks; then you would not have a heart to lead for the throw-in play.

#10	North
	♠ K Q 10 3
	♡ 8 5
	◇ A 8 5 4
Contract: six spades	♣ K 9 6
Opening Lead: queen of hearts	South
	♠ A J 9 7 6
	♡ A 2
	◇ K Q 7 3
	♣ A 8

You must lose a heart trick, so the contract hinges on avoiding a diamond loser. There is no problem if diamonds divide 3-2, so you should consider the possible 4-1 breaks. If either defender has J 10 9 x, the future is dismal; but if the jack, ten, or nine is singleton, you can make the contract by a throw-in play.

Suppose this is the layout:

	North	
	♠ K Q 10 3	
	♡ 8 5	
	◇ A 8 5 4	
	♣ K 9 6	
West		East
♠ 4		♠ 8 5 2
♡ Q J 10 3		♡ K 9 7 6 4
◇ J 9 6 2		◇ 10
♣ 7 5 4 2		♣ Q J 10 3
	South	
	♠ A J 9 7 6	
	♡ A 2	
	◇ K Q 7 3	
	♣ A 8	

Win the first trick with the ace of hearts, draw three rounds of trumps ending in dummy, and lead a diamond to your king. (The advantage of leading from dummy is that East may play the nine from J 10 9 x.) *Do not play any more diamonds.* Now strip the clubs—ace, king, and a ruff—and exit with a heart. If West wins the heart and leads any diamond, you can pick up the suit without loss by playing low from the dummy. If East wins the heart (or if West returns anything but a diamond), you will obtain a ruff and discard.

Note that the key play is to cash exactly one diamond honor (king or queen) before the throw-in. If you do anything else, you will be defeated by any 4-1 diamond split.

Multiple Tenace Positions

Sometimes you have more than one suit in which a trick can be gained from a lead by an opponent.

The next two deals illustrate this:

#11	**North**
	♠ 7 6
	♡ 8 4 2
	◊ K J 8 7 5
Contract: six diamonds	♣ A K 5
Opening Lead: ten of clubs	**South**
	♠ A Q 9
	♡ A K J
	◊ A Q 10 4 2
	♣ 6 3

If West has the king of spades and the queen of hearts, you will be set if you try both finesses; but that would be a foolish line of play. You can make the contract even if both finesses fail.

Suppose this is the layout:

```
                  North
                  ♠ 7 6
                  ♡ 8 4 2
                  ◊ K J 8 7 5
                  ♣ A K 5
   West                            East
   ♠ K J 4 2                       ♠ 10 8 5 3
   ♡ Q 7 5 3                       ♡ 10 9 6
   ◊ 9 6                           ◊ 3
   ♣ 10 9 8                        ♣ Q J 7 4 2
                  South
                  ♠ A Q 9
                  ♡ A K J
                  ◊ A Q 10 4 2
                  ♣ 6 3
```

The plan is to endplay West, but first you must remove his safe exit cards. Win the first trick with the ace of clubs, draw two rounds of trumps, cash the king of clubs, and ruff dummy's last club in your hand. Now play a third round of trumps to reach the dummy, and lead a spade toward your hand. If East plays low, finesse the *nine* (else cover the ten with your queen), and West will be endplayed; he must return a spade or a heart into one of your tenaces.

#12   North
                                        ♠ A 10 9 4
                                        ♡ A 9 6
                                        ♢ A 9 4
Contract: two spades   ♣ J 7 2

Opening Lead: queen of hearts   South
                                        ♠ K J 6 3
                                        ♡ 7 5 2
                                        ♢ K 10 5
                                        ♣ Q 8 4

There are seven possible losers (one spade, two hearts, one diamond, and three clubs), so you must eliminate two losers to make your bid. This time there are *three* suit combinations that you would like to have the opponents lead: spades, diamonds, and clubs. The best procedure is a throw-in play at *trick two*. Win with the ace of hearts and lead a heart right back.

Suppose the four hands are:

                            North
                            ♠ A 10 9 4
                            ♡ A 9 6
                            ♢ A 9 4
                            ♣ J 7 2
        West   East
        ♠ 8 5   ♠ Q 7 2
        ♡ Q J 10 8   ♡ K 4 3
        ♢ Q 8 2   ♢ J 7 6 3
        ♣ A 9 6 5   ♣ K 10 3
                            South
                            ♠ K J 6 3
                            ♡ 7 5 2
                            ♢ K 10 5
                            ♣ Q 8 4

Assume the opponents cash their two heart tricks, then West leads a trump. This solves your guess in spades, so draw the outstanding trumps. Now you are ready for a second throw-in play to guarantee your contract: Cash the ace and king of diamonds, and then lead a third diamond. No matter which opponent wins the trick, he must lead a club or give you a ruff and discard. In either case you will lose only two club tricks.

Choosing Your Victim

Sometimes you will have an option to throw in either defender, in which case you must decide which play is more likely to gain a trick.

For example:

#13

Contract: six spades

Opening Lead: nine of hearts

North
♠ A 9 7 5 4
♡ K 4 3
◇ K Q 10
♣ Q 2

South
♠ K Q J 8 3
♡ A 6 2
◇ A 7 6
♣ A 5

Hands with "mirror distribution" (exactly the same shape) are usually troublesome. Note that if either hand contained a doubleton heart or diamond (instead of a doubleton club), the contract would be cold. As it is, you have a losing heart and a losing club, so there is work to be done.

The first step is to draw trumps, and then to cash your heart and diamond winners. This turns out to be revealing: West shows out on the second lead in both spades and hearts, and East shows out on the third round of diamonds. You have learned the exact distribution of three suits, so now you can count the hand. West started with one spade, one heart, five diamonds, and therefore six clubs; East started with two spades, six hearts, two diamonds, and therefore three clubs.

You have two options for a throw-in play: If you think East has the king of clubs, play a heart and force him to lead a club from the king or give your a ruff and discard. If you think West has the king of clubs, play the ace and another club to force him to give you a ruff and discard.

Before looking at the four hands, which play would you choose?

North
♠ A 9 7 5 4
♡ K 4 3
◇ K Q 10
♣ Q 2

West
♠ 10
♡ 9
◇ J 9 8 5 2
♣ K 10 8 7 4 3

East
♠ 6 2
♡ Q J 10 8 7 5
◇ 4 3
♣ J 9 6

South
♠ K Q J 8 3
♡ A 6 2
◇ A 7 6
♣ A 5

As you can see, West has the king of clubs, so the winning choice is to throw West on lead by playing the ace and another club. Logically, the player who was dealt the greater number of clubs is more likely to have the king. You learned that West began with six clubs and East only three, so the odds are 6-to-3 (2-to-1) that West has the king.

Throw-In for a Trump Lead

In Chapter 6 you read about trump endplays when you know the exact enemy trump holding. In the next deal the strategy is to execute an endplay without knowing anything about the trump division.

#14   North
                                                ♠ K 9 2
                                                ♡ 8 7 5 4
                                                ◇ K 7 6 3
Contract: four spades   ♣ Q 10

Opening Lead: king of hearts   South
                                                ♠ A 10 8 5 4
                                                ♡ 6 3
                                                ◇ A 9 2
                                                ♣ A K J

West	North	East	South
			1 ♠
2 ♡	2 ♠	Pass	4 ♠
All Pass			

West leads the king, ace, and queen of hearts. On the third round, East discards a low club and you ruff with the four of spades. It appears that you must lose a diamond trick, so your goal is to avoid a spade loser. If you lead spades yourself, you will be set routinely unless you are lucky and find either West with a singleton honor (if you cash the king and West drops an honor, the percentages favor finessing East for the other honor), or East with a doubleton queen-jack. A better chance is to strip the hand *without* leading any trumps, and then to throw the opponents on lead with a diamond.

Suppose these are the four hands:

                                North
                                ♠ K 9 2
                                ♡ 8 7 5 4
                                ◇ K 7 6 3
                                ♣ Q 10
West   East
♠ Q 7   ♠ J 6 3
♡ A K Q J 9   ♡ 10 2
◇ Q 4   ◇ J 10 8 5
♣ 9 8 6 3   ♣ 7 5 4 2
                                South
                                ♠ A 10 8 5 4
                                ♡ 6 3
                                ◇ A 9 2
                                ♣ A K J

After ruffing the third heart lead, cash three top clubs and two top diamonds with the lead ending up in the *dummy*. Here is the end position:

```
                        North
                        ♠ K 9 2
                        ♡ 8
                        ◊ 7
                        ♣ —
      West                              East
      ♠ Q 7                             ♠ J 6 3
      ♡ J 9                             ♡ —
      ◊ —                               ◊ J 10
      ♣ 9                               ♣ —
                        South
                        ♠ A 10 8 5
                        ◊ —
                        ◊ 9
                        ♣ —
```

Lead the eight of hearts from dummy. Suppose East discards the ten of diamonds (if he ruffs, you can overruff and avoid a trump loser), and you ruff with the five of spades. Now exit with the nine of diamonds. Whether West ruffs or lets East win with the jack, you can win the rest of the tricks as long as you play for the spade honors to be divided.

Throw-In for an Entry

#15

Contract: six hearts

Opening Lead: nine of diamonds

North
♠ K Q J 7
♡ 9 6 3
◊ J 8 5 4
♣ K 10

South
♠ A
♡ A K Q J 4 2
◊ A 7 6 3 2
♣ A

The only diamonds you cannot see are the king, queen, and ten. Since West would not lead the nine of diamonds if he held any of those cards, he must have a singleton. Therefore, East has two natural diamond tricks. The only chance to make your bid is to get to dummy and discard four diamonds on the high spades and clubs. This will be easy if the ten of hearts drops, so win the ace of diamonds and cash *two* high hearts. No luck — East shows out on the second round.

Here are the four hands:

North
♠ K Q J 7
♡ 9 6 3
◇ J 8 5 4
♣ K 10

West   East
♠ 10 6 4 3   ♠ 9 8 5 2
♡ 10 8 5   ♡ 7
◇ 9   ◇ K Q 10
♣ Q 9 8 7 2   ♣ J 6 5 4 3

South
♠ A
♡ A K Q J 4 2
◇ A 7 6 3 2
♣ A

It is now impossible to reach dummy from your own hand, but you can get there with West's help. After cashing the two black aces, lead a *low heart* to endplay West. He must win with his ten and lead a spade or a club.

#16   North
                                       ♠ 5 4 2
                                       ♡ 8 7 5 3
                                       ◇ A 10 4
Contract: six spades   ♣ Q J 9

Opening Lead: king of clubs   South
                                       ♠ A K Q J 10 9
                                       ♡ A K 4 2
                                       ◇ K Q J
                                       ♣ —

Your only losers are two heart tricks, and there is no problem if that suit divides 3-2. Ruff the opening lead, draw trumps in three rounds, and cash the ace and king of hearts. West shows out on the second heart lead. Since East has two high hearts, the only chance now is to establish a club trick in dummy (so you can discard a heart loser); but you do not have enough entries to do this on your own. Again, you must enlist West's help.

Here are the four hands:

                          North
                          ♠ 5 4 2
                          ♡ 8 7 5 3
                          ◇ A 10 4
                          ♣ Q J 9

West   East
♠ 3   ♠ 8 7 6
♡ 6   ♡ Q J 10 9
◇ 9 8 7 6 3 2   ◇ 5
♣ A K 10 8 5   ♣ 7 6 4 3 2

                          South
                          ♠ A K Q J 10 9
                          ♡ A K 4 2
                          ◇ K Q J
                          ♣ —

If West has the ace of clubs, as his opening lead suggests, you can make this contract by a throw-in play. Cash the king of diamonds, then lead the queen of diamonds, and *overtake* with dummy's ace. Now lead the queen of clubs and *discard the jack of diamonds*. If West takes his ace of clubs, he must put you back in dummy and you will discard both of your heart losers on the jack of clubs and ten of diamonds. If West refuses to win with his ace of clubs, the lead remains in the dummy and you can discard one of your losing hearts on the ten of diamonds.

Throw-In at Notrump

Throw-in plays may occur at any contract (although they are ill-advised in a grand slam). Obviously, when a throw-in play occurs at a notrump contract, a ruff and discard is not possible; the sole purpose is to force an opponent to lead into one of your suit combinations.

Here are two examples:

#17   North
                                  ♠ Q 10 4
                                  ♡ 9 5 2
                                  ◇ A Q 6 3
Contract: three notrump   ♣ K 8 7

Opening Lead: four of hearts   South
                                  ♠ K J 3
                                  ♡ A Q 8
                                  ◇ 10 9 7 4
                                  ♣ A Q J

West	North	East	South
		1 ♡	1 NT
Pass	3 NT	All Pass	

You have six winners (two hearts, one diamond, and three clubs), and you can develop two more by driving out the ace of spades. The bidding marks East with all of the missing high cards, so the diamond finesse will surely fail. The best chance for a ninth trick is a throw-in play to force East to lead a diamond into dummy's ace-queen.

After winning the first trick by capturing East's ten of hearts with your queen, lead a spade. Assume East wins with the ace and leads the king of hearts to your ace, as West discards a low spade. You now know that East started with six hearts. Cash your spade and club winners to see what else you can learn. East discards a diamond on the third spade lead and a heart on the third club lead. So East began with six hearts, two spades, two clubs, and therefore three diamonds. Here is the complete deal:

```
                        North
                        ♠ Q 10 4
                        ♡ 9 5 2
                        ◇ A Q 6 3
                        ♣ K 8 7
West                                         East
♠ 9 7 6 5 2                                  ♠ A 8
♡ 4                                          ♡ K J 10 7 6 3
◇ 8 5                                        ◇ K J 2
♣ 10 6 4 3 2                                 ♣ 9 5
                        South
                        ♠ K J 3
                        ♡ A Q 8
                        ◇ 10 9 7 4
                        ♣ A Q J
```

Since East discarded one diamond and one heart, his last five cards must be three hearts and two diamonds. *Lead your losing heart.* After East cashes his heart winners, he must lead a diamond into dummy's ace-queen.

Note that if East's two discards were both diamonds, the winning play would be to cash the ace of diamonds and drop his blank king.

#18

Contract: three notrump

Opening Lead: king of spades

```
                        North
                        ♠ 8 7 6 3
                        ♡ 5 4
                        ◇ A Q J 5 4
                        ♣ 8 2

                        South
                        ♠ A 10 5
                        ♡ A Q 2
                        ◇ K 9 7 3
                        ♣ A Q 6
```

West	North	East	South
			1 ◇
1 ♠	2 ◇	Pass	3 NT
All Pass			

After you hold up your ace of spades at trick one, West continues with the queen of spades, East discards a heart, and you win with the ace. You have eight winners, and the ninth must come from winning a trick with the queen of hearts or the queen of clubs. Which finesse should you take? The answer is *neither* because a throw-in play is available.

Suppose these are the four hands:

North
♠ 8 7 6 3
♡ 5 4
♢ A Q J 5 4
♣ 8 2

West
♠ K Q J 9 4
♡ K 8
♢ 10 2
♣ K 9 7 3

East
♠ 2
♡ J 10 9 7 6 3
♢ 8 6
♣ J 10 5 4

South
♠ A 10 5
♡ A Q 2
♢ K 9 7 3
♣ A Q 6

As you can see, both finesses fail; but the contract can still be made. Your plan is to throw West on lead with the third round of spades (he cannot win enough spade tricks to set you), so he will have to lead a heart or a club into one of your ace-queen combinations. But first, you must *remove his safe exit cards*.

The correct play is to cash *two* (or three) diamond tricks and then lead a spade. As West cashes his remaining spades, discard one low heart and one low club from your hand. West must then give you your ninth trick.

Note that the contract is in jeopardy if you cash five diamond tricks before leading a spade. West's best defense would be to hold on to all of his spades and unguard one of his kings. You can still make the contract if you guess what to do. But suppose you misguess? The recommended play avoids any guesswork.

Quiz for Chapter Ten

1.
North
♠ A K 5
♡ K 10 8
◇ 7 4
♣ Q 9 6 3 2

South
♠ 4
♡ A 9 4 3
◇ A 8 2
♣ A K J 7 5

West	North	East	South
			1 ♣
Pass	3 ♣	Pass	6 ♣
All Pass			

West leads the queen of diamonds.

2.
North
♠ Q 8 7 6
♡ 7 6 3
◇ 8 7 5 2
♣ 10 4

South
♠ A K
♡ A 9 4
◇ A K Q 9
♣ A Q 6 2

West	North	East	South
			3 NT
All Pass			

West leads the five of hearts and East plays the queen. If you hold up your ace, East will return the ten of hearts.

3.
North
♠ A Q 8 7 2
♡ 3 2
◇ Q 5 4
♣ A 6 5

South
♠ K 10 9 6 4 3
♡ A Q
◇ J 7 2
♣ K 8

West	North	East	South
			1 ♠
Pass	3 ♠	Pass	4 ♠
All Pass			

West leads the jack of clubs.

4.
North
♠ A J 6 4
♡ K 9 6 3
◇ A K 7
♣ Q 2

South
♠ K Q 10 9 8 2
♡ 8 5 2
◇ 3 2
♣ A 5

West	North	East	South
	1 NT	Pass	3 ♠
Pass	4 ♠	All Pass	

West leads the jack of clubs.

5.

	North		
	♠ K 7 3		
	♡ K 10 9 2		
	◇ A K 4		
	♣ Q J 8		

	South		
	♠ Q 10 2		
	♡ A Q J 8 5		
	◇ 7 6		
	♣ 10 9 3		

West	North	East	South
1 ♠	1 NT	Pass	3 ♡
Pass	4 ♡	All Pass	

West leads the king, ace, and another club; East follows suit throughout.

6.

	North		
	♠ K Q 9 8		
	♡ A 5 3		
	◇ 6 4 2		
	♣ K Q 7		

	South		
	♠ A J 10 6 5 2		
	♡ Q		
	◇ A Q 5		
	♣ A 4 3		

West	North	East	South
			1 ♠
Pass	3 ♠	Pass	6 ♠
All Pass			

West leads the jack of clubs.

7.

	North		
	♠ A 2		
	♡ A Q 8 5 3 2		
	◇ 7 5 3		
	♣ 6 4		

	South		
	♠ 4		
	♡ K J 9 7 6		
	◇ A K J 8		
	♣ A Q 2		

West	North	East	South
			1 ♡
1 ♠	3 ♡	Pass	4 NT
Pass	5 ♡	Pass	6 ♡
All Pass			

West leads the king of spades.

8.

	North		
	♠ 10 9 8 7		
	♡ K Q 2		
	◇ A K		
	♣ 7 5 3 2		

	South		
	♠ A K 6 3 2		
	♡ A 4		
	◇ 5 3		
	♣ A K 8 4		

West	North	East	South
			1 ♠
Pass	3 ♠	Pass	4 ♣
Pass	4 ◇	Pass	6 ♠
All Pass			

West leads the jack of diamonds. When you cash the ace and king of spades, East discards a diamond on the second round.

Answers to Quiz for Chapter Ten

1.

```
                North
                ♠ A K 5
                ♡ K 10 8
                ◊ 7 4
                ♣ Q 9 6 3 2
West                            East
♠ Q 9 8 3                       ♠ J 10 7 6 2
♡ J 6 5                         ♡ Q 7 2
◊ Q J 10 6                      ◊ K 9 5 3
♣ 10 4                          ♣ 8
                South
                ♠ 4
                ♡ A 9 4 3
                ◊ A 8 2
                ♣ A K J 7 5
```

West	North	East	South
			1 ♣
Pass	3 ♣	Pass	6 ♣
All Pass			

West leads the queen of diamonds.

The success of this contract hinges on whether or not you lose a heart trick, and your chances are slim unless you can induce the opponents to lead the suit for you. This is an ideal situation for a throw-in play.

Win the first trick with the ace of diamonds, draw trumps in two rounds, cash the ace and king of spades (discarding a *diamond*), and ruff dummy's last spade. The hands are now stripped, so exit with a diamond. The defender who wins the trick must lead a heart, or give you a ruff and discard; in either case, you can win the rest of the tricks.

2.

```
                North
                ♠ Q 8 7 6
                ♡ 7 6 3
                ◊ 8 7 5 2
                ♣ 10 4
West                            East
♠ 5 4 3                         ♠ J 10 9 2
♡ K J 8 5 2                     ♡ Q 10
◊ J 10 6                        ◊ 4 3
♣ K 7                          ♣ J 9 8 5 3
                South
                ♠ A K
                ♡ A 9 4
                ◊ A K Q 9
                ♣ A Q 6 2
```

West	North	East	South
			3 NT
All Pass			

West leads the five of hearts and East plays the queen. If you hold up your ace, East will return the ten of hearts.

If diamonds break 3-2, you have eight winners in your hand; but there is no way to get to dummy's queen of spades. The best chance to make your bid is to endplay West. To do this, you must *win the second heart trick* (if you duck, the contract is hopeless — West will win the trick and lead a third heart). Next cash the ace and king of spades and three (or four) diamonds to remove West's safe exit cards. Now lead your last heart. After West cashes his heart tricks, he must put you in dummy with the queen of spades, or lead a club into your ace-queen.

3.

```
              North
              ♠ A Q 8 7 2
              ♡ 3 2
              ◇ Q 5 4
              ♣ A 6 5
West                        East
♠ J                         ♠ 5
♡ K 10 8 6 4                ♡ J 9 7 5
◇ A 9 3                     ◇ K 10 8 6
♣ J 10 9 2                  ♣ Q 7 4 3
              South
              ♠ K 10 9 6 4 3
              ♡ A Q
              ◇ J 7 2
              ♣ K 8
```

West	North	East	South
			1 ♠
Pass	3 ♠	Pass	4 ♠
All Pass			

West leads the jack of clubs.

The suit combination in diamonds should be familiar: If an opponent leads it first, you will lose only two tricks; if you lead it first, you probably will lose three tricks. The contract is ironclad if you ignore the heart finesse and use the queen of hearts to endplay whoever has the king.

Win the first trick with the king of clubs, draw trumps, cash the ace of clubs, ruff a club in your hand, cash the ace of hearts, and lead the queen of hearts. As the cards lie, West will win with the king, and then he must either break the diamond suit or give you a ruff and discard.

Observe that the contract can be set if you take the heart finesse. West can win with the king and return a *heart*, forcing you to break the diamond suit. The heart finesse is a sucker play. If it fails, you may be set; if it works, you will most likely win the same number of tricks as you can with the endplay.

4.

```
              North
              ♠ A J 6 4
              ♡ K 9 6 3
              ◇ A K 7
              ♣ Q 2
West                        East
♠ 5                         ♠ 7 3
♡ J 10 4                    ♡ A Q 7
◇ Q J 9 6                   ◇ 10 8 5 4
♣ J 10 9 8 6                ♣ K 7 4 3
              South
              ♠ K Q 10 9 8 2
              ♡ 8 5 2
              ◇ 3 2
              ♣ A 5
```

West	North	East	South
	1 NT	Pass	3 ♠
Pass	4 ♠	All Pass	

West leads the jack of clubs.

West is unlikely to lead a club away from the king, so presumably East has it. If so, the contract is assured without risking the heart finesse; you can endplay East provided you play a *low* club from dummy and win with the ace.

After drawing the enemy trumps and stripping the hands of diamonds, exit with a club. East will win with the king and must lead a heart or give you a ruff and discard.

Note that if you play the queen of clubs on the first trick, you cannot make the contract whether you win with the ace or duck. The opponents will eventually win a club and three hearts.

5.

	North		
	♠ K 7 3		
	♡ K 10 9 2		
	◇ A K 4		
	♣ Q J 8		

West		East	
♠ A J 9 6 5		♠ 8 4	
♡ 7 4		♡ 6 3	
◇ J 8 3		◇ Q 10 9 5 2	
♣ A K 4		♣ 7 6 5 2	

	South		
	♠ Q 10 2		
	♡ A Q J 8 5		
	◇ 7 6		
	♣ 10 9 3		

West	North	East	South
1 ♠	1 NT	Pass	3 ♡
Pass	4 ♡	All Pass	

West leads the king, ace and another club; East follows suit throughout.

6.

	North		
	♠ K Q 9 8		
	♡ A 5 3		
	◇ 6 4 2		
	♣ K Q 7		

West		East	
♠ 7		♠ 4 3	
♡ K J 6 4 2		♡ 10 9 8 7	
◇ K 10 9		◇ J 8 7 3	
♣ J 10 9 8		♣ 6 5 2	

	South		
	♠ A J 10 6 5 2		
	♡ Q		
	◇ A Q 5		
	♣ A 4 3		

West	North	East	South
			1 ♠
Pass	3 ♠	Pass	6 ♠
All Pass			

West leads the jack of clubs.

You can make your bid if you do not lose two spade tricks, but the normal play of finessing East for the jack should be rejected. Since West opened the bidding with one spade, he is much more likely to have the jack. West cannot be finessed out of his jack, but you can endplay him with the proper technique.

Draw two rounds of trumps, cash the ace and king of diamonds, ruff a diamond in your hand, and lead a heart to dummy. Now lead a spade to your *queen*—the key play. West can win only one spade trick: If he takes the queen with the ace, he must lead away from his jack; if he ducks the queen, you still have the king behind his ace.

If the king of diamonds is offside, you can still make this contract by endplaying West if either the diamonds divide favorably or there is a defensive error. The first step is to strip the hand. The best sequence of plays is this: Win the first trick with the ace of clubs, draw two rounds of trumps, cash the ace of hearts, ruff a heart, lead a club to the dummy, ruff the last heart, and lead a club to the dummy. Now play a diamond toward your hand, intending to duck. There is a fair chance that West will win the trick, either because his diamonds are all higher than East's, or (more likely) because East routinely plays "second hand low." Note that, with the diamond division in the diagram, East would have to play the *jack* to hold the lead and beat the contract.

If, when you lead the diamond from dummy, East plays a high diamond that you think will win the trick if you duck, there is an optional line of play that guards against West holding a doubleton king: Win with the ace of diamonds, return to dummy with a trump, and lead a diamond with the intention of putting up the queen unless East plays the king. If West began with a doubleton king, he will have to yield a ruff and discard.

7.

	North		
	♠ A 2		
	♡ A Q 8 5 3 2		
	◊ 7 5 3		
	♣ 6 4		
West		**East**	
♠ K Q J 7 5		♠ 10 9 8 6 3	
♡ 4		♡ 10	
◊ Q 10 9 4		◊ 6 2	
♣ K 10 3		♣ J 9 8 7 5	
	South		
	♠ 4		
	♡ K J 9 7 6		
	◊ A K J 8		
	♣ A Q 2		

West	*North*	*East*	*South*
			1 ♡
1 ♠	3 ♡	Pass	4 NT
Pass	5 ♡	Pass	6 ♡
All Pass			

West leads the king of spades.

There are three obvious chances to avoid losing a club and a diamond: the diamond finesse, a 3-3 diamond break, or the club finesse. If you try all three (diamonds first, of course) and fail, it would be bad luck—and bad play. A good player would see the throw-in play against West and make his bid without risk.

Win with the ace of spades, ruff a spade in your hand, and draw trumps ending in dummy. Now lead a diamond and finesse the *eight*; let West win the trick with the nine or ten. Whether West leads a diamond or a club into one of your tenaces, or a spade to give you a ruff and discard, you have the rest of the tricks.

Note that if East held the nine or ten of diamonds and played it when you led the diamond from dummy, you could achieve the same result by covering with the jack.

8.

	North		
	♠ 10 9 8 7		
	♡ K Q 2		
	◊ A K		
	♣ 7 5 3 2		
West		**East**	
♠ Q J 4		♠ 5	
♡ J 7 6 3		♡ 10 9 8 5	
◊ J 10 9 8		◊ Q 7 6 4 2	
♣ 9 6		♣ Q J 10	
	South		
	♠ A K 6 3 2		
	♡ A 4		
	◊ 5 3		
	♣ A K 8 4		

West	*North*	*East*	*South*
			1 ♠
Pass	3 ♠	Pass	4 ♣
Pass	4 ◊	Pass	6 ♠
All Pass			

West leads the jack of diamonds. When you cash the ace and king of spades, East discards a diamond on the second round.

West has a natural spade trick, so you cannot afford a club loser. Things appear gloomy. One of your club losers can be discarded on the third heart, but what about the other? Your only chance is to find West with two clubs or fewer; then you can endplay him and get a ruff and discard. Since West was dealt three spades to East's one, West is likely to be shorter than East in clubs. The odds are in your favor.

Cash your remaining diamond winner and three rounds of hearts. Next cash the ace and king of clubs, and lead a spade. West must win and lead a heart or a diamond, which you will ruff in dummy while you discard the last club from your hand.

11
Deception and Psychology

♣　　♢　　♡　　♠　　♣　　♢　　♡　　♠

Many contracts are made as a result of defensive errors. A good declarer is deceptive and reveals as little information as possible when he plays a hand. As a result, the defenders are given more problems and are more apt to make mistakes.

Many contracts hinge on making a winning guess. A good declarer analyzes the habits of the defenders to obtain clues. He knows that poor defenders are more reliable than good defenders because they "tip their mitt" by the tempo of their plays; they seldom false-card, or do anything to baffle the declarer.

The purpose of this chapter can be summarized as making deceptive plays to help the defenders do the *wrong* thing, and analyzing the defenders' plays to help you do the *right* thing.

False-carding

#1

Contract: four spades

Opening Lead: king of hearts

```
                    North
                    ♠ J 7 6 3
                    ♡ J 8 2
                    ◇ A Q 4
                    ♣ 9 5 2

                    South
                    ♠ A K Q 10 2
                    ♡ Q 5
                    ◇ K 9
                    ♣ K J 10 3
```

West	North	East	South
			1 ♠
Double	2 ♠	Pass	4 ♠
All Pass			

If the opponents do not take their two heart tricks immediately, you will be able to discard your second heart on the third round of diamonds and make your bid even if you lose two club tricks. The play to discourage West from cashing the ace of hearts is to drop the *queen* to give the impression that you have a singleton.

Suppose this is the full deal:

```
                        North
                        ♠ J 7 6 3
                        ♡ J 8 2
                        ◇ A Q 4
                        ♣ 9 5 2
        West                            East
        ♠ 5                             ♠ 9 8 4
        ♡ A K 10 4                      ♡ 9 7 6 3
        ◇ J 10 8 3                      ◇ 7 6 5 2
        ♣ A Q 7 6                       ♣ 8 4
                        South
                        ♠ A K Q 10 2
                        ♡ Q 5
                        ◇ K 9
                        ♣ K J 10 3
```

West will almost surely lead the ace of hearts at trick two if you play the five on the first trick, but he may decide to lead the jack of diamonds if you drop the queen. Note that cashing the ace of hearts would give you the contract if you held

♠ A K Q 10 4 2 ♡ Q ◇ 9 2 ♣ K J 10 3,

or a similar hand (you could discard a diamond on the jack of hearts). The false-card does give West a legitimate problem.

#2

Contract: four hearts

Opening Lead: five of spades

```
                        North
                        ♠ J 7 6 4 3
                        ♡ K 9 4
                        ◇ A K
                        ♣ 5 3 2

                        South
                        ♠ K 2
                        ♡ A Q J 10 6 3
                        ◇ 4
                        ♣ A 9 7 4
```

West	North	East	South
		1 ♠	2 ♡
Pass	3 ♡	Pass	4 ♡
All Pass			

The bidding makes it clear that West has led a singleton, and the contract is likely to fail if East gives West a spade ruff at trick two. If you play the two of spades on the first trick, East will know that his partner has led a singleton (West would not lead the five from king-five). The play to confuse East is to drop the *king* of spades under the ace. East probably will conclude that West led from the five-two, in which case a spade return at trick two will allow you to obtain a discard on dummy's jack.

Here is a predictable layout:

North
♠ J 7 6 4 3
♡ K 9 4
◇ A K
♣ 5 3 2

West
♠ 5
♡ 8 7 2
◇ J 9 8 5 3 2
♣ 10 8 6

East
♠ A Q 10 9 8
♡ 5
◇ Q 10 7 6
♣ K Q J

South
♠ K 2
♡ A Q J 10 6 3
◇ 4
♣ A 9 7 4

If East is clairvoyant and sees through your false-card, he can beat the contract by returning a *low* spade. But in the real world, you can expect East to lead a club, and then you will make your bid by discarding your losing spade on the king of diamonds.

#3

Contract: four spades

Opening Lead: ace of clubs

North
♠ A Q 5
♡ K Q J 10 4
◇ 7 3 2
♣ Q 8

South
♠ K J 10 9 3
♡ A
◇ Q 9 6
♣ K 9 3 2

West	North	East	South
			1 ♠
Pass	2 ♡	Pass	2 ♠
Pass	4 ♠	All Pass	

East plays the seven of clubs on the first trick, and West must decide whether to lead a club or a diamond at trick two. Which club should you play from your hand to encourage West to continue leading clubs?

Suppose these are the four hands:

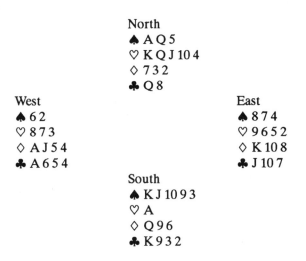

North
♠ A Q 5
♡ K Q J 10 4
◇ 7 3 2
♣ Q 8

West
♠ 6 2
♡ 8 7 3
◇ A J 5 4
♣ A 6 5 4

East
♠ 8 7 4
♡ 9 6 5 2
◇ K 10 8
♣ J 10 7

South
♠ K J 10 9 3
♡ A
◇ Q 9 6
♣ K 9 3 2

You should play the *nine* of clubs. West may think that East has the two and three (perhaps K 7 3 2), in which case he will judge East's seven to be a come-on signal. If you were to play the two or three of clubs, West is more likely to read the seven as a discouraging signal and make the killing switch to a low diamond.

False-carding tip: When you want to *encourage* your left-hand opponent to continue leading a suit, usually play the card that is closest to, *but above*, the card played by your right-hand opponent. For example, if East plays the six, your best false-card from K 9 7 2 is the *seven* (not the nine). The logic is that East would play the seven from any seven-six combination if he were giving an encouraging signal. Hence, West already knows you have the seven; so if you play the nine, he will know you are false-carding.

#4

North
♠ Q 9 6
♡ K 10 3 2
◇ J 7 4
♣ 8 5 3

Contract: four hearts

Opening Lead: king of spades

South
♠ 8 7 5 2
♡ A Q J 9 8
◇ K Q 10
♣ A

West	North	East	South
			1 ♡
1 ♠	2 ♡	Pass	4 ♡
All Pass			

On the first trick, East plays the four of spades, which you know to be a singleton, but West does not. You can make your bid if West does not give his partner a spade ruff, so your goal is to *discourage* West from leading a spade at trick two. Which spade should you play from your hand?

Here is the full deal:

<pre>
                              North
                              ♠ Q 9 6
                              ♡ K 10 3 2
                              ◇ J 7 4
                              ♣ 8 5 3
          West   East
          ♠ A K J 10 3   ♠ 4
          ♡ 4   ♡ 7 6 5
          ◇ 9 6 5   ◇ A 8 3 2
          ♣ Q J 7 2   ♣ K 10 9 6 4
                              South
                              ♠ 8 7 5 2
                              ♡ A Q J 9 8
                              ◇ K Q 10
                              ♣ A
</pre>

You should play the *two* of spades. West will then recognize the four to be East's lowest card – the one he would normally play to discourage the continuation of the suit. Since another spade lead could cost a trick if East held three or four spades, West may decide to switch suits.

If you play any spade but the two on the first trick, West is likely to continue spades; he will think that East may have played the four from four-two doubleton.

When you want to *discourage* your left-hand opponent from continuing the suit led, do *not* false-card if you hold a card that is lower than the card played by your right-hand opponent.

Winning with the Right Card

#5   North
                                                 ♠ Q J 9
                                                 ♡ A 6 5
                                                 ◇ A J 9
Contract: four spades   ♣ K J 10 2

Opening Lead: two of hearts   South
                                                 ♠ K 10 8 6 2
                                                 ♡ K Q 9
                                                 ◇ Q 7
                                                 ♣ 9 8 3

West	*North*	*East*	*South*
	1 NT	Pass	3 ♠
Pass	4 ♠	All Pass	

Three notrump is the best contract, but you have reached four spades. On the first trick you play a low heart from dummy and East plays the jack. If you win with the queen,

West will know that you also have the king (East would not play the jack from king-jack). The deceptive play is to win with the *king*. West cannot tell who has the queen, and he might conclude East has it. This play could decide your fate on a layout such as:

```
                    North
                    ♠ Q J 9
                    ♡ A 6 5
                    ◊ A J 9
                    ♣ K J 10 2
    West                            East
    ♠ A 7 3                         ♠ 5 4
    ♡ 10 8 4 2                      ♡ J 7 3
    ◊ 10 6 5                        ◊ K 8 4 3 2
    ♣ 6 5 4                         ♣ A Q 7
                    South
                    ♠ K 10 8 6 2
                    ♡ K Q 9
                    ◊ Q 7
                    ♣ 9 8 3
```

You win the second trick by leading a spade to dummy's queen, and then play the jack of spades, which West wins with the ace. At this point, West must lead a *diamond* to beat the contract (otherwise you will have time to establish dummy's fourth club and discard your losing diamond). But how does West know this? If East has the queen of hearts instead of the king of diamonds, the winning play is to lead another heart. No one knows what a defender might do, but winning the first trick with the king of hearts gives West an option to do the wrong thing.

Note that it would not help to win the first trick with the ace of hearts. East would play the three as a discouraging signal, and then West would know not to lead another heart. The only play to deceive West is to capture the jack with the king.

#6

Contract: three notrump

Opening Lead: four of spades

```
                    North
                    ♠ 8 7
                    ♡ 9 5
                    ◊ K Q J 10 8 6
                    ♣ A 4 3

                    South
                    ♠ A K 5
                    ♡ K 8 4
                    ◊ 7 3 2
                    ♣ K Q J 5
```

If East has the ace of diamonds and West has the ace of hearts, this contract is in jeopardy—East may shift to a heart when he wins with the ace of diamonds. You would like to persuade East to return a spade (his partner's suit) so you will have eleven easy tricks. On the first trick East plays the jack of spades, and you must decide whether it will be more deceptive to win with the ace or the king.

Suppose this is the full deal:

<pre>
                              North
                              ♠ 8 7
                              ♡ 9 5
                              ◇ K Q J 10 8 6
                              ♣ A 4 3
West   East
♠ Q 10 6 4 3   ♠ J 9 2
♡ A 7 3 2   ♡ Q J 10 6
◇ 5 4   ◇ A 9
♣ 10 6   ♣ 9 8 7 2
                              South
                              ♠ A K 5
                              ♡ K 8 4
                              ◇ 7 3 2
                              ♣ K Q J 5
</pre>

When East gets the lead with his ace of diamonds, he should realize that the diamond suit will provide enough tricks for you to make your bid; so his only chance to beat the contract is to win the next four tricks. As the cards lie, he must lead a heart. But if South's spades and hearts are reversed, he must lead a spade. How can East tell which to lead?

Suppose you win the first trick with the ace of spades. East should judge that you have another spade stopper because you would hold up your ace with A x x. This reasoning suggests that the only chance is that West has the ace of hearts, so a thoughtful East would switch to the queen of hearts and beat the contract.

The correct play is to win the first trick with the *king* of spades. East then has no clue to indicate that he should lead a heart. He probably will return his partner's suit, which would be correct if you started with K x x or K Q x in spades.

There is no general rule as to which of equal honors you should win. You must judge each case individually, with the basic intention of concealing your actual holding from the defenders.

In the next deal, you must decide which card to win from *unequal* honors.

#7

<pre>
                              North
                              ♠ 10 9 8
                              ♡ Q 4
                              ◇ Q J 10 9 3
Contract: three notrump   ♣ K J 5

Opening Lead: three of spades   South
                              ♠ A Q
                              ♡ 8 6 3
                              ◇ A 8 7 2
                              ♣ A Q 4 3
</pre>

You have received a favorable lead and can win eleven tricks if the diamond finesse works — but if it *fails*, the opponents can run the heart suit and set you. On the first trick, East plays the jack of spades. Now is the time for subterfuge: You should win with the *ace* to give West the impression that East has the queen of spades.

Suppose these are the four hands:

                           North
                           ♠ 10 9 8
                           ♡ Q 4
                           ◇ Q J 10 9 3
                           ♣ K J 5
        West   East
        ♠ K 7 6 3 2   ♠ J 5 4
        ♡ A 5 2   ♡ K J 10 9 7
        ◇ K 4   ◇ 6 5
        ♣ 10 8 6   ♣ 9 7 2
                           South
                           ♠ A Q
                           ♡ 8 6 3
                           ◇ A 8 7 2
                           ♣ A Q 4 3

After winning the first trick with the ace of spades, lead a club to the king, and take the diamond finesse. When West wins with the king of diamonds, he will almost surely lead a low spade, expecting his partner to win with the queen. Then you will make your bid with an overtrick.

It should be fun to see the shocked look on West's face when you produce the queen. You might tell him: "I pulled the wrong card. I meant to play the queen on the first trick."

Note that if you win the first trick with the queen of spades, West will know you have the ace. He will reason that a heart switch is the only chance to beat the contract, and you will be set two tricks.

Tempting a Defender to Cover an Honor

#8   North
                                 ♠ Q 7 6 3
                                 ♡ 8 7 5 2
                                 ◇ 10 9 8
Contract: four spades   ♣ A Q

Opening Lead: king of diamonds   South
                                 ♠ J 10 9 8 5 2
                                 ♡ K Q
                                 ◇ A 4
                                 ♣ K J 4

You have four losers and the only chance to make your bid is to eliminate one of your trump losers; that is, you must hope for a defensive error. A good tactic would be to lead the queen of spades from dummy, hoping to crash the enemy trump honors. East will be put to the test if the spades are divided as follows:

```
                              North
                              ♠ Q 7 6 3
                              ♡ 8 7 5 2
                              ◇ 10 9 8
                              ♣ A Q
        West                                      East
        ♠ A                                       ♠ K 4
        ♡ 9 6 4 3                                 ♡ A J 10
        ◇ K Q 2                                   ◇ J 7 6 5 3
        ♣ 10 8 7 5 3                              ♣ 9 6 2
                              South
                              ♠ J 10 9 8 5 2
                              ♡ K Q
                              ◇ A 4
                              ♣ K J 4
```

Win the first trick with the ace of diamonds, play a club to the dummy, and lead the queen of spades. East must play his low spade to set you, but many players are brainwashed into thinking it is always right to cover an honor with an honor. East probably will cover with the king and have his regrets when his partner plays the ace on the same trick.

Technically, it is wrong for East to cover in this situation. He would gain by covering if West has J x and South A 10 9 8 x; but in that event, the correct play by declarer is not to lead the queen, but to cash the *ace* (see the note following illustration 12 on page 9).

#9

Contract: six hearts

Opening Lead: jack of diamonds

```
                              North
                              ♠ A Q 9
                              ♡ K J 5
                              ◇ A 8 7 3
                              ♣ Q 6 2

                              South
                              ♠ 3
                              ♡ A Q 10 9 8 7 4
                              ◇ 6 5
                              ♣ A J 10
```

You have two losers: one diamond and one club. If you take the club finesse and it fails, you will be set. If you try the spade finesse (to discard your losing diamond) and it fails, you will be set. Therefore, you have only a 50-50 chance to make your bid if you try one finesse or the other.

The way to improve the odds is to give the opponents a chance to help you. Win the first trick with the ace of diamonds, draw the trumps, and lead the *queen* of clubs from dummy. If East covers with the king, your problem is solved. A vast majority of players, experts included, would cover the queen of clubs if they held the king; in this case, it is the normal play. If East does not cover the queen of clubs, you should be confident that he does not have the king. Since the club finesse is bound to lose, go up with the ace and take the spade finesse.

Suppose this is the layout:

North
♠ A Q 9
♡ K J 5
◇ A 8 7 3
♣ Q 6 2

West
♠ K 8 6 5 4
♡ 6
◇ J 10 2
♣ K 8 7 3

East
♠ J 10 7 2
♡ 3 2
◇ K Q 9 4
♣ 9 5 4

South
♠ 3
♡ A Q 10 9 8 7 4
◇ 6 5
♣ A J 10

Since West has the king of spades, you will make your bid. The recommended line of play will cost you the contract only if East has both black kings and does not cover the queen of clubs when you lead it.

Tempting a Defender to Play Second Hand Low

#10

North
♠ K 8 5 2
♡ Q 10 7 2
◇ A
♣ Q 6 4 3

Contract: three notrump

Opening Lead: six of diamonds

South
♠ A 6
♡ K 5 3
◇ Q 9 4
♣ A K J 9 2

West	North	East	South
			1 NT
Pass	2 ♣	Pass	2 ◇
Pass	3 NT	All Pass	

You have eight winners and need one heart to make your bid. The contract is in jeopardy if West has the king of diamonds and East has the ace of hearts, but even then East must win the *first* heart trick to set you. The best way to discourage East from playing the ace of hearts is to lead a low heart from dummy at trick two.

Suppose these are the four hands:

North
♠ K 8 5 2
♡ Q 10 7 2
◇ A
♣ Q 6 4 3

West
♠ 9 7 4
♡ 9 4
◇ K 10 8 6 3
♣ 10 7 5

East
♠ Q J 10 3
♡ A J 8 6
◇ J 7 5 2
♣ 8

South
♠ A 6
♡ K 5 3
◇ Q 9 4
♣ A K J 9 2

East can beat the contract by going up with the ace of hearts and leading a diamond. But he probably will play "second hand low" since he doesn't know that you need only one heart trick or that you have no other diamond stopper. If you run five club tricks before leading a heart, East is more likely to see the need to grab the ace of hearts and lead a diamond.

#11

Contract: four spades

Opening Lead: king of hearts

North
♠ J 10 8 4
♡ 9 7 5 2
◇ 6
♣ K J 10 8

South
♠ A K Q 7 6
♡ 4
◇ K Q J 10 9
♣ 3 2

West	*North*	*East*	*South*
			1 ♠
Pass	2 ♠	Pass	4 ♠
All Pass			

West wins the first trick with the king of hearts and leads a second heart, which you ruff. Your plan is to drive out the ace of diamonds and discard dummy's clubs on the diamond suit. The defense you are worried about is West winning with the ace of diamonds and leading a club, subjecting you to two club losers before you regain the lead.

You can increase your chance of success by leading the *nine* of diamonds from your hand *before* drawing trumps.

Suppose this is the layout:

North
♠ J 10 8 4
♡ 9 7 5 2
♢ 6
♣ K J 10 8

West
♠ 5 2
♡ K Q J 3
♢ A 8 5 4
♣ 9 7 6

East
♠ 9 3
♡ A 10 8 6
♢ 7 3 2
♣ A Q 5 4

South
♠ A K Q 7 6
♡ 4
♢ K Q J 10 9
♣ 3 2

Diamonds have not been bid and West may decide to duck his ace, expecting his partner to be able to beat the nine; you must admit the actual diamond situation is extraordinary. Even if West wins with the ace, a club shift is not obvious. He may think you are planning to ruff losing diamonds, so he may lead a trump to cut down your ruffs in dummy; or he may lead another heart.

From an expert standpoint, West should realize that you are destined to make this contract unless East can win two tricks in the black suits. Therefore, he should win with the ace of diamonds and lead a club to cater to the actual layout. But there is a big difference between what an opponent *should* do and what he *does* do; you have nothing to lose and everything to gain by your deceptive play.

Tempting a Defender to Play Second Hand High

#12

North
♠ Q J 7 4
♡ K Q
♢ K Q 6 3
♣ 10 9 5

Contract: six spades

Opening Lead: queen of clubs

South
♠ A K 10 9 8 5 3
♡ J 10 2
♢ —
♣ A 6 2

West	North	East	South
			1 ♠
Pass	3 ♠	Pass	6 ♠
All Pass			

It is unlucky that partner has the king-queen of diamonds instead of the king-queen of clubs, but here you are in a nearly hopeless slam. The only chance to make your bid is to discard *two* club losers on the diamond suit; hence, you must force out the ace of diamonds without wasting the king or queen. The situation that offers a glimmer of hope is to find East with the ace of diamonds (but not the jack), as in the following layout:

```
                        North
                        ♠ Q J 7 4
                        ♡ K Q
                        ◇ K Q 6 3
                        ♣ 10 9 5
    West                                    East
    ♠ 2                                      ♠ 6
    ♡ A 7 6 3                                ♡ 9 8 5 4
    ◇ J 9 7 5                                ◇ A 10 8 4 2
    ♣ Q J 8 4                                ♣ K 7 3
                        South
                        ♠ A K 10 9 8 5 3
                        ♡ J 10 2
                        ◇ —
                        ♣ A 6 2
```

Win the first trick with the ace of clubs, play a spade to dummy, and lead a *low* diamond. If East puts up his ace, you will ruff and then be able to discard two club losers on the king and queen. You cannot make the contract if East plays low, but this is your only chance. If you lead the king or queen of diamonds first, you can never make your contract.

Note that East has a legitimate problem. If you held the singleton jack of diamonds and one fewer club, you would play the same way. A good defender would reason that a void suit is more likely because of your gambling six-spade bid (with a singleton diamond, it would be foolish to bid a slam without investigation). East may analyze this correctly and play a low diamond, but at least you gave him a chance to go wrong.

Tempting a Defender Not to Ruff

#13   North
                                            ♠ 10 7 6 2
                                            ♡ A 4
                                            ◇ K J 10 5
Contract: four spades   ♣ 8 6 3

Opening Lead: queen of clubs   South
                                            ♠ A K 8 4
                                            ♡ 9 6 2
                                            ◇ A Q 7
                                            ♣ A 9 5

You allow West to win the first trick, but he persists with the jack of clubs to your ace. Next you cash the ace and king of spades and both opponents follow suit. You must lose one spade and one heart, so your only chance is to discard your remaining club loser on the fourth round of diamonds. If the player with the high trump has three or more diamonds, the contract is safe. But suppose the cards are as shown below:

North
♠ 10 7 6 2
♡ A 4
◇ K J 10 5
♣ 8 6 3

West
♠ 5 3
♡ K 10 8 3
◇ 9 8 4 2
♣ Q J 10

East
♠ Q J 9
♡ Q J 7 5
◇ 6 3
♣ K 7 4 2

South
♠ A K 8 4
♡ 9 6 2
◇ A Q 7
♣ A 9 5

When you lead the third round of diamonds, East can ruff and cash his club trick. If you could entice East *not* to ruff the third diamond, you can discard a club on the fourth diamond and make your contract. You must be deceptive in your play of the diamond suit.

The proper technique is to cash the ace of diamonds, lead a *low* diamond to dummy's *king*, and then lead the jack or ten of diamonds. East has not seen the queen, so he may conclude that his partner has it and not ruff. If so, you will win with the queen, return to dummy with the ace of hearts, and discard a club on the fourth diamond.

Discouraging the Defenders from Leading a Suit

#14

Contract: three notrump

Opening Lead: two of clubs

North
♠ J 7 4
♡ 10 5
◇ K 10 7 3
♣ K J 9 8

South
♠ 10 9 3
♡ Q J 6
◇ A Q J 2
♣ A Q 7

Pushing to three notrump with these cards is clear overbidding, and you appear to be in an impossible contract. You have eight winners and the only chance for a ninth is to establish a heart trick. But you have no spade stopper. If you go after your heart trick directly, or cash your winners first, the opponents surely will shift to spades and set you.

The best chance is to encourage the opponents to lead hearts for you. To do this, you must discourage them from leading spades by *leading spades yourself*. Win the first trick with the jack of clubs, and lead dummy's four of spades to your ten.

Suppose the four hands are:

<pre>
                          North
                          ♠ J 7 4
                          ♡ 10 5
                          ◊ K 10 7 3
                          ♣ K J 9 8
        West   East
        ♠ A Q 8   ♠ K 6 5 2
        ♡ A 4 2   ♡ K 9 8 7 3
        ◊ 9 5 4   ◊ 8 6
        ♣ 10 6 3 2   ♣ 5 4
                          South
                          ♠ 10 9 3
                          ♡ Q J 6
                          ◊ A Q J 2
                          ♣ A Q 7
</pre>

When West wins the second trick with the queen of spades, he is unlikely to lead another spade. In view of dummy, he probably will switch to hearts; as soon as you win a heart trick, you will scamper home with nine tricks.

The spades may be divided in such a way that the opponents can see through your deception, in which case you will probably be set an extra trick. But it is surprising how often this scheme works—and it is the only realistic chance to make your contract.

Reading Defensive Carding

#15   North
                                  ♠ K 10 5 4
                                  ♡ K Q 9 2
                                  ◊ K 5
Contract: four spades   ♣ 8 6 3

Opening Lead: king of clubs   South
                                  ♠ A Q 9 6
                                  ♡ A 5
                                  ◊ A Q 8 2
                                  ♣ J 7 4

West wins the first three tricks with top clubs and then leads the ten of diamonds; East follows suit throughout. The contract is safe if trumps divide 3-2; but if either defender has J x x x, you must guess how to play. If you think West is more likely to have four spades, your first two plays should be the ace and queen. If you think East is more likely to have four spades, you should win with the ace (or queen) and then the king.

You dare not play the side suits to find out how they divide (one of your winners may get ruffed), so you must use other means to decide which player is more likely to have four spades. Suppose you win with the king of diamonds at trick four and lead a spade to the ace; East plays the seven and West the two. Which spade honor should you play next?

The following logic assumes you are playing against average players: If spades are 4-1, either East has played the seven from J 8 7 3 or West the two from J 8 3 2. You should assume that East would not play the seven from J 8 7 3 and therefore does not have the four spades, so your second spade play should be the *queen*.[1]

Suppose this is the full deal:

```
                      North
                      ♠ K 10 5 4
                      ♡ K Q 9 2
                      ◇ K 5
                      ♣ 8 6 3
       West                              East
       ♠ J 8 3 2                         ♠ 7
       ♡ 7 6 4                           ♡ J 10 8 3
       ◇ 10 9 3                          ◇ J 7 6 4
       ♣ A K Q                           ♣ 10 9 5 2
                      South
                      ♠ A Q 9 6
                      ♡ A 5
                      ◇ A Q 8 2
                      ♣ J 7 4
```

If East and West are experts, the above logic does not hold. Experts know how and when to false-card, and they vary their tactics so a clever declarer cannot gain by analyzing their plays. Consequently, declarer is left with little more than a guess in most situations of this kind. For example, in the above diagram, West's first spade play might be the *eight*. Then declarer knows that *someone* is false-carding (probably with J x x x), but he cannot tell who.

#16

Contract: six notrump

Opening Lead: eight of clubs

```
                      North
                      ♠ K Q 10
                      ♡ K J 2
                      ◇ K 10 8
                      ♣ A Q 10 3

                      South
                      ♠ 4 3 2
                      ♡ A Q 9
                      ◇ A Q 6
                      ♣ K J 9 7
```

You have ten winners and the only chance to make the slam is to win two spade tricks. If you lead spades toward dummy twice, you will make your bid if West has the ace and

---

1. You may think that many players would play the seven from J 8 7 3, but *this is not true*. I have run this test with thousands of students and a vast majority always play their lowest card; they virtually never false-card. But after they read this book, look out!

jack, but you will be set if East has both honors. If the ace and jack are divided (West has one and East the other), then you will have to guess how to play.

You may decide to cash some side winners first, but eventually you lead a low spade: West plays low, you call for dummy's king, and East plays low. Next you play another suit to get to your hand, lead a second spade, and West plays low again. Now you must guess. If West has the ace, you must put up the queen; if West has the jack, you must finesse the ten.

Here is the layout:

```
                         North
                         ♠ K Q 10
                         ♡ K J 2
                         ◇ K 10 8
                         ♣ A Q 10 3
         West                              East
         ♠ ? 6 5                           ♠ ? 9 8 7
         ♡ 10 5 3                          ♡ 8 7 6 4
         ◇ J 7 5 4                         ◇ 9 3 2
         ♣ 8 4 2                           ♣ 6 5
                         South
                         ♠ 4 3 2
                         ♡ A Q 9
                         ◇ A Q 6
                         ♣ K J 9 7
```

It may seem like a pure guess whether to play the ten or queen, but maybe not. Consider that one defender has played well so far by concealing his ace. If one defender is a much better player than the other, play him for the ace: If West is better, go up with the queen; if East is better, finesse the ten.

Another possible clue is the tempo. The player with the ace may have thought for a while before deciding to play a low spade, while the player with the jack had no problem and played without pause. Declarer is entitled to take advantage of a defender's hesitation; but *he does so at his own risk*. Not all players are completely honest (that might be the understatement of the year); an unethical player might violate the proprieties of the game and hesitate when he has no problem, just to mislead you. Therefore, to be a good guesser, you also must be a good psychologist; you must judge whether you are playing against an honest player or one whose ethics are suspect.

Let me tell you about a very good player with whom I used to play a lot of rubber bridge for high stakes. When defending a hand, he always would hesitate if he had no problem, and he was clever enough not to hesitate if he did have a problem. For example, if he held the ace in the above hand, he would play a low spade very smoothly to give the impression that he did not have the ace; the card would float out of his hand. To the contrary, if he did not have the ace, he would hesitate very briefly and maybe fumble with the cards before playing a low spade. His hesitation was not long enough that anyone could formally complain about his ethics, but he was clearly dishonest because his actions were meant to mislead the declarer. He always did these things — he could not help himself — so his larcenous behavior made him an open book for a good psychologist.

Quiz for Chapter Eleven

1.

	North
	♠ A 7 6
	♡ K 7 5
	◇ A Q 4
	♣ 10 8 3 2

	South
	♠ K 2
	♡ A 8 4
	◇ K 9 8 3
	♣ Q J 9 5

West	North	East	South
	1 ♣	Pass	2 NT
Pass	3 NT	All Pass	

West leads the five of spades and you allow East to win with the ten. East leads the jack of spades at trick two and West plays the four.

2.

	North
	♠ 9 8 5
	♡ A Q J
	◇ 10 4 2
	♣ J 8 6 3

	South
	♠ K 4
	♡ K 5 3
	◇ A 8 7
	♣ A K 10 9 2

West	North	East	South
			1 NT
Pass	2 NT	Pass	3 NT
All Pass			

West leads the six of diamonds and East plays the queen.

3.

	North
	♠ 7 5 2
	♡ K J 3
	◇ A K Q J 10
	♣ J 8

	South
	♠ J 10 9
	♡ A Q 10 8 6
	◇ 2
	♣ K 6 4 3

West	North	East	South
	1 ◇	Pass	1 ♡
Pass	2 ♡	Pass	4 ♡
All Pass			

West leads the ace of clubs and East plays the five.

4.

	North
	♠ A J 7 3
	♡ J 10 2
	◇ A 8
	♣ K J 6 5

	South
	♠ K Q 10 9 8 4
	♡ K 7 6
	◇ K 2
	♣ A Q

West	North	East	South
	1 ♣	Pass	1 ♠
2 ♡	2 ♠	Pass	4 NT
Pass	5 ♡	Pass	6 ♠
All Pass			

West leads the ace of hearts and East plays the four.

5.   North
          ♠ J 9 3 2
          ♡ Q J 10
          ◊ A K
          ♣ J 6 5 4

        South
          ♠ A K 8 7 5 4
          ♡ 6 3 2
          ◊ 10 7
          ♣ A 2

West	North	East	South
			1 ♠
Pass	3 ♠	Pass	4 ♠
All Pass			

West leads the king of clubs.

6.   North
          ♠ 9 5 2
          ♡ A K 5 3
          ◊ 6 3
          ♣ Q J 9 4

        South
          ♠ Q 8
          ♡ Q J 4
          ◊ A K J
          ♣ A 10 7 6 2

West	North	East	South
			1 NT
Pass	2 ♣	Pass	2 ◊
Pass	3 NT	All Pass	

West leads the five of diamonds and East plays the ten.

7.   North
          ♠ A 7
          ♡ 8 5 4
          ◊ A Q 9 3
          ♣ Q J 10 2

        South
          ♠ 8 4 3
          ♡ A J 6
          ◊ J 10 7 5
          ♣ A K 9

West	North	East	South
			1 ◊
1 ♡	3 ◊	Pass	3 NT
All Pass			

West leads the king of hearts and East plays the three.

8.   North
          ♠ A Q 8 3
          ♡ K 10 9 5
          ◊ Q 7
          ♣ 7 4 2

        South
          ♠ J 4
          ♡ A Q J 8 3
          ◊ K 10 9
          ♣ A 6 5

West	North	East	South
		1 ♣	1 ♡
Pass	3 ♡	Pass	4 ♡
All Pass			

West leads the jack of clubs, and will lead another club if you hold up the ace.

Answers to Quiz for Chapter Eleven

1.

	North	
	♠ A 7 6	
	♡ K 7 5	
	◇ A Q 4	
	♣ 10 8 3 2	

West		East
♠ Q 9 8 5 4		♠ J 10 3
♡ Q 9 6 3		♡ J 10 2
◇ 6 2		◇ J 10 7 5
♣ A 7		♣ K 6 4

	South	
	♠ K 2	
	♡ A 8 4	
	◇ K 9 8 3	
	♣ Q J 9 5	

West	North	East	South
	1 ♣	Pass	2 NT
Pass	3 NT	All Pass	

West leads the five of spades and you allow East to win with the ten. East leads the jack of spades at trick two and West plays the four.

The plays to the first two tricks indicate that West began with five (or six) spades. You have only seven winners and must establish the club suit to make your bid. If West has the ace and king of clubs, you will surely fail; if East has both of these cards, you will succeed. The critical situation arises when the club honors are divided and West has exactly five spades. Then you must try to force out West's club honor while you still have the ace of spades in dummy.

As the cards lie, you can always be set — and you *will* be if you lead a club from your hand at trick three. East will win with the king and return a spade, leaving West with the ace of clubs and two good spade tricks.

The play that is likely to succeed is to cross to dummy and lead a *low* club. East is now second-hand and is unlikely to rise with the king of clubs — a difficult play that few players would make. Once East ducks the club lead, you cannot be prevented from establishing two club winners and making your bid.

2.

	North	
	♠ 9 8 5	
	♡ A Q J	
	◇ 10 4 2	
	♣ J 8 6 3	

West		East
♠ A 3 2		♠ Q J 10 7 6
♡ 10 8 7 4		♡ 9 6 2
◇ K J 9 6 3		◇ Q 5
♣ 5		♣ Q 7 4

	South	
	♠ K 4	
	♡ K 5 3	
	◇ A 8 7	
	♣ A K 10 9 2	

West	North	East	South
			1 NT
Pass	2 NT	Pass	3 NT
All Pass			

West leads the six of diamonds and East plays the queen.

It is a very good idea to win the first trick with the ace of diamonds, as a spade switch from East could be disastrous. You need five club tricks to make your bid. The percentage play with nine clubs missing the queen is to cash the ace or king and, if both opponents follow suit, to cash the other honor, hoping the queen will drop.

You intend to play this way, but *first* give East a chance to help you. Play a heart over to dummy and lead the *jack of clubs*. If East covers — as most players will if they have the queen — you have nine tricks. If East does not cover, you should follow the normal percentage play and cash the ace and king.

```
3.                  North
                    ♠ 7 5 2
                    ♡ K J 3
                    ◇ A K Q J 10
                    ♣ J 8
     West                          East
     ♠ A Q 6                       ♠ K 8 4 3
     ♡ 5 4 2                       ♡ 9 7
     ◇ 8 5 3                       ◇ 9 7 6 4
     ♣ A 9 7 2                     ♣ Q 10 5
                    South
                    ♠ J 10 9
                    ♡ A Q 10 8 6
                    ◇ 2
                    ♣ K 6 4 3


     West      North     East      South
               1 ◇       Pass      1 ♡
     Pass      2 ♡       Pass      4 ♡
     All Pass
```

West leads the ace of clubs and East plays the five.

With the solid diamond suit in dummy, West should reason that he must win the first four tricks to beat the contract. The best hope is to find East with a king. If East has the king of clubs, he should continue leading clubs; if East has the king of spades, he should shift to a spade.

The only thing West has to guide him is East's signal on the first trick. Since you want West to continue leading clubs, you should false-card with the *six*. West will notice that the three and four are missing, and he may conclude that East is encouraging from K 5 4 3. If you play the three or four on the first trick, West is likely to read the five of clubs as discouraging and switch to a spade.

```
4.                  North
                    ♠ A J 7 3
                    ♡ J 10 2
                    ◇ A 8
                    ♣ K J 6 5
     West                          East
     ♠ 2                           ♠ 6 5
     ♡ A Q 9 8 5 3                 ♡ 4
     ◇ Q J 7 6                     ◇ 10 9 5 4 3
     ♣ 10 4                        ♣ 9 8 7 3 2
                    South
                    ♠ K Q 10 9 8 4
                    ♡ K 7 6
                    ◇ K 2
                    ♣ A Q


     West      North     East      South
               1 ♣       Pass      1 ♠
     2 ♡       2 ♠       Pass      4 NT
     Pass      5 ♡       Pass      6 ♠
     All Pass
```

West leads the ace of hearts and East plays the four.

Perhaps you should have bid six notrump, but it is too late now. The bidding indicates that West has a six-card heart suit (it is very unlikely that he would overcall at the two-level with a mediocre five-card suit and a maximum of nine high-card points); therefore, East has a singleton. West has made the killing opening lead; he obviously plans to lead another heart in the hope that his partner can ruff. The play to change his mind is to drop the *king* of hearts under the ace. You will be set an extra trick if West continues with the queen, but he is more likely to believe you have a singleton and lead another suit.

Even an expert West is likely to be fooled by this play. Note that if you did have a singleton heart, West would establish a heart trick in dummy if he played the suit again. If your gambit works, you can discard your heart losers on the club suit and make your bid.

```
5.                North
                  ♠ J 9 3 2
                  ♡ Q J 10
                  ◇ A K
                  ♣ J 6 5 4
West                                East
♠ —                                 ♠ Q 10 6
♡ 9 8 5 4                           ♡ A K 7
◇ J 9 8 4 3                         ◇ Q 6 5 2
♣ K Q 10 7                          ♣ 9 8 3
                  South
                  ♠ A K 8 7 5 4
                  ♡ 6 3 2
                  ◇ 10 7
                  ♣ A 2

West      North      East      South
                                1 ♠
Pass      3 ♠        Pass       4 ♠
All Pass
```

West leads the king of clubs.

You must lose one club and two heart tricks, so the contract hinges on avoiding a spade loser. There is a 78-percent chance that spades will divide 2-1, so the normal play is to cash the ace and king. But you can increase your chances further by giving East a chance to make a mistake if he holds three trumps. Win the first trick with the ace of clubs, play a diamond to dummy, and lead the *jack* of spades. If East covers with the queen, you can avoid a spade loser by subsequently finessing him out of his ten. Of course, if East does not cover, you have no intention of finessing because the odds are heavily in favor of a 2-1 split.

Defensive tip: East should know from the bidding that his partner has at most a singleton spade. Therefore he cannot gain by covering the jack with the queen. Besides the actual layout, covering would cost a trick if West held a singleton king. Would you have covered?

```
6.                North
                  ♠ 9 5 2
                  ♡ A K 5 3
                  ◇ 6 3
                  ♣ Q J 9 4
West                                East
♠ A 6 4                             ♠ K J 10 7 3
♡ 10 8 7                            ♡ 9 6 2
◇ Q 9 7 5 2                         ◇ 10 8 4
♣ K 8                               ♣ 5 3
                  South
                  ♠ Q 8
                  ♡ Q J 4
                  ◇ A K J
                  ♣ A 10 7 6 2

West      North      East      South
                                1 NT
Pass      2 ♣        Pass       2 ◇
Pass      3 NT       All Pass
```

West leads the five of diamonds and East plays the ten.

You have eight winners: four hearts, three diamonds, and one club. If the club finesse works, you can win twelve tricks. If the club finesse fails, you can be set if West switches to a spade. The play to discourage West from leading a spade is to win the first trick with the *king* (or ace) of diamonds instead of the jack. Next lead the four of hearts to dummy's king and finesse the queen of clubs.

Suppose you were sitting West and saw your partner's ten of diamonds force out the king. Wouldn't you be convinced that partner has the jack of diamonds? If so, when you regain the lead, you would reason that a diamond continuation will establish the suit and offers the best chance to defeat the contract.

To the contrary, if declarer wins the first trick with the *jack* of diamonds, he is marked with the ace and king. West will realize the futility in continuing diamonds, and he will shift to a spade.

7.   North
             ♠ A 7
             ♡ 8 5 4
             ◇ A Q 9 3
             ♣ Q J 10 2

West   East
♠ K Q 10   ♠ J 9 6 5 2
♡ K Q 10 9 2   ♡ 7 3
◇ 6 4   ◇ K 8 2
♣ 8 7 5   ♣ 6 4 3

             South
             ♠ 8 4 3
             ♡ A J 6
             ◇ J 10 7 5
             ♣ A K 9

West	North	East	South
			1 ◇
1 ♡	3 ◇	Pass	3 NT
All Pass			

West leads the king of hearts and East plays the three.

You cannot be set if the diamond finesse works, so the sensible thing to do is to organize a plan that may succeed even if the finesse fails.

Consider what will happen with the cards as shown in the diagram. If you win the first trick with the ace of hearts, East will return a heart when he wins with the king of diamonds and you will be set. If you play the six of hearts on the first trick, West will see his partner's discouraging three-spot (East should not play his lowest card if he holds the ace or jack) and switch to the king of spades—now the opponents can set you by running the spade suit.

It may seem that you are damned if you do and damned if you don't; but there are *three* choices, not two. The best play is to drop the *jack* of hearts on the first trick. West can beat you if he switches to a spade, but he has been led to believe that you have a doubleton ace-jack of hearts. West will almost surely lead another heart, which you will win with the ace and take the diamond finesse. The contract is now safe, even if East happens to have another heart.

8.   North
             ♠ A Q 8 3
             ♡ K 10 9 5
             ◇ Q 7
             ♣ 7 4 2

West   East
♠ 7 5 2   ♠ K 10 9 6
♡ 7 6   ♡ 4 2
◇ 8 6 4 3 2   ◇ A J 5
♣ J 10 9   ♣ K Q 8 3

             South
             ♠ J 4
             ♡ A Q J 8 3
             ◇ K 10 9
             ♣ A 6 5

West	North	East	South
		1 ♣	1 ♡
Pass	3 ♡	Pass	4 ♡
All Pass			

West leads the jack of clubs, and will lead another club if you hold up the ace.

You have two losing clubs and one losing diamond, so you will be set if you lose a spade trick. There are so few high cards missing that East must have the king of spades for his opening bid. Unless the king of spades is singleton, your only chance is to hoodwink East into thinking that you have a singleton spade.

Win the second club lead with your ace, play the four of spades to the ace, and lead a low spade from the dummy. If East takes his king of spades, you will be set; but he cannot see your hand, and he may opt to duck. Note that if you hold ♠ 4 ♡ A Q J 8 7 3 ◇ 10 9 2 ♣ A 6 5 (or similar), East will give you the contract if he goes up with the king. Nobody knows what East will do, but this line of play is your only hope.

12

Matchpoint Strategy

♣　　◇　　♡　　♠　　♣　　◇　　♡　　♠

Matchpoints is the scoring method generally used in duplicate pair events, and it is quite different from the methods used in rubber bridge, Chicago bridge, and most team events. Throughout the chapter, these other methods will be referred to as "total-point scoring," which implies that the goal is to win as many *points* as possible. The goal at matchpoint scoring is to beat as many other *pairs* as possible; it does not matter whether you beat them by 10 points or 1000 points—you get exactly one point for each pair that you beat.

The strategy for playing the hand sometimes depends on the form of scoring. Total-point scoring was presumed in the previous eleven chapters. This chapter explains the differences created by matchpoint scoring.

Overtricks

#1

Contract: four hearts

Opening Lead: queen of diamonds

North
♠ 10 7 4 3
♡ 8 6 5 2
◇ A K 5
♣ 9 2

South
♠ K Q
♡ A K Q J 9
◇ 9 8 3
♣ A J 10

You have only three losers (one spade, one diamond, and one club), so your contract is virtually assured. But you are playing in a duplicate pair event (matchpoint scoring) and many other pairs will reach the same contract. The difference between a good score and a bad score may depend on whether you make an overtrick.

Win the first diamond trick, lead a club from dummy, and finesse the jack (or ten). Suppose West wins with the king or queen and leads the jack of diamonds to dummy's king. If you take a second club finesse and it works, you will be able to discard a diamond from dummy on the ace of clubs and make an overtrick. If the second club finesse fails

(West has both the king and queen), West will cash his diamond trick and set the contract. Should you risk the second finesse? At matchpoints, yes, because the odds are 2-to-1 that it will work (see Restricted Choice on page 12).

Here is a likely layout:

```
                         North
                         ♠ 10 7 4 3
                         ♡ 8 6 5 2
                         ◊ A K 5
                         ♣ 9 2
        West                              East
        ♠ 8 6 5                           ♠ A J 9 2
        ♡ 7 4                             ♡ 10 3
        ◊ Q J 10 7                        ◊ 6 4 2
        ♣ Q 6 4 3                         ♣ K 8 7 5
                         South
                         ♠ K Q
                         ♡ A K Q J 9
                         ◊ 9 8 3
                         ♣ A J 10
```

The other declarers who play this hand will be confronted with the same problem. Those who win eleven tricks will be tied for the top score, while those who win ten tricks will be tied for bottom. The reverse would be true if West had the king and queen of clubs, but the odds are against it.

At total points you should win the first trick and draw trumps immediately. Do not play for overtricks at total points if it puts your contract in jeopardy.

#2

Contract: three notrump

Opening Lead: six of spades

```
                         North
                         ♠ A Q 10 7
                         ♡ 9 5
                         ◊ A K Q 4
                         ♣ A J 3

                         South
                         ♠ 8 3 2
                         ♡ Q 7 3
                         ◊ 9 5
                         ♣ K Q 10 6 4
```

West	North	East	South
	1 ◊	Pass	1 NT
Pass	3 NT	All Pass	

You have nine sure tricks if you win the first trick with the ace of spades. But if West has led his fourth-best spade, East has no card above the six (see the Rule of Eleven on page 184) and you can win the first trick with the seven or eight of spades. By taking three spade finesses, you can win twelve tricks: four spades, three diamonds, and five clubs.

Suppose these are the four hands:

North
♠ A Q 10 7
♡ 9 5
◇ A K Q 4
♣ A J 3

West
♠ K J 9 6 4
♡ K J 4
◇ 8 6 2
♣ 8 7

East
♠ 5
♡ A 10 8 6 2
◇ J 10 7 3
♣ 9 5 2

South
♠ 8 3 2
♡ Q 7 3
◇ 9 5
♣ K Q 10 6 4

Play the seven of spades from dummy, overtake with your eight, and then finesse the ten. You will eventually finesse the queen and win four spade tricks. The three overtricks will reward you with an excellent matchpoint score.

But suppose the East-West cards are divided as follows:

North
♠ A Q 10 7
♡ 9 5
◇ A K Q 4
♣ A J 3

West
♠ 6 5 4
♡ K J 4
◇ J 8 6 2
♣ 8 7 5

East
♠ K J 9
♡ A 10 8 6 2
◇ 10 7 3
♣ 9 2

South
♠ 8 3 2
♡ Q 7 3
◇ 9 5
♣ K Q 10 6 4

The six-of-spades opening lead is reasonable with the West hand, and many players would choose it. If you now play low from dummy (or any spade but the ace), you figure to be set two tricks in a laydown contract. East will win the first trick and shift to the six of hearts; then the opponents can run five heart tricks.

How do you know what to do? You *don't*. But West's lead is more likely to be fourth-best, so at matchpoints you should gamble for the overtricks. At total points, go up with the ace of spades and take your nine sure tricks.

#3   North
                                                  ♠ 6 4
                                                  ♡ 9 8 7
                                                  ◇ K 9
Contract: three notrump   ♣ A Q J 10 6 5

Opening Lead: king of hearts   South
                                                  ♠ A K 3 2
                                                  ♡ A 6 5
                                                  ◇ A Q 4
                                                  ♣ 9 8 7

You correctly hold up the ace of hearts on the first trick, and West continues with the queen of hearts. (East follows with the two and three.) Should you hold up a second time?

At matchpoints, most emphatically, *no*. Assume that West has the longer hearts (evident from East's discouraging signal). Winning the *second* heart will gain either when the club finesse works—you will win twelve tricks—or if the club finesse fails and East began with two hearts—you will win eleven tricks instead of ten. Winning the *third* heart will gain if the club finesse fails and East has three hearts—you will win ten tricks instead of nine. Clearly, there is more potential to gain by winning the *second* heart lead. Suppose this is the full deal:

                                                  North
                                                  ♠ 6 4
                                                  ♡ 9 8 7
                                                  ◇ K 9
                                                  ♣ A Q J 10 6 5

West   East
♠ 8 7 5   ♠ Q J 10 9
♡ K Q J 10   ♡ 4 3 2
◇ 7 5 3 2   ◇ J 10 8 6
♣ 4 2   ♣ K 3

                                                  South
                                                  ♠ A K 3 2
                                                  ♡ A 6 5
                                                  ◇ A Q 4
                                                  ♣ 9 8 7

Tilt! You will win only nine tricks if you take the second heart trick, but you would win ten if you held up again. Nevertheless, at matchpoints you should hold up only once; the percentage play does not always work.

Note that after winning the second trick the contract is in jeopardy only if West has a doubleton king-queen of hearts. This possibility is so remote (especially in view of East's discouraging signal) that it is a reasonable decision to win the second trick at total points too.

#4

Contract: four spades

Opening Lead: eight of diamonds

North
♠ K Q 8 2
♡ K Q J 10
◇ 10 3
♣ Q J 8

South
♠ A 10 9 6 4
♡ 8 7
◇ A K J 7
♣ 10 5

If West is making a normal lead, East has the queen and nine of diamonds, and you have a golden opportunity to score an overtrick. You can win four diamond tricks and discard two clubs from dummy. Here are the four hands with the expected diamond distribution:

North
♠ K Q 8 2
♡ K Q J 10
◇ 10 3
♣ Q J 8

West
♠ J 7 3
♡ A 9 6 2
◇ 8 2
♣ A 7 6 3

East
♠ 5
♡ 5 4 3
◇ Q 9 6 5 4
♣ K 9 4 2

South
♠ A 10 9 6 4
♡ 8 7
◇ A K J 7
♣ 10 5

The first important play is to *cover* the eight of diamonds with the ten; otherwise East will play low and limit you to three diamond tricks. East covers the ten with the queen, and you win with the ace. Draw trumps with the king, ace, and queen (in that order), then lead the three of diamonds from dummy. When East plays low, finesse the *seven*. Now you can discard two of dummy's clubs and win eleven tricks — a fine matchpoint score.

Obviously, it would be foolish to try for this overtrick at total points. You would be set if West made the unorthodox lead of the eight from nine-eight — and your partner would never speak to you again.

#5   North
                                               ♠ 9 7 6
                                               ♡ 5 3 2
                                               ◊ A K Q 4 3
Contract: three notrump   ♣ 8 5

Opening Lead: seven of hearts   South
                                               ♠ A K Q
                                               ♡ A Q
                                               ◊ 8 2
                                               ♣ A 10 7 4 3 2

   East plays the king of hearts on the first trick, and you win with the ace. You have nine solid tricks and may win one or two overtricks, depending on how the diamond suit divides. You have no side entries to dummy, so you have two options: Cash the ace, king, and queen of diamonds—you will win two overtricks only if the suit divides 3-3; or concede the first diamond trick—you will win one overtrick if the suit divides 3-3 or 4-2. Which would you do?
   Here are the four hands:

                                               North
                                               ♠ 9 7 6
                                               ♡ 5 3 2
                                               ◊ A K Q 4 3
                                               ♣ 8 5

West   East
♠ 4 2   ♠ J 10 8 5 3
♡ J 9 8 7 4   ♡ K 10 6
◊ J 9 6 5   ◊ 10 7
♣ K 6   ♣ Q J 9
                                               South
                                               ♠ A K Q
                                               ♡ A Q
                                               ◊ 8 2
                                               ♣ A 10 7 4 3 2

   There is only a 36-percent chance that a suit will divide 3-3 and a 48-percent chance that it will divide 4-2 (see the percentage table on page 172). Therefore, the better play is to concede the first diamond trick and try for just one overtrick. Even at matchpoints, it is not always right to try for the maximum number of tricks.

Overtricks versus Safety Plays

#6   North
                                          ♠ 6 2
                                          ♡ 8 5 2
                                          ◊ 10 7 4
Contract: three notrump   ♣ A K Q 6 3

Opening Lead: queen of spades   South
                                          ♠ A K
                                          ♡ A K Q
                                          ◊ J 9 8 6 3
                                          ♣ 7 4 2

You need four club tricks to make your bid. At total points the right play is to cash one high club and, if both opponents follow suit, duck the second club trick. This safety play squanders an overtrick if the suit divides 3-2, but it insures the contract against a 4-1 break.

At matchpoints you should try for the extra trick because a suit will divide 3-2 68 percent of the time. Before committing yourself, however, there is a way to find out if *West* has a singleton club.

Suppose these are the four hands:

```
                          North
                          ♠ 6 2
                          ♡ 8 5 2
                          ◊ 10 7 4
                          ♣ A K Q 6 3
          West                              East
          ♠ Q J 10 9 8                      ♠ 7 5 4 3
          ♡ J 9 7 4 3                       ♡ 10 6
          ◊ K 5                             ◊ A Q 2
          ♣ 5                               ♣ J 10 9 8
                          South
                          ♠ A K
                          ♡ A K Q
                          ◊ J 9 8 6 3
                          ♣ 7 4 2
```

Win the first trick, lead a club to dummy's queen, return to your hand with a heart, and lead a second club. When West shows out, you know that East has a club stopper; so it is obvious that you must duck this trick in order to make your contract.

Note that if West followed suit to the second club lead, you should cash the high clubs and hope for a 3-2 break. You are a big favorite to score an overtrick, but you would be set if West began with four clubs.

#7   North
                                          ♠ Q 2
                                          ♡ A 4
                                          ◇ K Q 10 8 5 3
Contract: three notrump   ♣ 7 6 3

Opening Lead: six of spades   South
                                          ♠ K 7 4
                                          ♡ K 10 3 2
                                          ◇ A 9
                                          ♣ A J 8 5

You correctly play the queen of spades from dummy and it wins the first trick. If you cash your high diamonds, you can win ten tricks if the suit divides 3-2 or the jack is singleton. But you will probably go down if East has a diamond stopper; he will be able to get the lead and play a spade through your king before you can establish the diamond suit. There is a safety play to insure the contract if East has four diamonds to the jack.

Suppose these are the four hands:

```
                           North
                           ♠ Q 2
                           ♡ A 4
                           ◇ K Q 10 8 5 3
                           ♣ 7 6 3
        West                                   East
        ♠ A 10 8 6 5                           ♠ J 9 3
        ♡ 9 7 6 5                              ♡ Q J 8
        ◇ 4                                    ◇ J 7 6 2
        ♣ 9 4 2                                ♣ K Q 10
                           South
                           ♠ K 7 4
                           ♡ K 10 3 2
                           ◇ A 9
                           ♣ A J 8 5
```

Lead a low diamond from dummy at trick two and finesse the nine. This play is clearly right at total points because it gives you an extra chance to make your bid, but it is *wrong* at matchpoints. The correct play at matchpoints is to cash the ace, king, and queen of diamonds because the safety play will cost you an overtrick if West holds one, two, or three diamonds headed by the jack. This is much more likely than East having four to the jack. Note also that if *West* has four to the jack, you will win nine tricks with either line of play.

Playing for an overtrick when it risks your contract is good matchpoint strategy if you are in a *normal* contract and you are a *favorite* to win the overtrick. If you have bid to an excellent contract that you do not expect other pairs to reach, disregard overtricks and play as safely as possible to make your bid.

#8

Contract: six notrump

Opening Lead: ten of hearts

North
♠ A Q 10 6 4
♡ A 3
◇ Q 9 2
♣ J 8 5

South
♠ K 2
♡ K Q J
◇ A K J 10
♣ A 7 4 3

You have eight winners outside the spade suit, and need *four* spade tricks to make your bid. Suppose you win the first trick with the ace of hearts and lead a spade to your king, both opponents playing low spades. Now you lead a spade toward dummy and West follows with another low spade. The slam is ironclad if you make the safety play of finessing the ten of spades.

Here is the layout you are guarding against:

North
♠ A Q 10 6 4
♡ A 3
◇ Q 9 2
♣ J 8 5

West
♠ J 9 8 7 3
♡ 10 9 8
◇ 7 5 4
♣ 6 2

East
♠ 5
♡ 7 6 5 4 2
◇ 8 6 3
♣ K Q 10 9

South
♠ K 2
♡ K Q J
◇ A K J 10
♣ A 7 4 3

You definitely should finesse the ten of spades at total points because it insures the contract. But at matchpoints you should not be concerned with the slim chance that West has five spades to the jack. Instead, you should consider the better chance to win the maximum number of spade tricks.

If you finesse the ten of spades, you gain when West has J x x x or J x x x x. If you cash the three top spades, you gain when West has x x x or x x x x (East's jack will drop). The latter holdings are more likely; by cashing the three top spades you will gain more often. Note that the percentage play at matchpoints is usually *not* to take the safety play. Tough luck — if the cards lie as in the diagram.

The Wrong Contract

#9

North
♠ J 7
♡ K J 10 9 5 4
◇ K J 3
♣ J 8

Contract: three notrump

Opening Lead: ten of spades

South
♠ K Q
♡ A 7 3
◇ Q 10 8 6 4
♣ A Q 10

West	*North*	*East*	*South*
			1 NT
Pass	3 NT	All Pass	

This deal is from the 1957 National Championship (altered slightly to make a better lesson hand). The scoring was "board-a-match," which is the same as matchpoints, except your score is compared only with the team you are playing against. You gain one point if you beat them, half a point if you tie, and zero points if you lose.

I was the declarer and my partner was Helen Sobel, one of the best woman players of all time and Charles Goren's favorite partner. Nonetheless, she was an unorthodox bidder, as you can see from the diagramed deal. The normal response with the North hand is four hearts (or three hearts, in which case I would have bid four hearts).

I was confident our opponents would reach four hearts, and here I was in three notrump. East won the first trick with the ace of spades and returned a spade. The only chance to win the board was to take as many tricks at notrump as the opponents could take at hearts. If the queen of hearts dropped under the ace-king and the club finesse worked, I would wind up with ten tricks. But with this good luck, five hearts is cold — the opponents would score 450 to my 430 (neither side was vulnerable). After due thought, it became clear that we were going to lose this board unless West had three hearts to the queen. So, at trick three, I cashed the ace of hearts and led another heart. When West followed suit, I took a deep breath and finessed the jack.

This was the full deal:

North
♠ J 7
♡ K J 10 9 5 4
◇ K J 3
♣ J 8

West
♠ 10 9 8 4 3
♡ Q 6 2
◇ A 7
♣ 9 6 5

East
♠ A 6 5 2
♡ 8
◇ 9 5 2
♣ K 7 4 3 2

South
♠ K Q
♡ A 7 3
◇ Q 10 8 6 4
♣ A Q 10

The heart finesse worked, so I ran the hearts and took the successful club finesse for a total of ten tricks and a score of 430. As expected, the opponents bid four hearts and took the percentage play in hearts by cashing the ace and king. They made their bid exactly and scored 420. Our team won the board by 10 points, and I won my first National Team-of-Four Championship.

#10

North
♠ 8 6 5
♡ A J
◇ K 9 7 4 2
♣ A Q 3

Contract: six spades

Opening Lead: jack of clubs

South
♠ A K J 10 2
♡ K Q 9 3
◇ A 8
♣ K 7

West	North	East	South
			1 ♠
Pass	2 ◇	Pass	2 ♡
Pass	3 ♠	Pass	4 NT
Pass	5 ♡	Pass	5 NT
Pass	6 ◇	Pass	6 ♠
All Pass			

North and South did not bid this hand very well. The six-spade contract is reasonable at total points, but horrible at matchpoints; you can win the same number of tricks at notrump. The most common contract should be six notrump, and some pairs may bid a grand slam. If East has the queen of spades (or West the singleton queen), those declarers will win all thirteen tricks. The difference in trick score—220 for notrump and 210 for a major suit—will give you a well-deserved bottom for playing in spades instead of no-trump.

Consequently, to get a decent score, you must hope that West has the queen of spades (not singleton). If West has Q x x, you will beat those who bid grand slams; and if West has Q x, you can beat everyone — provided you do not take the losing finesse.

This is the layout you must hope for:

North
♠ 8 6 5
♡ A J
◇ K 9 7 4 2
♣ A Q 3

West
♠ Q 4
♡ 8 7 6 4
◇ 6 5 3
♣ J 10 9 2

East
♠ 9 7 3
♡ 10 5 2
◇ Q J 10
♣ 8 6 5 4

South
♠ A K J 10 2
♡ K Q 9 3
◇ A 8
♣ K 7

Win the first trick and cash the ace and king of spades. Since the queen of spades falls, you will win all thirteen tricks. Other declarers will finesse for the queen and win only twelve tricks. Your trick score of 210 will beat the six-notrump bidders' score of 190, so *you* will get the top.

Note that there is little to lose by choosing the inferior percentage play. If you win one trick less than you could by taking the spade finesse, it will not affect your score when compared to the pairs who bid six notrump or a grand slam.

#11

Contract: one notrump

Opening Lead: queen of diamonds

North
♠ A J
♡ J 5 3 2
◇ 7 6 4
♣ 9 8 5 3

South
♠ K 8 3
♡ A K 7 6 4
◇ A 9
♣ Q 6 2

West	North	East	South
			1 NT
	All Pass		

Your one-notrump opening bid is a reasonable choice, but this time it is unfortunate. The players who open with one heart figure to be playing in a heart partscore, which is clearly a better contract than one notrump. Your only chance to get a good score is to make as many tricks in notrump as those who play in hearts.

Win the first trick with the ace of diamonds, and cash the ace and king of hearts. Good news — the queen drops. You now have eight tricks, but that is not enough; those who play in hearts will win nine tricks, simply by ruffing a spade in dummy. So you must try for nine tricks, and your only resource is the spade finesse. Suppose the four hands are:

```
                          North
                          ♠ A J
                          ♡ J 5 3 2
                          ◊ 7 6 4
                          ♣ 9 8 5 3
        West                                    East
        ♠ Q 9 5 2                               ♠ 10 7 6 4
        ♡ Q 8                                   ♡ 10 9
        ◊ Q J 10 3                              ◊ K 8 5 2
        ♣ K 10 7                                ♣ A J 4
                          South
                          ♠ K 8 3
                          ♡ A K 7 6 4
                          ◊ A 9
                          ♣ Q 6 2
```

Lead the three of spades and finesse dummy's jack, then cash the rest of your winners. Your score of 150 will beat all those who score 140 for making three hearts. If the spade finesse failed, you would be set; but you were going to get a poor score anyway if you won only eight tricks for a score of 120.

As you can see from the last three hands, it is sometimes possible to salvage a good matchpoint score when you have reached a bad contract. You must choose a different line of play from the other declarers, usually a poor percentage play, and hope for the best.

Whose Hand Is It?

#12

Contract: three hearts

Opening Lead: king of spades

```
                          North
                          ♠ 7 2
                          ♡ 9 8 5 2
                          ◊ A J 6 4
                          ♣ 9 6 3

                          South
                          ♠ Q 3
                          ♡ A K Q 7 4
                          ◊ K 10 2
                          ♣ J 8 5
```

West	North	East	South
			1 ♡
1 ♠	2 ♡	2 ♠	3 ♡
All Pass			

Both sides are vulnerable. West wins the first two tricks with the king and ace of spades, then he leads the ten of hearts to your queen. You next cash the ace and king of hearts and West discards two spades. If you take time to analyze how the opponents would fare in spades, you will notice they can win nine or ten tricks, depending on how the diamonds divide. So it is their hand; they have misbid. Most of the East-West pairs will bid three spades and score 140 or 170, so you can achieve a good score for anything better than minus 140.

Contrary to the other deals in this book, your goal here should not be to make your bid, but to be sure that you are not set more than one trick. The difference between making three hearts and going down one will not affect your score sizably (either plus 140 or minus 100 should be a good score), but down *two* (minus 200) will be a disaster.

Suppose these are the four hands:

```
                        North
                        ♠ 7 2
                        ♡ 9 8 5 2
                        ◊ A J 6 4
                        ♣ 9 6 3
        West                                    East
        ♠ A K 10 6 5                            ♠ J 9 8 4
        ♡ 10                                    ♡ J 6 3
        ◊ Q 9 7 3                               ◊ 8 5
        ♣ K 10 4                                ♣ A Q 7 2
                        South
                        ♠ Q 3
                        ♡ A K Q 7 4
                        ◊ K 10 2
                        ♣ J 8 5
```

Note that the East-West cards merit a bid of three spades over three hearts. West, in particular, was very conservative, and you are headed for a good matchpoint result.

At trick six you should lead a *club* from your hand, settling for down one. After winning their club tricks, the opponents must lead a diamond or give you a ruff and discard; in either case, you will avoid a diamond loser.

It is wrong to try the diamond finesse because you will be set *two* tricks if it loses. It is true that you can make your bid if you guess which player has the queen of diamonds and if that player has three or fewer diamonds; but the risk is not justified. In the actual layout note that you cannot make your contract even if you *guess* the queen of diamonds — West has a fourth-round stopper. So you will do just as well by leading a club.

The vulnerability on this deal is important. If you were non-vulnerable, you could afford to try the diamond finesse — if it failed, down two would cost only 100 points. But since you are vulnerable, you must be careful — the matchpoint score of minus 200 is disastrous when the opponents can make only a partscore.

Stealing a Trick

#13   North
                                        ♠ A 10 7 2
                                        ♡ Q 10 6 5
                                        ◇ J 9 3
Contract: four spades   ♣ A K

Opening Lead: queen of clubs   South
                                        ♠ K Q J 8 5
                                        ♡ A 3
                                        ◇ K Q 2
                                        ♣ 7 6 4

This looks like a flat board. Practically everyone will bid to four spades and win eleven tricks. At total points you might put your cards on the table and claim; but at matchpoints you should turn your thoughts to stealing an extra trick. The best chance (after drawing trumps) is to lead the *three* of hearts from your hand.

Suppose this is the full deal:

                        North
                        ♠ A 10 7 2
                        ♡ Q 10 6 5
                        ◇ J 9 3
                        ♣ A K
West   East
♠ 9   ♠ 6 4 3
♡ K 8 7 4   ♡ J 9 2
◇ 10 6 5 4   ◇ A 8 7
♣ Q J 9 2   ♣ 10 8 5 3
                        South
                        ♠ K Q J 8 5
                        ♡ A 3
                        ◇ K Q 2
                        ♣ 7 6 4

West can hold you to eleven tricks if he goes up with his king of hearts, but that is not obvious. From West's point of view, you might hold A x x and misguess by playing dummy's ten; or his partner might hold ace-jack doubleton or a blank ace.

The recommended play sacrifices a legitimate chance to win a twelfth trick — a singleton king of hearts — but that will occur less than one percent of the time. There is no way to calculate the chances of stealing the trick; but if West has the king, he will duck a reasonable portion of the time. Ironically, your chances are better against a *good* defender because he is aware of the cases in which he will benefit by ducking. If West is a bad defender, he is more likely to grab his trick.

Shooting

Suppose you are playing in a one-session duplicate pair game and the schedule is for twenty-six boards. Ten or twelve boards have been played so far and you have two bad results and no good results. If you don't get a good score pretty soon to turn things around, you will have no chance to finish near the top. This is a time for "shooting."

#14

North
♠ A K 7 3 2
♡ 7
◇ A K J 10 5 4
♣ 9

Contract: six spades

Opening Lead: king of hearts

South
♠ Q J 10 9 6
♡ A 4
◇ 8 3
♣ K Q J 10

West	North	East	South
			1 ♠
Pass	4 NT	Pass	5 ◇
Pass	6 ♠	All Pass	

It is hard to imagine that any North-South pair will fail to reach six spades on these cards, and West's opening lead appears to be routine. Therefore, you are headed for an average result. The normal line of play is to draw trumps and cash the ace and king of diamonds. If the queen drops, you can discard four clubs and win all thirteen tricks; if the queen does not drop, you must lose a trick to the ace of clubs.

But you are not interested in an average score. Instead you should try a gambling play that may earn you a top (or a bottom).

Here is the layout you are hoping for:

North
♠ A K 7 3 2
♡ 7
◇ A K J 10 5 4
♣ 9

West
♠ 8
♡ K Q 10 5 2
◇ Q 9 7 6
♣ 5 4 3

East
♠ 5 4
♡ J 9 8 6 3
◇ 2
♣ A 8 7 6 2

South
♠ Q J 10 9 6
♡ A 4
◇ 8 3
♣ K Q J 10

Win the first trick with the ace of hearts, draw two rounds of trumps ending in your hand, and *take a first-round diamond finesse*. Now play a trump to your hand, and repeat the diamond finesse. The rest of the diamonds are good, so you can discard four clubs and win all thirteen tricks for a top score.

Due to this good luck, you may score well during the rest of the session and win the tournament. Of course, if East had the queen of diamonds, you would be set in a cold slam. You would receive a bottom score and probably be out of contention.[1]

---

1. Continuous shooting, when you have no chance to win, is poor sportsmanship, as your extreme results will affect the other pairs in contention. Sometimes you have to accept defeat and use the balance of the session just to practice good bridge technique.

Quiz for Chapter Twelve

This is a quiz for matchpoint scoring. The vulnerability is immaterial in many cases, but assume both sides are vulnerable throughout the quiz.

1.
    North
    ♠ K Q 10 2
    ♡ A 7 4 3
    ◇ 6 5
    ♣ J 10 9

    South
    ♠ A J
    ♡ K 2
    ◇ A 10 7
    ♣ A Q 8 6 5 3

West	North	East	South
			1 ♣
Pass	1 ♡	Pass	2 NT
Pass	3 NT	All Pass	

West leads the three of diamonds and East plays the queen.

2.
    North
    ♠ 8 3 2
    ♡ 9 6 5
    ◇ A K 7 4 2
    ♣ 10 3

    South
    ♠ A Q 4
    ♡ A K 3
    ◇ Q 6 5
    ♣ A 7 4 2

West	North	East	South
			1 ♣
Pass	1 ◇	Pass	2 NT
Pass	3 NT	All Pass	

West leads the jack of spades, East plays the king, and you win with the ace.

3.
    North
    ♠ K 8 7 5 2
    ♡ J 6
    ◇ 10 6 4 3 2
    ♣ 9

    South
    ♠ A Q 6 4 3
    ♡ A K 8
    ◇ 7 5
    ♣ K Q 2

West	North	East	South
			1 ♠
Pass	4 ♠	All Pass	

West leads the nine of hearts.

4.
    North
    ♠ A K Q J 8 5
    ♡ 9
    ◇ Q 2
    ♣ A 6 3 2

    South
    ♠ 10 3
    ♡ K J 4
    ◇ A 9 7 5
    ♣ J 10 9 8

West	North	East	South
	1 ♠	Pass	1 NT
Pass	3 ♠	Pass	3 NT
All Pass			

West leads the five of hearts and East plays the queen.

5.

	North		
	♠ K 10 5		
	♡ K J 9 2		
	◇ A 7 3		
	♣ A J 4		

	South		
	♠ A Q J 8 3		
	♡ A 7 4		
	◇ K 5		
	♣ K Q 2		

West	North	East	South
	1 NT	Pass	3 ♠
Pass	4 ♠	Pass	4 NT
Pass	5 ♡	Pass	6 ♠
All Pass			

West leads the ten of clubs.

6.

	North		
	♠ 8		
	♡ 10 9 8 5		
	◇ 8 4 2		
	♣ A 10 7 6 2		

	South		
	♠ K Q J		
	♡ A Q 7 6 4 3		
	◇ 9 3		
	♣ 5 4		

West	North	East	South
1 ♠	Pass	3 ♠	4 ♡
4 ♠	5 ♡	Dbl	All Pass

West wins the first two tricks with the king and queen of diamonds, and leads a third diamond.

7.

	North		
	♠ A J 8 5 4		
	♡ K 6 3		
	◇ 10 7 3		
	♣ 7 2		

	South		
	♠ K Q 2		
	♡ Q J 10		
	◇ A K Q		
	♣ A K Q 4		

West	North	East	South
			2 ♣
Pass	2 ♠	Pass	2 NT
Pass	3 NT	Pass	6 NT
All Pass			

West leads the jack of clubs.

8.

	North		
	♠ Q 7 2		
	♡ 5 4 3		
	◇ A Q 10 9 7 6		
	♣ 8		

	South		
	♠ A 6		
	♡ A K 9 2		
	◇ J 8 3		
	♣ A 7 6 5		

West	North	East	South
			1 NT
Pass	3 NT	All Pass	

West leads the five of spades.

Answers to Quiz for Chapter Twelve

1.   **North**
                            ♠ K Q 10 2
                            ♡ A 7 4 3
                            ◇ 6 5
                            ♣ J 10 9

West   **East**
♠ 8 6 3   ♠ 9 7 5 4
♡ J 9 5   ♡ Q 10 8 6
◇ K J 8 3 2   ◇ Q 9 4
♣ 7 4   ♣ K 2

                            South
                            ♠ A J
                            ♡ K 2
                            ◇ A 10 7
                            ♣ A Q 8 6 5 3

West	*North*	*East*	*South*
			1 ♣
Pass	1 ♡	Pass	2 NT
Pass	3 NT	All Pass	

West leads the three of diamonds and East plays the queen.

This is a pretty good slam hand, but difficult to bid. Most pairs will stop at three notrump, so you must strive to win as many tricks as you can. The problem is whether you should win the first, second, or third diamond trick.

The three-of-diamonds lead suggests that West has four or five diamonds. Since West will gain the lead if the club finesse loses, there is almost no advantage in holding up the ace of diamonds. Win the *first* trick, cross to dummy in hearts or spades, and take the club finesse. As the cards lie, you will win all thirteen tricks. If West had the king of clubs, you would be set; but a holdup play would not have helped.

There is a slight advantage in holding up the ace of diamonds at *total points*. Win the third round of diamonds and, assuming West appears to have the diamond length, cash the ace of clubs to guard again his winning with a singleton king.

2.   **North**
                            ♠ 8 3 2
                            ♡ 9 6 5
                            ◇ A K 7 4 2
                            ♣ 10 3

West   **East**
♠ J 10 9 7   ♠ K 6 5
♡ Q 4   ♡ J 10 8 7 2
◇ J 9 8 3   ◇ 10
♣ 8 6 5   ♣ K Q J 9

                            South
                            ♠ A Q 4
                            ♡ A K 3
                            ◇ Q 6 5
                            ♣ A 7 4 2

West	*North*	*East*	*South*
			1 ♣
Pass	1 ◇	Pass	2 NT
Pass	3 NT	All Pass	

West leads the jack of spades, East plays the king, and you win with the ace.

You need four diamond tricks to make your bid, and you can win five if the suit divides 3-2. The problem is that the dummy has no side entries. If you cash the high diamonds in an attempt to win five tricks, you will win only three if the suit divides 4-1.

At total points, you should make a safety play: Win with the *queen* of diamonds and duck the second round. This ensures four diamond tricks (and your contract) against a 4-1 diamond split.

At matchpoints the safety play should be made only if West *shows out* on the second diamond lead, in which case you will know that East began with four diamonds. If West *follows* to the second diamond lead, you should win the trick in dummy and hope for a 3-2 break. Note that you will be set as the cards lie, but the odds are heavily in your favor. Ducking the second diamond lead usually will result in winning only nine tricks when you could have won ten.

```
3.                North
                  ♠ K 8 7 5 2
                  ♡ J 6
                  ◇ 10 6 4 3 2
                  ♣ 9
West                              East
♠ 10 9                           ♠ J
♡ 9 4                            ♡ Q 10 7 5 3 2
◇ K J 9 8                        ◇ A Q
♣ A 8 7 5 3                      ♣ J 10 6 4
                  South
                  ♠ A Q 6 4 3
                  ♡ A K 8
                  ◇ 7 5
                  ♣ K Q 2
```

West	North	East	South
			1 ♠
Pass	4 ♠	All Pass	

West leads the nine of hearts.

Unless West has made an unorthodox lead, he has led his highest heart and East has the queen and ten. This affords you a chance to score an overtrick. Your first play should be the jack from dummy; East covers with the queen, and you win with the ace. After drawing trumps, lead a heart from dummy and finesse the *eight*. Now you can eliminate dummy's club loser by discarding it on the king of hearts.

Note that you would be set in a laydown contract if West had the ten of hearts. But the lead of the nine makes this very unlikely, so gambling for the overtrick is good matchpoint strategy.

At total points, the risky finesse is not advisable because you gain 30 points if you are right and lose 720 points (620 for a vulnerable game plus 100 for down one) if you are wrong.

I remember once when the great Howard Schenken made the deceptive lead of the nine from 10 9 x in a world championship match. The dummy had J x x x and the declarer had A Q 8 x x. Thinking Schenken's partner held the king-ten, declarer played dummy's jack. As a result, he lost a trick to the ten and went down in a slam that he would have made with any other lead.

```
4.                North
                  ♠ A K Q J 8 5
                  ♡ 9
                  ◇ Q 2
                  ♣ A 6 3 2
West                              East
♠ 6 2                            ♠ 9 7 4
♡ A 10 8 5 2                     ♡ Q 7 6 3
◇ K 6 3                          ◇ J 10 8 4
♣ Q 7 4                          ♣ K 5
                  South
                  ♠ 10 3
                  ♡ K J 4
                  ◇ A 9 7 5
                  ♣ J 10 9 8
```

West	North	East	South
	1 ♠	Pass	1 NT
Pass	3 ♠	Pass	3 NT
All Pass			

West leads the five of hearts and East plays the queen.

Three notrump is the wrong contract. Most North-South pairs will bid to four spades and win ten (or eleven) tricks with normal breaks. Therefore, you will get a poor matchpoint score if you win only your nine top tricks in three notrump. The best chance to get a tenth trick is to find West with the king of diamonds. Win the first trick with the king of hearts and lead a *low diamond* from your hand. If West wins the trick, your J x of hearts serves as a second stopper. You cannot be prevented from winning 10 tricks and may win more (if West continues hearts).

If East happens to have the king of diamonds, he will capture the queen, lead a heart through your jack, and set the contract. But this will not cost much since three notrump making *three* was destined to be a bad score anyway.

5.
        North
        ♠ K 10 5
        ♡ K J 9 2
        ◇ A 7 3
        ♣ A J 4

West   East
♠ 7 4   ♠ 9 6 2
♡ 10 6 5   ♡ Q 8 3
◇ Q 8 4 2   ◇ J 10 9 6
♣ 10 9 8 7   ♣ 6 5 3

        South
        ♠ A Q J 8 3
        ♡ A 7 4
        ◇ K 5
        ♣ K Q 2

West	*North*	*East*	*South*
	1 NT	Pass	3 ♠
Pass	4 ♠	Pass	4 NT
Pass	5 ♡	Pass	6 ♠
All Pass			

West leads the ten of clubs.

Six spades is a bad contract at matchpoints because the same number of tricks can be won at notrump. There are twelve top tricks, so your only chance to get a good score is to make an overtrick when the six-notrump bidders do not. If West has the queen of hearts, you can win thirteen tricks with the normal heart finesse; but so will the notrump declarers. The only hope to beat them is to find the heart honors divided as shown, in which case you will succeed with a backward finesse.

After drawing trumps and cashing your minor-suit winners if desired, your first heart play should be the *jack* from dummy. If East plays low, let the jack ride; if East plays the queen, win with the ace and finesse West for the ten.

Note that your result (twelve or thirteen tricks) makes no difference when compared to those who bid a grand slam — *the only thing that matters is whether they make their bid.*

6.
        North
        ♠ 8
        ♡ 10 9 8 5
        ◇ 8 4 2
        ♣ A 10 7 6 2

West   East
♠ A 7 6 5 2   ♠ 10 9 4 3
♡ —   ♡ K J 2
◇ K Q J 10   ◇ A 7 6 5
♣ Q 9 8 3   ♣ K J

        South
        ♠ K Q J
        ♡ A Q 7 6 4 3
        ◇ 9 3
        ♣ 5 4

West	*North*	*East*	*South*
1 ♠	Pass	3 ♠	4 ♡
4 ♠	5 ♡	Dbl	All Pass

West wins the first two tricks with the king and queen of diamonds, and leads a third diamond.

South's four-heart bid is questionable; the proper call is to pass because of the spade strength and the weakness of the heart suit. Most East-West pairs will be allowed to play in four spades, a contract that will be set if hearts divide 2-1. Therefore, you must assume that West is *void* in hearts — else your five-heart bid will be a phantom sacrifice. Furthermore, you must not go down more than two tricks (minus 500) to achieve a better score than minus 620. Since you must lose one spade, two diamonds, and one club, you cannot afford to lose any heart tricks.

Ruff the third diamond trick and lead the jack of spades — it never hurts to try, but assume West wins with the ace. As soon as you get to dummy, lead the ten of hearts. If East plays low (as he should), let it ride. Repeat the finesse and you will be set two tricks — a good result since the opponents can make four spades. Finally, note that if West had the king or jack of hearts, you would be set three tricks for minus 800. But in that case the opponents could not make four spades and you would have a bad score regardless of your play.

7.

```
North
♠ A J 8 5 4
♡ K 6 3
◇ 10 7 3
♣ 7 2
```

```
West                              East
♠ 2                               ♠ 10 7 6 3
♡ A 7 5 2                         ♡ 9 8 4
◇ 9 8 6 4                         ◇ J 5 2
♣ J 10 9 8                        ♣ 6 5 3
```

```
South
♠ K Q 2
♡ Q J 10
◇ A K Q
♣ A K Q 4
```

West	North	East	South
			2 ♣
Pass	2 ♠	Pass	2 NT
Pass	3 NT	Pass	6 NT
All Pass			

West leads the jack of clubs.

Six notrump is a normal contract and you have twelve cold tricks, so your goal is to make an overtrick. The best chance is to steal a heart trick and then play for a squeeze.

Win the first trick with the ace of clubs and lead the *jack* of hearts. West may well decide to duck, on the chance that his partner has the queen and you will finesse. If he does duck, you have the rest of the tricks. Cash your high diamonds and run four of your five spade tricks, to reach this ending:

```
North
♠ 8
♡ K 6
◇ —
♣ 7
```

```
West                              East
♠ —
♡ A                               (immaterial)
◇ —
♣ 10 9 8
```

```
South
♠ —
♡ Q
◇ —
♣ K Q 4
```

Now cash dummy's last spade and discard your queen of hearts to squeeze West.

8.

```
North
♠ Q 7 2
♡ 5 4 3
◇ A Q 10 9 7 6
♣ 8
```

```
West                              East
♠ K J 9 5 4                       ♠ 10 8 3
♡ J 10 8                          ♡ Q 7 6
◇ 4 2                             ◇ K 5
♣ 9 4 3                           ♣ K Q J 10 2
```

```
South
♠ A 6
♡ A K 9 2
◇ J 8 3
♣ A 7 6 5
```

West	North	East	South
			1 NT
Pass	3 NT	All Pass	

West leads the five of spades.

At total points, you should play a low spade from dummy and win the first trick with the ace. The queen of spades then insures that the opponents cannot run the spade suit if the diamond finesse loses to East. This technique guarantees the contract (unless East has all four diamonds).

At matchpoints, however, you have an excellent chance to score one or more overtricks if you play the *queen* of spades on the first trick. As the cards lie, you will win ten tricks (but only nine if you play low—when East wins with the king of diamonds, he will shift to the king of clubs). Also observe that, if the diamond finesse works and hearts are divided 3-3, playing the queen of spades allows you to win twelve tricks by establishing your fourth heart (but only eleven tricks if you play low).

Note that you would be set if you played the queen of spades and East held the king of spades and the king of diamonds; but the odds are very much against that. You definitely should try for the overtricks at matchpoints.